Luce Irigaray and the Philosophy of Sexual Difference

This book offers a feminist defence of the idea that sexual difference is natural. Providing a new interpretation of the later philosophy of Luce Irigaray, Alison Stone defends Irigaray's unique form of essentialism and her rethinking of the relationship between nature and culture. She also shows how Irigaray's ideas can be reconciled with Judith Butler's performative conception of gender by rethinking sexual difference in relation to German Romantic philosophies of nature. This is the first sustained attempt to connect feminist conceptions of embodiment to German Idealist and Romantic accounts of nature. Not merely an interpretation of Irigaray, this book also presents an original feminist perspective on nature and the body. It will encourage debate on the relations among sexual difference, essentialism, and embodiment.

Alison Stone is Senior Lecturer in Philosophy at Lancaster University and the author of *Petrified Intelligence: Nature in Hegel's Philosophy* (2004).

T0370843

Luce Irigaray and the Philosophy of Sexual Difference

ALISON STONE

Lancaster University

CAMBRIDGE
UNIVERSITY PRESS

CAMBRIDGE UNIVERSITY PRESS
Cambridge, New York, Melbourne, Madrid, Cape Town, Singapore, São Paulo, Delhi

Cambridge University Press
32 Avenue of the Americas, New York, NY 10013-2473, USA

www.cambridge.org
Information on this title: www.cambridge.org/9780521118101

First published 2006
This digitally printed version 2009

A catalog record for this publication is available from the British Library

Library of Congress Cataloging in Publication data
Stone, Alison, 1972–
Luce Irigaray and the philosophy of sexual difference / Alison Stone.
p. cm.
Includes bibliographical references and index.
ISBN 0-521-86270-1 (hardcover)
1. Irigaray, Luce. 2. Feminist theory. 3. Sex role. I. Title.
HQ1190.S77 2006
305.4201–dc22   2005027577

ISBN 978-0-521-86270-7 hardback
ISBN 978-0-521-11810-1 paperback

Contents

Acknowledgements

I am grateful to many people who have helped me in writing this book. Firstly, I thank the Leverhulme Trust, who awarded me a Research Fellowship which enabled me to complete the book. Secondly, I thank my colleagues in the Institute for Environment, Philosophy, and Public Policy at Lancaster University (now the Institute for Philosophy and Public Policy) for providing a stimulating and supportive environment for carrying out this research.

I thank all those who have commented on chapters or sections of this book at various stages: these include Emily Brady, Andrew Chitty, Sarah Cooper, Paul Davies, Simon Gillham, Susan James, Rachel Jones, Clare Palmer, Stella Sandford, Andrew Sayer, and John Varty. Kimberly Hutchings, Susan James, and John O'Neill have been encouraging and supportive of the project and have provided valuable advice. Many others have responded helpfully to papers, based on chapters of the book, presented to the Philosophy departments at the Universities of Dundee, Durham, Glasgow, and Lancaster, and to the History of Philosophy seminar at the Institute for Historical Research. I am particularly grateful to the anonymous referees for Cambridge University Press, from whose suggestions and comments I have benefited greatly. I also thank my editor at Cambridge University Press, Beatrice Rehl, for her support of this project.

Earlier versions of parts of this book have been published as journal articles. An earlier version of some of Chapter 1 appeared as 'From Political to Realist Essentialism: Rereading Luce Irigaray', in *Feminist Theory* 5: 1 (2004), pp. 5–23. Parts of Chapter 2 appeared in 'Towards a Genealogical Feminism: A Reading of Judith Butler's Political Thought', in *Contemporary Political Theory* 4: 1 (2005), pp. 4–24. Chapter 3 draws on material from 'The Sex of Nature: A Reinterpretation of Irigaray's Metaphysics and Political Thought', in *Hypatia: A Journal of Feminist Philosophy* 18: 3 (2003), pp. 60–84. An earlier version of part of Chapter 4 was published as 'Irigaray and Hölderlin on the Relation Between Nature and Culture', in *Continental Philosophy Review* 36: 4 (2003), pp. 415–32. An earlier version of part of Chapter 5 appeared in 'Sexing the State: Familial and Political Form in Irigaray and Hegel', in *Radical Philosophy* 113 (2002), pp. 24–36.

Finally, my special thanks to John Varty for his care and support.

Abbreviations

References to all repeatedly cited works by Irigaray are parenthetical and to standard English translations where available. In the case of all citations from translations from the French, English pagination precedes the pagination to the French original, a slash separating the two. I have sometimes amended these translations, without special notice, following the French originals. References to repeatedly cited works by other authors – Judith Butler, G. W. F. Hegel, and F. W. J. Schelling – are also parenthetical. I use the following abbreviations.

Works by Luce Irigaray

S	*Speculum of the Other Woman.* Translated by Gillian C. Gill. Ithaca: Cornell University Press, 1985.
	Speculum de l'autre femme. Paris: Minuit, 1974.
TS	*This Sex Which Is Not One.* Translated by Catherine Porter with Carolyn Burke. Ithaca: Cornell University Press, 1985.
	Ce sexe qui n'en est pas un. Paris: Minuit, 1977.
FA	*The Forgetting of Air in Martin Heidegger.* Translated by Mary Beth Mader. Austin: University of Texas Press, 1999.
	L'oubli de l'air, chez Martin Heidegger. Paris: Minuit, 1983.
E	*An Ethics of Sexual Difference.* Translated by Carolyn Burke. London: Athlone, 1993.
	Éthique de la différence sexuelle. Paris: Minuit, 1984.
SG	*Sexes and Genealogies.* Translated by Gillian C. Gill. New York: Columbia University Press, 1993.
	Sexes et parentés. Paris: Minuit, 1987.

TD   *Thinking the Difference: For a Peaceful Revolution.* Translated by
         Karin Montin. London: Athlone, 1994.
         Le temps de la différence: Pour une révolution pacifique. Paris:
         Librairie Générale Française, 1989.
JTN   *Je, Tu, Nous: Toward a Culture of Difference.* Translated by Alison
         Martin. London: Routledge, 1993.
         Je, tu, nous: Pour une Culture de la Différence. Paris: Grasset,
         1990.
ILTY   *I Love to You: Sketch for a Possible Felicity in History.* Translated by
         Alison Martin. London: Routledge, 1996.
         J'aime à toi: Esquisse d'une félicité dans l'histoire. Paris: Grasset,
         1992.
DBT   *Democracy Begins Between Two* (1994). Translated by Kirsteen
         Anderson. London: Athlone, 2000.
TBT   *To Be Two* (1994). Translated by Monique M. Rhodes and
         Marco F. Cocito-Monoc. London: Athlone Press, 2000.
JLI   ' "Je–Luce Irigaray": A Meeting with Luce Irigaray'. Interview
         with Elizabeth Hirsh and Gary A. Olson. In *Hypatia* 10: 2
         (1995), pp. 93–114.
BEW   *Between East and West: From Singularity to Community.* Translated
         by Stephen Pluháček. New York: Columbia University Press,
         2002.
         Entre Orient et Occident: De la singularité à la communauté. Paris:
         Grasset, 1999.
WD   *Why Different? A Culture of Two Subjects: Interviews with Luce
         Irigaray.* Edited by Sylvère Lotringer. Translated by Camille
         Collins. New York: Semiotext(e), 2000.
WL   *The Way of Love.* Translated by Heidi Bostic and Stephen
         Pluháček. London: Continuum, 2002.
KW   *Key Writings.* Edited by Luce Irigaray. London: Continuum,
         2004.

Works by Judith Butler

SD   *Subjects of Desire: Hegelian Reflections in Twentieth-Century France.*
         New York: Columbia University Press, 1987.
VSG   'Variations on Sex and Gender: Beauvoir, Wittig and
         Foucault'. In *Feminism as Critique*, edited by Seyla Benhabib
         and Drucilla Cornell. Cambridge, U.K.: Polity Press, 1987.

GT   *Gender Trouble: Feminism and the Subversion of Identity.* London: Routledge, 1990.

BTM   *Bodies That Matter: The Discursive Limits of 'Sex'.* London: Routledge, 1993.

FC   'Contingent Foundations: Feminism and the Question of "Postmodernism"' and 'For a Careful Reading'. In Seyla Benhabib et al., *Feminist Contentions.* London: Routledge, 1995.

PL   *Precarious Life: The Powers of Mourning and Violence.* London: Verso, 2004.

UG   *Undoing Gender.* London: Routledge, 2004.

Works by G. W. F. Hegel

Werke   *G. W. F. Hegel: Werke in zwanzig Bänden.* Edited by Eva Moldenhauer and Karl Markus Michel. Frankfurt: Suhrkamp, 1969–72. Works cited below by volume number.

PhG   *Phenomenology of Spirit.* Translated by A. V. Miller. Oxford: Oxford University Press, 1977. Cited with English pagination preceding German.
Phänomenologie des Geistes. 1807. *Werke* 3.

PR   *Elements of the Philosophy of Right.* Edited by Allen Wood, translated by H. B. Nisbet. Cambridge: Cambridge University Press, 1991. Cited with paragraph number preceding English pagination.
Grundlinien der Philosophie des Rechts, oder Naturrecht und Staatswissenschaft im Grundrisse. 1821. *Werke* 7.

Works by F. W. J. Schelling

Werke   *Historisch-kritische Ausgabe Reihe 1.* Edited by Hans Michael Baumgartner, Wilhelm G. Jacobs, Jörg Jantzen, Hermann Krings, Francesco Moiso, and Hermann Zeltner. Stuttgart: Frommann-Holzboog, 1976–. Works cited below by volume number.

IPN   *Ideas for a Philosophy of Nature.* Translated by Errol E. Harris and Peter Heath. Cambridge: Cambridge University Press, 1988. Cited with English pagination before German.
Ideen zu einer Philosophie der Natur. 1797. Edited by Manfred Durner. *Werke* 5. Stuttgart: Frommann-Holzboog, 1994.

FO   *First Outline of a System of the Philosophy of Nature.* Translated by
            Keith R. Petersen. Albany: SUNY Press, 2004. Cited with
            English pagination before German.
            Erster Entwurf eines Systems der Naturphilosophie. 1799. Edited by
            Wilhelm G. Jacobs and Paul Ziche. *Werke* 7. Stuttgart:
            Frommann-Holzboog, 2001.

I   'Introduction to the Outline of a System of the Philosophy of
            Nature, or, On the Concept of Speculative Physics and the
            Internal Organization of a System of this Science'. 1799.
            Translated by Keith R. Petersen in *First Outline of a System of the
            Philosophy of Nature.* Albany: SUNY Press, 2004. Cited with
            English pagination before German.
            'Einleitung zu dem Entwurf eines Systems der
            Naturphilosophie'. In *Schriften (1799–1800). Werke* 8. Edited
            by Manfred Durner and Wilhelm G. Jacobs. Stuttgart:
            Frommann-Holzboog, 2004.

Luce Irigaray and the Philosophy of Sexual Difference

Introduction

Luce Irigaray and the Nature of Sexual Difference

This book defends an understanding of sexual difference as natural, challenging the prevailing consensus within feminist theory that sexual difference is a culturally constructed and symbolically articulated phenomenon. The book supports this challenge with a distinctive interpretation and critical rethinking of Luce Irigaray's later philosophy of sexual difference. According to my interpretation, the later Irigaray sees sexual difference as a natural difference between the sexes, which should receive cultural and social expression. Opposing the dominant view that any idea that sexual difference is natural must be politically conservative and epistemologically naïve, I want to show that Irigaray's later conception of sexual difference is philosophically sophisticated and coherent, and supports a politics of change which – importantly – aspires not only to improve women's situations but also to revalue nature and to improve humanity's relations with the natural world. However, I will not simply defend the later Irigaray but will criticise her for overlooking what I call the natural multiplicity within each of our bodies: a multiplicity of forces and capacities such that we are never simply sexually specific. Given this problem, I shall argue, Irigaray's philosophy must be fundamentally rethought within the framework of a theory of nature as self-differentiating, a theory which can recognise the reality and value of bodily multiplicity as well as that of sexual duality. Thus, this book is not merely an exposition of Irigaray but also the development of an original position within feminist thought – a philosophy of self-differentiating nature.

Although Irigaray's earlier thought has exerted immense influence on
feminist theory, her later philosophy has proved considerably less popular.[1] As one feminist critic writes: 'Irigaray's later work is far more problematic with respect to the charge of essentialism, and her deployment
of sexual difference has seemed increasingly to suggest certain pre-given
and determinant qualities of the feminine'.[2] The later Irigaray assumes
that men and women naturally have different characters, implying that
they are qualified for distinct ranges of activities. This looks troublingly
close to the traditional view that women's natural character predisposes
them to childrearing and the domestic sphere. In attempting to identify
and describe the natural characters of the sexes, Irigaray appears to overlook how deeply any perceptions of their characters must be shaped by
existing cultural prescriptions, prescriptions which she can only end up
reproducing. Moreover, to support her account of the natural differences
between the sexes, she appeals to an understanding of nature as a whole:
seemingly, for her, 'the fixity of the natural, material world is the ground
of the fixity of the social world', whereas, for most feminists: 'Any theory
of women's liberation . . . must certainly abandon the belief that nature is
immutable and fixed; otherwise, no liberation is possible'.[3]

Against these criticisms, my first aim in this book is to show that
Irigaray's later philosophy has underappreciated strengths. Her focus on
nature is valuable in reminding us that we are natural beings, surrounded
and shaped by natural environments. Moreover, she sees nature not as a
static realm of fixed forms but, rather, as a process (or set of processes)
of open-ended growth and unfolding. By stressing that human beings
belong to nature so conceived, Irigaray can maintain that human beings
have natures which need to grow and express themselves culturally. She
thereby links feminist and ecological politics, by arguing that the pursuit

---

[1] Despite Irigaray's influence on feminism, she herself avoids the label, instead professing
support for 'movements of liberation of women' ('Women's Exile', trans. Couze Venn, in
Ideology and Consciousness 1 (1977), p. 67). I take this to reflect not a substantial rejection
of feminism by Irigaray but her desire to mark that her feminism takes an original and
unusual form.

[2] Margrit Shildrick, *Leaky Bodies and Boundaries: Feminism, Postmodernism and (Bio)ethics*
(London: Routledge, 1997), p. 227. Even Penelope Deutscher's sustained examination
of Irigaray's later thought in *A Politics of Impossible Difference: The Later Work of Luce Irigaray*
(Ithaca: Cornell University Press, 2002) is premised on the view that her recourse to natural reality is *prima facie* problematic; for discussion of Deutscher's reading, see Chapter 1,
note 33.

[3] Dorothea Olkowski, *Gilles Deleuze and the Ruin of Representation* (California: University
of California Press, 1999), pp. 5, 7. Olkowski is not explicitly discussing Irigaray's later
position here but a (comparable) position which she calls 'naturalism'.

of our own flourishing as sexed beings must be based on recognition of our dependence on, and responsibilities to, the natural environment. As for her belief that humans naturally have sexually specific characters which need to unfold and develop culturally, this need not be conservative; it enables her to criticise existing society on the grounds that women's nature has never been allowed expression. Admittedly, this would hardly appease critics if women's nature gave them a need to express themselves only in the activities traditionally allotted to them, such as childrearing. But Irigaray distinguishes her account of women's (and men's) nature from traditional views by deriving her account from her novel conception of nature as processual.[4] This conception leads her to rethink sexed individuals as differing, fundamentally, in respect of certain rhythms which (as I will explain later) she takes to regulate the circulation of the fluid materials composing individuals' bodies.[5] (Throughout, when I refer to 'bodies', this denotes specifically human bodies, not natural bodies generally.) Irigaray maintains that these fluid materials enter into transient bodily forms, which give rise to sexually specific bodily capacities and forms of experience and perception.

In claiming that men and women have inherently different characters as an effect of their location within nature, Irigaray can be seen to use the concept of nature in two main senses. Firstly, the 'nature' of something, for her, denotes its defining character or essence – in this sense, men and women are said to have different natures. Secondly, for Irigaray, 'nature' designates the material world or environment as a whole, which is understood to exist, and to pursue patterns of development, independently

---

[4] Irigaray demarcates her view of nature from that of 'patriarchal' (*patriarcal*) cultures, which interpret nature 'in accordance with a *human nature* that they have themselves defined' (SG, 129/143). That is, patriarchal cultures interpret nature in a way which supports belief in fixed, hierarchical, sexual difference. So: 'We need to reinterpret the idea of nature' (4/16); Irigaray reinterprets nature as 'in the first instance . . . earth, water, wind, fire, plants, living bodies, which precede any definition or fabrication that tear them away from roots and origins existing independently of man's transforming activity' (129/143).

[5] Alison Martin notes that Irigaray's 'philosophy of two [is] a philosophy of two *rhythms*... [which] emphasizes that the structures of sexual difference she envisages are primarily structures of process, flow, and becoming in which form and content are united in a regulated harmony' (*Luce Irigaray and the Question of the Divine* (Leeds: Maney Publishing, 2000), p. 123). One might ask why Irigaray thinks that rhythms regulate the circulation of bodily fluids rather than thinking that some other factor (perhaps chromosomal and genetic material) causes this circulation, with rhythms as a side effect. Irigaray will argue against that alternative on the grounds that any potentially causal factor within bodies must itself result from a process of growth which must already have a rhythm. See Chapter 3, Section IV.

of human transformative activities. This material world includes human beings insofar as they have natures (and act according to those natures), but it excludes humans insofar as they are distinctively cultural beings, engaged in activities of transforming themselves and the material world around them.

The idea that Irigaray's descriptions of nature and sexed humanity differ from traditional – patriarchal – descriptions may seem problematic. Is Irigaray hereby claiming to 'leap to a pre-linguistic, pre-metaphysical, pre-cultural description of nature that would deny our unavoidable situation in language, culture, and metaphysics'?[6] Irigaray does not deny that she claims knowledge of nature and human bodies from a culturally specific standpoint; rather, in her view, her cultural location within the European philosophical tradition gives her epistemic access to nature and to the natural reality of human bodies. This location offers her the resources to reconceive nature in a novel way and, on that basis, to offer a correspondingly novel – and socially critical – account of sexual difference.[7]

The feminism of sexual difference which Irigaray espouses in her later work differs significantly, I believe, from that of her earlier work.[8] This earlier work understands sexual difference as the difference between 'male' and 'female' as identities or positions made available within the symbolic order (that is, broadly, the linguistically articulated realm of culture and meaning). On this understanding, sexual difference differs importantly from both *sex* difference – the biological difference between the sexes – and *gender* difference – the difference between masculinity and femininity

---

[6] Stacy Keltner, 'The Ethics of Air: Technology and the Question of Sexual Difference', in *Philosophy Today* Suppl. 45:5 (2001), p. 60.

[7] As Sally Haslanger argues, it does not 'follow from the fact that our epistemic relation to the world is mediated (by language, by concepts, by our sensory system, etc.) that we cannot refer to things independent of us . . . Intermediaries do not necessarily block access' ('Feminism in Metaphysics: Negotiating the Natural', in *The Cambridge Companion to Feminism in Philosophy*, ed. Miranda Fricker and Jennifer Hornsby (Cambridge: Cambridge University Press, 2000), p. 121). For example, spectacles and telephones are intermediaries which enable us to know about things which really, independently, exist.

[8] Irigaray herself periodises her work into an 'early' phase, criticising the 'monosexuate' character of western culture, a 'middle' phase, creating the conditions for female subjectivity, and a 'later' phase, encouraging dialogic relations between the sexes (JLI, 96–97; DBT, 121–41). As Chapter 1 will explain, I think that it is in her middle phase that Irigaray introduces the idea that sexual difference is natural, which persists in her self-proclaimed later phase. Thus, when I refer to Irigaray's later thought, I take this to encompass both her self-proclaimed middle and later phases.

as roles embodied in social practices.[9] According to the earlier Irigaray, western culture persistently defines the female as the inferior counterpart of the male, establishing patterns of symbolism which are more fundamental and all-pervasive than the contingent, varying, gender roles which result from social practices. Irigaray's early form of sexual difference feminism is important in focusing attention on the symbolic constitution of sexual difference and in opening up the project of transforming received patterns of symbolism by reconceiving female identity positively.[10] But, although sexual difference feminism is usually understood consistently with Irigaray's earlier position, she herself moves away from this position, which she comes to find incoherent.[11] This position aims to revalue female identity and, also, nature, matter, and embodiment – with which the female is traditionally aligned – yet it attempts to revalue these only as culturally conceived and symbolised, presupposing, all along, the validity of the conceptual hierarchy which privileges (symbolically male) culture over (symbolically female) nature. Irigaray rightly moves on to espouse her later form of sexual difference feminism, which, preferably, does not devalue nature and matter relative to culture and meaning. One might object that she has reverted to focusing on biological *sex* difference, not sexual difference. But she insists that sexual difference, as a difference in rhythms which (among other things) regulate sexual energy and forms of perception and experience, remains culturally significant

---

[9] As Judith Butler (not, herself, a sexual difference feminist) explains, '"gender" is...opposed in the name of sexual difference precisely because gender endorses a socially constructivist view of masculinity and femininity, displacing or devaluing the *symbolic* status of sexual difference' (UG, 185).

[10] Irigaray's earlier form of sexual difference feminism is distinct from the kinds of difference feminism better known in Anglo-American contexts. These aim to recognise and revalue feminine character traits and abilities which have traditionally been disparaged or neglected. For example, Carol Gilligan recognises and revalues the caring, contextualist, ethical standpoint of women, which influential taxonomies of moral development had ranked as mere immaturity; see Gilligan, *In a Different Voice* (Cambridge, Mass.: Harvard University Press, 1982). Whereas approaches like Gilligan's presume that a sex or gender difference *already* exists in some domain (for example, in moral reasoning), Irigaray holds that traditional symbolic structures deny sexual difference by regarding the female as merely an inferior approximation of the male. She therefore seeks recognition of an as yet *non*-existent female identity, seeing herself as pursuing a transformation of culture's basic symbolism.

[11] For an exemplary definition of sexual difference feminism following the earlier Irigaray, see Rosi Braidotti, 'Sexual Difference Theory', in *A Companion to Feminist Philosophy*, ed. Alison M. Jaggar and Iris Marion Young (Malden, Mass.: Blackwell, 1998), pp. 298–306.

and erotically charged, and hence is a sex*ual*, not narrowly biological, difference.

Insofar as I am defending Irigaray's later philosophy of sexual difference, I am also – unusually within feminist theory – defending essentialism as it figures in her later thought. Although Irigaray explicitly denies being an essentialist, her later view that men and women have natural characters which need and strive for expression is identifiably essentialist.[12] Generally in philosophy, essentialism is the belief that things have essential properties or characters which are necessary to their being the (kind of) things they are. A stronger variant of philosophical essentialism holds that the essences of things consist in their spontaneous tendencies to develop in certain ways – to exhibit certain distinctive patterns of unfolding.[13] Within feminism, essentialism denotes the view that women and men are constituted as such by certain essential characteristics. For simplicity, whenever I discuss essentialism, I will understand it in this intra-feminist sense.[14] Irigaray's (feminist) essentialism is of a strong form, holding that women's and men's essential characters consist in the rhythms which ensure that their bodies and experiences grow and unfold in distinctive ways. In attributing this form of essentialism to Irigaray, I have no intention of discrediting her later philosophy; rather, I think that the intricacy and fruitfulness of this philosophy shows that essentialism has underexplored potential which feminists should tap.

Although I shall defend Irigaray's focus on the natural reality of bodies against many of the criticisms levied against it, I nonetheless believe that her later philosophy has serious problems. To name the most salient:

---

[12] In defence of this point, see Chapter 3, Section IV.

[13] Both weaker and stronger variants of essentialism can be found in Aristotle's concept of form. He regards form as that in any thing which makes it a member of a given species. But also, more strongly, he holds that form exists within any entity as a striving towards full realisation. See Jonathan Lear, *Aristotle: The Desire to Understand* (Cambridge: Cambridge University Press, 1988), pp. 28, 35–6.

[14] My arguments in this book could be redescribed based on a broader philosophical definition of essentialism. As currently described, I criticise Irigaray's 'essentialism', arguing that individual women (and men) have diverse capacities and forces such that they are never constituted merely as women (or men). In proposing that these diverse capacities and forces exist and should be expressed and developed, I am, in intra-feminist terms, advocating a synthesis of 'essentialism' and 'anti-essentialism'. If redescribed in broader philosophical terms, though, my position – that all individuals have not only sexed but also diverse, non-sexed forces and capacities – would remain 'essentialist'. In this, I follow Andrew Sayer's principle that 'if social science [or philosophy] is to be critical of oppression, it must be essentialist insofar as it has to invoke ... extra-discursive human capacities for suffering' or flourishing (*Realism and Social Science* (London: Sage, 2000), p. 99).

this philosophy is heterosexist, assuming that, being naturally different, men and women are naturally attracted to one another. Irigaray cannot, either, acknowledge deep differences between women but considers them to differ only as particular members of a common kind. She therefore regards sexual difference as more fundamental than other differences, such as race. She also asserts that all individuals are naturally either male or female, implicitly denying – or dismissing as aberrant – the intersexed (those whose bodies have ambiguous sex characteristics, such as testes and a vagina). These problems all stem from Irigaray's conception of natural sexual difference, and so they cannot be resolved unless we fundamentally rethink her later philosophy. Nevertheless, given the attractions of this philosophy – its connection of feminist to ecological politics, and its provision of an original, socially critical, form of essentialism – this rethinking is worthwhile.

Accordingly, I aim to rethink Irigaray's later philosophy, by synthesising it with two other currents of thought: Judith Butler's 'performative' theory of gender and the idea of self-differentiating nature articulated within the German tradition of philosophy of nature. Butler's approach to gender becomes important for my argument because it is strong in the very areas where Irigaray's later philosophy is most problematic. Butler argues that gender, sex division, and heterosexuality are (in a sense to be explained) culturally produced and can, as cultural artefacts, be subverted and dismantled. Accommodating differences among women, she argues that norms concerning gender are continually changing and do not confer on women any common identity or experience. Moreover, she denies that sex difference is more fundamental than other differences, construing it merely as a transient artefact of these shifting gender norms. Despite these advantages, Butler's thought is problematic in that her stress on the cultural production of sex and gender privileges culture over matter and nature. A viable synthesis of her thought with that of Irigaray must therefore considerably revise Butler's thought too, specifically (I will argue) by predicating Butler's claims on the idea that bodies do have a natural character, but one of *multiplicity*. By this, I mean that each body is naturally composed of multiple forces (pre-conscious impulses to pursue particular kinds of activity), where this character of multiplicity is universally shared by all bodies. This idea of bodily multiplicity conflicts with Irigaray's belief in sexual duality in several ways. One is that multiplicity is common to all bodies, so it cannot serve as a principle which introduces sexual differentiation between them. Being universal to all bodies, there is nothing in multiplicity as such which could cause these bodies to become specified into two sexually different forms.[15]

How, then, can this idea of bodily multiplicity be reconciled with Irigaray's belief in natural duality? For this, we can turn to the tradition of philosophy of nature.[16] F. W. J. Schelling and, to a lesser extent, the poet/thinker Friedrich Hölderlin propose that nature is a process of self-differentiation, endlessly dividing into polar oppositions, then seeking to go beyond these oppositions by subdividing each of their poles. Nature, so understood, generates the difference between the sexes but, once realised in this form, passes beyond it by introducing subdifferentiations into each sexed individual, so that individuals are never simply sexed but always have an internal multiplicity of characteristics as well. Since natural duality can be fully realised only when it is expressed culturally, a culture

[15] For further reasons why the beliefs in multiplicity and duality are opposed, see Chapter 2, Section IV; Chapter 3, Section V; and Chapter 6, Section II, this volume. The notion of 'multiplicity' may seem obscure. I derive it from scholarship on Irigaray, within which there has been considerable discussion about how far her philosophy of sexual difference celebrates multiplicity. See: Moira Gatens, *Imaginary Bodies: Ethics, Power and Corporeality* (London: Routledge, 1996), p. 43; Elizabeth Grosz, *Jacques Lacan: A Feminist Introduction* (London: Routledge, 1990), p. 173; Alison Martin, *Luce Irigaray and the Question of the Divine*, pp. 124–5; Judith L. Poxon, 'Corporeality and Divinity: Irigaray and the Problem of the Ideal', in *Religion in French Feminist Thought: Critical Perspectives*, ed. Morny Joy, Kathleen O'Grady, and Judith L. Poxon (London: Routledge, 2003), p. 48; Margaret Whitford, *Luce Irigaray: Philosophy in the Feminine* (London: Routledge, 1991), p. 23. Poxon writes, for instance, of the 'importance of "corporeal multiplicity" . . . [T]hat bodies not be conceived as only masculine or feminine is . . . important. . . . [F]eminist theory [should] . . . theorise the multiplicity of bodily differences that keep "women" from being (simply) "woman"' (p. 48). Within Poxon's and other discussions, multiplicity has three main connotations: differences between women; the presence within each woman, or each individual, of a plethora of forces whose diversity disrupts any identity that the individual assumes; and an indefinite process of becoming and change within both individuals and society. Multiplicity has acquired these meanings, in part, from debates within literary theory about whether 'female'/'feminine' writing expresses women's nature or a profusion of changing bodily rhythms and forces (which are female only symbolically, in being bodily and passionate). The apparently heterogeneous senses of multiplicity actually interrelate and, I aim to show, can be derived from a basic understanding of bodies as composed of diverse, non-sexuate – 'multiple' – forces.

[16] 'Philosophy of nature' translates the German *Naturphilosophie*, a tradition normally taken to include Goethe, Schelling, Hegel, and their scientific followers. On this tradition as a whole, see Robert J. Richards, *The Romantic Conception of Life* (Chicago, Ill.: University of Chicago Press, 2002). Hölderlin, whom I also discuss, is not usually included in this tradition, since his discussions of nature are highly fragmentary and cast in a literary register with little overt reference to science. However, the continuities between his view of nature and those of the *Naturphilosophen* mean that he can reasonably be located in this tradition, as I shall do here.

of sexual difference is the precondition for the full development of multiplicity within individuals (although, because sexual duality is already partially realised, varying degrees of multiplicity must already co-exist with duality in all individuals). However, any legitimate culture of sexual difference must be of a *self-critical* kind which permits the expression of our accompanying multiplicity as well. According to my rethinking of Irigaray's later philosophy, then, sexual difference remains natural, but it is merely one manifestation of a broader natural process of self-differentiation, and so it should be culturally expressed in a self-critical, self-limiting, form.

Evidently, my approach to Irigaray is not simply expository but is also informed by the aim of working out a viable, substantive position in feminist philosophy – namely, a conception of nature as self-differentiating and manifesting itself in both duality and multiplicity. Given this orientation, I shall explain Irigaray's claims in a critical and analytic style distinct from her own. Her later writing style is less allusive and opaque than that of her earlier texts, yet it often remains evocative and politically inspirational rather than precise. My relatively exact language may seem incapable of doing justice to her thought. Against this, I would stress that readers whose intellectual and cultural standpoints differ from those of a text can, because of this difference, illuminate previously occluded aspects of the text. This principle is familiar from feminist history of philosophy: current feminist concerns can unearth dimensions in earlier texts – for example, the sexed connotations of their concepts – which have always been present but can be articulated and more explicit only in the context of subsequent feminist movements.[17] Similarly, predominantly English-speaking feminist debates around nature, essentialism, and sexual diversity enable us to analyse critically the strengths and weaknesses of Irigaray's later philosophy and so, too, to ascertain how it can be resituated within a framework that recognises bodily multiplicity as well as duality.

Complicating the question of the appropriate language for discussing Irigaray's ideas is the untranslatability of some of her terms, conspicuously her distinction between *masculin* and *féminin*. She speaks of a *féminin* sex, desire, language, and cultural world (TS, 149/146, 30/29; DBT, 131), whereas English speakers, informed by the sex/gender distinction, would

---

[17] See Genevieve Lloyd, 'Introduction' to *Feminism and History of Philosophy*, ed. Lloyd (Oxford: Oxford University Press, 2002), esp. pp. 7–9.

probably call sex and desire female, language and culture feminine. Irigaray's usage reflects the fact that the French *féminin* covers all aspects of human being, the predicates *mâle* and *femelle* generally applying only to nonhuman animals and plants.[18] To confuse matters further, Irigaray asserts the need for a *genre féminin*; by this, she means not a social feminine role but a culturally recognised female identity with its own specific worth, which all women could see themselves as embodying.[19] In general, the wider scope of the French *féminin* facilitates Irigaray's postulation of a natural sexual difference in humans which is rhythmic and processual, rather than narrowly biological, and which realises itself in sexual, psychical, and, ideally, cultural forms. In turn, whenever I explicate or draw on Irigaray, I will speak indifferently of men and males, or women and females. I shall use the adjective 'female' (or 'male') to translate Irigaray's *féminin* (or *masculin*), given her view that the various manifestations of sexual difference ultimately derive from nature.[20]

My aim of rethinking Irigaray in terms of ideas from the philosophy of nature may seem idiosyncratic, since her more obvious reference points lie in the traditions of phenomenology and psychoanalysis – although her references to other authors and texts generally tend to be oblique and indirect. Still, there are some elements of the tradition of philosophy

[18] See Stella Sandford, 'Feminism Against "The Feminine"', in *Radical Philosophy* 105 (2001), p. 6. Because French *femelle/féminin* do not correspond to English female/feminine, it is sometimes held that – for better or worse – the sex/gender distinction is unavailable in French (see, for example, Christine Battersby, *The Phenomenal Woman: Feminist Metaphysics and the Patterns of Identity* (Cambridge, U.K.: Polity Press, 1998), pp. 19–22). However, some French materialist feminists, such as Christine Delphy, do speak of *genre* and *rapports de genre* (not *sexe*) to denote social relations of gender (see Gill Allwood, *French Feminisms: Gender and Violence in Contemporary Theory* (London: UCL Press, 1998), pp. 89–91). Although French thus does permit at least some distinction between sex and gender, Irigaray avoids any such distinction because she thinks that it would implicitly privilege culture over nature (for a comparable Anglophone criticism of the distinction, see Moira Gatens, *Imaginary Bodies*, pp. 3–20).

[19] The French *genre* means, among other things, kind, as in the *genre humain*; for Irigaray, *genre* must become *sexué* (JTN, 13/14) – humankind must be seen as dual; that is, culture must conceptualise two different sexuate identities (so recognising the difference between the sexes' natural characters). On *genre* as kind, see Whitford, ed., *The Irigaray Reader* (Oxford: Blackwell, 1991), p. 17; for more on Irigaray's concept of *genre*, see Chapter 5, Section IV, and Chapter 6, Section IV.

[20] Some recent translations on which Irigaray has partially collaborated render *féminin* as 'feminine', but I remain convinced on philosophical grounds that 'female' better captures the sense of her *féminin*. Occasionally, though, I will use 'feminine' in translating Irigaray, when 'female' would read oddly; in such cases I will note that *féminin* remains Irigaray's term.

of nature which Irigaray knowingly, and relatively overtly, adopts in her later work. Firstly, she is explicit that she draws some support for her conception of natural duality from Hegel's account of nature, specifically his view that mind, and social institutions and relationships, emerge from and must reflect our nature. (Irigaray criticises other aspects of Hegel's philosophy of nature, though, as we will see.) Secondly, Irigaray also – but usually less explicitly – draws support for her particular understanding of natural duality from Hölderlin's idea that nature divides against itself through the medium of humanity. Thirdly, Irigaray openly appropriates aspects of Heidegger's rethinking of nature as a process of growth, a rethinking which is itself deeply influenced by Hölderlin, as Irigaray is well aware. In part, therefore, I turn to philosophy of nature in this book because Irigaray herself builds more or less explicitly on ideas from Hegel, Hölderlin, and Heidegger; by filling in more of the detail and background of these ideas, I can clarify and amplify her later views. But, in addition, I turn to other elements of the philosophy of nature which Irigaray ignores – namely, Hölderlin's and Schelling's conception of nature as a process of unending self-differentiation. This conception does not support Irigaray's later philosophy of duality (which is, perhaps, why she ignores it). Rather, this conception of nature supports the view that sexual duality and multiplicity co-exist within bodies. Thus, looking at how Irigaray adapts ideas from philosophy of nature provides us with a vantage point from which we can proceed to identify alternative elements in this tradition, elements which enable us to rethink and go beyond Irigaray's own position.

Although there are these elements of philosophy of nature on which Irigaray draws, it must be admitted that many of her most sustained textual discussions are actually of writings from the rather different traditions of phenomenology and psychoanalysis. However, Irigaray's engagements with philosophy of nature are more sustained than it might at first appear, since they sometimes inform her reflections on other topics or run like undercurrents through those reflections. This has been largely overlooked by scholars of her work, perhaps owing to the widespread unease about her later focus on nature. As for her relation to phenomenology, this itself is contested. Her evocations of our embodiment and situatedness within the material world are usually thought to reflect the influence of phenomenology. But Dorothea Olkowski has recently argued that Irigaray breaks with the phenomenological project of describing experience, instead offering an ontology of the fluid – that is, a theory according to which fluid processes are fundamentally real.[21] Here, I will take the different view that Irigaray's notion of natural and human rhythms remains, broadly, phenomenological because, although she intends this notion to capture the processual character of reality, she thinks that we are made directly aware of this character in the structure of our pre-theoretical, perceptual, experience.[22]

With respect to psychoanalysis, the early Irigaray's background in Lacanian psychoanalysis is well-known and will receive scant attention here.[23] My account of the early Irigaray presupposes that she aims for the creation of a new symbolic order which recognises the sexes as equiv-alent in value. It appears, though, that the later Irigaray removes herself further from any Lacanian framework. From the perspective of Lacanian psychoanalysis, male and female are symbolic positions which individu-als must take up, at the cost of repressing the multiple drives and dimen-sions of experience which, in their very diversity, are inconsistent with any coherent sexed identity.[24] From this perspective, therefore, sexed iden-tity is always problematic, disturbed by promptings and residues from the unconscious. In contrast, the later Irigaray assumes that men and women, boys and girls, are naturally sexed and have direct experience of their sexual specificity. On that basis, she argues that infant girls and boys develop different relationships to their maternal origin, which lead

---

[21] Olkowski, 'The End of Phenomenology: Bergson's Interval in Irigaray', in *Hypatia* 15: 3 (2000), pp. 75–7. As Naomi Schor says: 'The real in Irigaray is neither impossible, nor unknowable: it is the fluid' ('This Essentialism Which Is Not One: Coming to Grips with Irigaray', in *Engaging with Irigaray*, ed. Carolyn Burke, Naomi Schor, and Margaret Whitford (New York: Columbia University Press, 1994), p. 69).

[22] Irigaray's attention to rhythm reflects a wider preoccupation with this notion within phenomenologically informed French thought. Gaston Bachelard's *The Dialectic of Dur-ation* (1950), trans. Mary McAllester Jones (Manchester, U.K.: Clinamen Press, 2000), ch. 8, and Henri Lefebvre's *Rhythmanalysis: Space, Time, and Everyday Life* (1985–92), trans. Stuart Elden and Gerald Moore (London: Continuum, 2004) are in the background here. For Lefebvre, all natural things, including human bodies, are composed of inter-woven, cyclical, rhythms which co-exist – often uneasily – with the linear rhythms of soci-ety. For Lefebvre, we all concretely experience our bodies, and other entities (p. 80), as 'rhythmed', although this experience gives us access to a dimension of reality which pre-exists human consciousness (p. 18). Two other theorists who address rhythm, and to whom Irigaray refers explicitly, are the linguist Emile Benveniste and the psychoanalyst Nicolas Abraham: see Chapter 3.

[23] On how Irigaray's early thought arises from, and against, Lacanian psychoanalysis, see Margaret Whitford, *Luce Irigaray*.

[24] On this, see Jacqueline Rose, 'Introduction – II' to Jacques Lacan, *Feminine Sexuality*, ed. Juliet Mitchell and Jacqueline Rose (New York: Norton, 1982), esp. p. 28: 'Sexual difference is constructed at a price and . . . it involves subjection to a law which exceeds any natural or biological division'.

them to acquire different psychical dispositions (and pathologies). Since Irigaray emphasises the importance of early infantile relationships to the mother, her later perspective remains broadly psychoanalytic, but some feminists may be unhappy about her shift away from the Lacanian insistence that sexed identities can never be completely or stably achieved. I shall not directly address this issue in this book because it can be satisfactorily resolved only once Irigaray's later philosophical approach is thoroughly understood. However, inasmuch as I criticise her exclusive belief in natural duality and attempt to show that sexual difference invariably co-exists with – and becomes disturbed by – multiple bodily drives, I hope, at least, to open up a perspective from which we can rethink Irigaray's later ideas consistently with a more Lacanian emphasis on the instability of any sexed identity.

My defence, criticism, and rethinking of Irigaray's later philosophy of sexual difference will be developed in the following stages. I begin, in Chapter 1, by reviewing feminist debates around essentialism, tracing how they intersected with the Anglophone reception of Irigaray's work, which early critics perceived as essentialist. More recent scholars have reinterpreted Irigaray as employing traditional essentialist notions of women merely 'strategically', to transform their meaning and revalue female identity. These reinterpretations make good sense of her earlier texts but are less well supported by her later writings, which claim that men and women naturally have different characters and abilities which deserve realisation and expression through a culture of sexual difference. Most scholars have assumed that this position, being realist, is unacceptably naïve epistemologically. In contrast, I will argue that Irigaray's later 'realist essentialism' (as I will call it) is more coherent than merely 'strategic' essentialism, since the latter aims to revalue female identity and bodies only as imagined and symbolised, reinforcing the conceptual hierarchy of culture over nature.

It might be argued, though, that even if bodies really have different characters which require expression, these characters need not be sexually *dual* as Irigaray holds. To bring out this point, Chapter 2 re-examines Butler's theory of gender. On my analysis, Butler's theory has three central components: an account of how bodies are shaped by socio-cultural norms concerning gender, a claim that there is constant slippage in the meaning of gender norms (leading to continual differences in women's and men's experiences and identities), and a political recommendation to subvert and dissolve dualistic gender norms. I argue, though, that Butler's account of bodies problematically privileges culture over nature and matter, a problem which vitiates her politics, since she justifies this politics in terms of an ethic of protecting bodies from harms to which they are vulnerable *qua* culturally formed entities. I conclude that Butler's theory should be reformulated as premised on the view that bodies naturally have multiple forces and capacities which require cultural realisation and expression, the subversion of dualistic gender norms being justified to promote this expression.

As Chapter 3 explores, the key question now becomes: which conception of bodies is true – the conception of bodily multiplicity which can be derived from Butler or Irigaray's conception of sexual duality? To support her belief in natural duality, Irigaray develops a philosophy on which all of nature follows polar rhythms, which come to their fullest realisation in human sexual dimorphism. This account of nature underpins her rethinking of sexual difference as a difference in rhythms which regulate the growth of male and female bodies. So defined, sexual difference is (Irigaray maintains) 'ontological'; this, one of her least understood claims, means that sexual difference exists at the level of 'being' or, what for her is equivalent, of nature as *physis*, open-ended growth into presence. She defends both her account of nature and her rethinking of sexual difference phenomenologically, on the grounds that they articulate embodied, pre-theoretical, experience. Yet belief in bodily multiplicity has phenomenological support from other aspects of our embodied experience, specifically our sense of having diverse, pre-volitional, motivations and potentials. In addition, the idea of bodily multiplicity better accommodates intersexed bodies, seeing them as manifesting, unusually clearly, the multiplicity inherent in all bodies. I conclude that both conceptions of bodies must be synthesised, a project which the remaining chapters pursue.

Sexual duality and multiplicity can be reconciled if they are reconceived as stages in an ongoing movement of nature towards increasing differentiation. I move towards this idea of self-differentiating nature, which is outlined by Schelling above all, by assessing Irigaray's own engagements with philosophy of nature, beginning in Chapter 4 with her reading of Hölderlin's and Heidegger's accounts of the relation between humanity and nature. Adapting their idea that nature is self-dividing, she argues that *male* nature originally tends to divide itself. Men naturally tend to react against the threat of sexual difference by denying this difference and, with it, nature and embodiment. Irigaray does not think that this self-dividing tendency is what makes men naturally male; rather, for her, men are male independently, in virtue of their distinctive natural rhythm. But because this rhythm leads men to experience the world in a specifically male way, they become aware – beginning with their relationship to their mothers in early infancy – that women have a different mode of experience, a difference which males perceive as a threat, and against which they tend to react (self-)divisively. If actualised, men's self-dividing tendency generates a patriarchal culture which is hostile to nature; however, Irigaray argues, this culture also can act back against male nature to redirect men's self-destructive tendencies against themselves and instil respect for sexual difference.[25] By appreciating how Irigaray adapts Hölderlin (and Heidegger), we see how she can claim that all cultures – including patriarchal culture – express our natures, without implying that patriarchal culture is immutable. On the negative side, her adaptation of Hölderlin presumes that there is an original, fixed, sexual duality in nature, overlooking his productive suggestion that nature originally undergoes a process of self-differentiation.

Chapter 5 turns to Irigaray's related engagement with Hegel's idea that social institutions can educate and redirect natural desires, an idea which arises out of his philosophy of nature and, specifically, his account of the relation between nature and mind. Building on Hegel, Irigaray proposes that the state should re-educate men's naturally self-opposing tendencies by introducing legal recognition of 'sexuate rights' – which are best understood as rights of all individuals to cultural self-expression as sexually specific beings. If legally enshrined, these rights would enable the emergence of a generalised culture of sexual difference, a culture which would inspire men to redirect their hostility against itself, enabling relations of respect between men and women. Irigaray's readings of Hegel thus underpin her controversial proposals for the legalisation of sexuate rights. These proposals are marred, I suggest, by their overestimation of the power of law and by Irigaray's assumption that the heterosexual

---

[25] The question arises of whether Irigaray believes that *all* men actualise these tendencies to (self-)destructive behaviour, or, rather, since manifestly there is considerable variation in male behaviour, how her thesis about male (self-)destructiveness can accommodate this variation. She might argue that some aspects of western culture must already be instilling a respect for sexual difference which serves to avert and redirect men's destructive tendencies. But this would conflict with her claim that our culture universally suppresses sexual difference (see Chapter 1, Section V). To explain the variations within male identity and behaviour, then, Irigaray would need to admit greater diversity in western culture, and this – as I will argue over the course of this book – would be possible only if she also acknowledged the reality of bodily multiplicity alongside that of duality.

family would remain the primary site for men and women to display their newly mutual respect.

Chapter 6 returns to Hölderlin's suggestion that nature is self-differentiating, elaborating this suggestion via Schelling's idea that nature spontaneously and continuously divides into 'productive' and 'inhibiting' forces. As I noted before, Irigaray herself ignores Schelling and to my knowledge never refers to or discusses him; but my claim is that his philosophy of nature provides a basis for rethinking her later ideas. For Schelling, all natural phenomena are polarised between productive and inhibiting forces, each pole embodying a determinate equilibrium between these forces. Schelling's thought implies that, as a movement of self-division, nature then pushes beyond each polarity by subdividing each pole from within. Accordingly, we can argue that nature first realises its polarity in human sexual duality then pushes on to give each individual body a character of internal diversity which conflicts with its sexual specificity. Recasting Irigaray, we may say that the denial and repression of sexual difference within patriarchal culture has, equally, repressed this self-differentiating movement of nature, which a culture of sexual difference would release. Consequently, a sexuate culture (*culture sexuée*) ought to express multiplicity as well, by promoting representations of sexed identities which embody a recognition that these identities are partial and limited.[26]

My proposal is that we should rethink sexual duality as a manifestation of self-differentiating nature, concomitantly rethinking sexuate culture as expressing a nature which necessarily also requires expression in its multiplicity. This rethinking of the nature and politics of sexual difference builds on the later Irigaray, retaining her valuable ideas that nature, as a process of growth, surrounds and shapes our bodies and that these bodies require a cultural expression which also brings nature to full realisation. But since the rethinking of sexual difference which I propose reconciles difference with multiplicity, it can combine these valuable Irigarayan ideas with Butler's equally valuable stress on differences among women (and among men) and on the need to dismantle constricting, dualistic, gender norms. I will conclude by bringing together the worthwhile elements of both Irigaray's and Butler's thought and explaining how my conception of self-differentiating nature retains and reconciles

---

[26] Irigaray uses the adjective 'sexuate' (*sexué*) – as I will throughout – in three main senses: (1) of law and rights, in the sense noted earlier; (2) of a culture insofar as it recognises sexual difference; and (3) of our natures *qua* sexed.

these. This idea of self-differentiating nature, I believe, enables a fruitful rethinking of Irigaray's later philosophy of sexual difference, which allows feminist thinkers to revalue nature, bodies, and sexual difference while, simultaneously, aiming for a culture which expresses the multiple forces within our bodies and allows us to develop these forces beyond the confines of fixed sexed identities.

1

Rereading Irigaray

Realism and Sexual Difference

The question of Irigaray's 'essentialism' has long been at the centre of controversy over the value of her work to feminist theory and politics. Yet the long-standing debates around Irigaray's essentialism may seem recently to have been laid to rest by the proliferation of scholarly investigations of the philosophical underpinnings of her thought, especially her thorough engagement with central themes from the history of philosophy.[1] One might imagine this research to have decisively superseded tired discussions of Irigaray's essentialism, which, one might suppose, were insufficiently philosophically informed to yield significant insight into her work. Actually, though, preceding debates over Irigaray's work have generated a network of now-standard assumptions about essentialism which continue to inform the otherwise diverse ways in which she is currently read.

In particular, those earlier debates have inspired a now-widespread assumption that no *realist* form of essentialism is acceptable and that, accordingly, Irigaray can only be read as essentialist in some distinctively non-realist sense.[2] By 'realism', I mean the view that we can know about

---

[1] For some examples, see: the essays in Burke et al., eds., *Engaging with Irigaray: Feminist Philosophy and Modern European Thought*; Tina Chanter, *Ethics of Eros: Irigaray's Rewriting of the Philosophers* (London: Routledge, 1995); Alison Martin, *Luce Irigaray and the Question of the Divine*; and Margaret Whitford, *Luce Irigaray.*

[2] See, for instance, Ellen T. Armour, *Deconstruction, Theology and the Problem of Difference: Subverting the Race/Gender Divide* (Chicago, Ill.: University of Chicago Press, 1999), ch. 4; Summers-Bremner, 'Reading Irigaray, Dancing', in *Hypatia* 15: 1 (2000), p. 112; Cathryn Vasseleu, *Textures of Light: Vision and Touch in Irigaray, Levinas and Merleau-Ponty* (London: Routledge, 1998), p. 9; Ping Xu, 'Irigaray's Mimicry and the Problem of Essentialism', in *Hypatia* 10: 4 (1995), pp. 76–89.

the world as it is independently of our practices and modes of representation. I therefore understand a realist form of essentialism to consist of the view that male and female bodies can be known to have essentially different characters, different characters which really exist, independently of how we represent and culturally inhabit these bodies. Realist essentialism, then, can equally be expressed as the view that natural differences between the sexes exist, prior to our cultural activities. The standard assumption which has come to guide Irigaray's readers is that such a realist form of essentialism can be neither philosophically tenable nor politically fruitful. This assumption is unhelpful, I wish to suggest in this chapter, since Irigaray's work displays a deepening commitment to just such a specifically realist essentialism, a position which she conceives to have transformative political implications.

A realist rereading of Irigaray's thought is unlikely to appear plausible or attractive unless it arises from sustained engagement with the dominant assumptions deposited by previous receptions of her work. We therefore need to re-examine the history of Irigaray's reception by (chiefly Anglophone) feminist thinkers, with reference to interwoven debates about essentialism. In the first and second sections of this chapter, I reconstruct how it became standard for scholars to assume that the only philosophically viable form of essentialism is a 'political', non-realist, essentialism, in terms of which Irigaray must therefore be read.[3] Then, in Section III, I argue that, far from being uniquely philosophically viable, the merely political essentialism now usually attributed to Irigaray is internally unstable. Political essentialism contains an internal tension insofar as it pursues the revaluation of femaleness and the body only as culturally imagined and symbolised, thereby reinforcing the very valorisation of symbolic over corporeal, cultural over natural, which it seeks to contest. I argue, therefore, that feminist essentialism can become coherent only if it seeks to revalue and transfigure *real* – and sexually different – bodies, by pursuing their cultural expression and enhancement.[4] Feminist

---

[3] My distinction between 'political' and 'realist' essentialism may seem confusing, since I will defend realist essentialism partly for its transformative political implications. So, to clarify, I am using the term 'realist essentialism' to mean a form of essentialism which is both realist *and also* political, whereas what I call 'political essentialism' is non-realist and so *merely* political.

[4] Whenever Irigaray claims that our natures need cultural expression, she relies on a complex conception of culture which she never really unpacks. 'Culture', generally, refers to: the process of intellectual development and education; a people's way of life; and intellectual and artistic activity and its products. See Raymond Williams, *Keywords: A Vocabulary of Culture and Society* (revised edn.; London: Flamingo, 1983), pp. 87–93. Irigaray's

essentialism, that is, must become realist.[5] This argument makes it possible to reread Irigaray as essentialist in this realist sense – as advocating, as she says, the 'cultivation of the real, a natural real: . . . the real of nature itself and all the living beings' (KW, 148).

Before defending such a rereading of Irigaray, it is important to acknowledge the complexity of her thought, which does not always straightforwardly support my interpretation. Irigaray's work is grounded in sustained engagement with psychoanalysis and the history of philosophy, and she never uses the terms 'political' or 'realist' essentialism. I have distilled these terms from Anglophone debates about essentialism, rather than from the philosophical traditions which Irigaray primarily addresses. Nonetheless, the terms 'political' and 'realist' essentialism demarcate substantive theoretical positions, where the latter position can be recognised as identical to the philosophical standpoint which Irigaray's work increasingly adopts. Thus, although Irigaray does not call herself a realist essentialist, this term may still be fruitfully applied in understanding her thought.

It must also be admitted that Irigaray's thought has changed considerably over time and does not unvaryingly support a realist construal. Rather, as Irigaray's thought develops, we see her move from political to realist essentialism. She passes from her early project of reimagining the symbolically female (in *Speculum* of 1974 and *This Sex Which Is Not One* of 1977) to an increasing recognition that this reimagining must, simultaneously, involve revaluing the body. She also increasingly recognises that this revaluation requires the elaboration of a new ontology in which bodies are active, self-expressive, and have naturally determinate

---

understanding of culture incorporates all these connotations, besides focusing – in her earlier work – on the role of symbolic patterns in organising culture.

5 I should clarify how my understanding of realist essentialism relates to Locke's distinction between real and nominal essences, which several feminist thinkers have appropriated. For Locke, real essences are the unknowable physical constitutions of things, from which their perceptible qualities derive. Nominal essences are our complex, culturally varying, definitions of those things, formed as we select from among their perceptible qualities: see Locke, *An Essay Concerning Human Understanding* (1690), ed. John W. Yolton (London: J. M. Dent, 1976), pp. 217–19, 229–44. Following Locke, Teresa de Lauretis argues that feminist essentialists do not attempt to describe women's real essence but to redefine women's nominal essence, by transforming accepted ideas about women's 'qualities, properties, and attributes' ('The Essence of the Triangle or, Taking the Risk of Essentialism Seriously: Feminist Theory in Italy, the U.S., and Britain', in *The Essential Difference*, ed. Schor and Weed, p. 3). It can be seen that, in my terms, de Lauretis is espousing a version of merely political essentialism. Irigaray differs from both Locke and de Lauretis in that, on her realist essentialism, the real characters of sexed bodies are not an imperceptible substratum but can be known and given cultural expression.

features which exist independently of any processes of cultural construction (throughout, I use 'ontology' simply to mean a theory or view about the nature of reality, and about what types of thing really exist).[6] Irigaray outlines such an ontology of active, self-expressive, bodies in *An Ethics of Sexual Difference* (1984) – the text which marks the transition to her later belief in real, naturally existing, sexual difference. In subsequent works, she sees – as I trace in Section IV – that her notion of self-expressive bodies entails a revised analysis of cultural structures and institutions as expressing, more or less well, our real, active, and sexually different bodies. She concludes that existing cultural structures fail to express female bodies, making it imperative that we transform those structures to enable women's greater bodily self-expression and development. Irigaray articulates these claims in her later, politically focused, writings, from *Sexes and Genealogies* (1987) onwards.

Some scholars view Irigaray's later work as relatively naïve, precisely in virtue of its belief that sexual difference is natural and exists independently of culture.[7] In contrast, I hope to suggest that this later work is ultimately *more* philosophically coherent, representing Irigaray's most consistent working-through of the essentialism which she has endorsed from her earliest writings. Nonetheless, in defending the philosophical coherence of Irigaray's realist essentialism, I do not mean to portray it as unproblematic. Section V surveys some immediately pressing problems with Irigaray's belief in natural sexual difference. This overview forms the point of departure for the deeper critical examination of Irigaray's philosophy of natural sexual difference which I pursue in subsequent chapters.

I. Early Criticisms of Irigaray's Essentialism

Early receptions of Irigaray in the late 1970s and 1980s were dominated by often-virulent criticism of her 'essentialism'.[8] Critics focused

---

[6] Other feminists have spoken of sexual difference as 'ontological' in a more specialised sense, drawing on Heidegger's distinction between the 'ontological' (which concerns being) and the 'ontic' (which concerns entities); see, for instance, Joanna Hodge, 'Irigaray Reading Heidegger', in *Engaging with Irigaray*, ed. Burke et al. I explain Heidegger's distinction, and Irigaray's take-up of it, in Chapter 3. An 'ontology', in the more general sense in which I use the term here, is equally a 'metaphysics' – an account of the nature of reality.

[7] For the charge of naïvety, see, for example, Cornell, *At the Heart of Freedom: Feminism, Sex, and Equality* (Princeton: Princeton University Press, 1998), pp. 119–23.

[8] Classic critiques are by Toril Moi, *Sexual/Textual Politics: Feminist Literary Theory* (London: Methuen, 1985), pp. 139–47; Monique Plaza, ' "Phallomorphic Power" and the Psychology of "Woman" ', in *Ideology and Consciousness* 4 (1978), pp. 5–36; Janet Sayers, *Sexual*

especially on the essentialism which they detected within certain essays in Irigaray's *This Sex Which Is Not One*. Its closing essay, 'When Our Lips Speak Together', poetically evokes the female body and female auto- and homo-eroticism, stressing the interplay between two sets of lips as the principle for a distinctive style of exchange and speech, which she calls a 'speaking (as) woman' (*parler-femme*) (TS, 135/133). Earlier in *This Sex*, Irigaray offers a more theoretical description of this female mode of speech and eroticism:

> Woman's autoeroticism is very different from that of man. In order to touch himself, he needs an instrument: his hand, a woman's genitals, language . . . As for woman, she touches herself in and of herself without the need for a mediation . . . Woman 'touches herself' all the time, . . . for her genitals [*sexe*] are formed of two lips that embrace continuously. (24/24)

Likewise, she refers to 'that touching of *at least two* (lips) which keeps woman in touch with herself, but without any possibility of distinguishing what is touching from what is touched' (26/26). She appears to be claiming that female anatomy engenders a particularly direct form of autoeroticism, which, in turn, can ground a distinctively female form of diffuse and polyvalent communication. Seemingly, too, Irigaray maintains that western culture has repressed the possibility of these distinctively female forms, validating only male forms of desire and speech. Culture should therefore be transformed so that each woman may 'articulat[e] the reality [*réalité*] of [her] sex' (149/145).

What did Irigaray's early critics mean when they castigated this position as 'essentialist'? To answer this question clearly, we must address four interrelated issues. Firstly, what was generally understood by 'essentialism' within contemporary feminist theory and philosophy? Secondly, why was essentialism generally found problematic? Thirdly, in what specific way did critics judge Irigaray's work to exemplify essentialism? Finally, what did critics find wrong with Irigaray's alleged version of essentialism?

Within philosophy generally, essentialism is the view that things have essential properties, properties that are necessary to those things being what they are. Recontextualised within feminist philosophy, essentialism comes to denote the view that there are properties which are essential to women (or men, although feminist discussion has generally focused on women). These properties are essential in that any woman must

Contradictions: Psychology, Psychoanalysis, and Feminism (London: Tavistock, 1986), pp. 42–7. For a recent reformulation, see Abigail Bray, 'Not Woman Enough: Irigaray's Culture of Difference', in *Feminist Theory* 2: 3 (2001), pp. 314–15.

necessarily have those properties to be a woman at all. So defined, essentialism entails a closely related view, *universalism*: that there are some properties which are shared by, or common to, all women – since without those properties they could not be women in the first place. Essential properties, then, are also universal. 'Essentialism' as generally debated in feminist contexts embraces this composite view: that there are properties essential to women and which all women therefore share.[9]

Although many prominent second-wave feminist theorists endorsed forms of essentialism, subsequent critics argued that claims about women's universal features are invariably false, as women do not really share any unitary pattern of experience, psychic identity, or position within social and cultural relations.[10] According to anti-essentialists, any generalisations about women only tacitly project particular forms of feminine experience as the norm, thereby duplicating the patterns of exclusion and oppression which feminism should contest.[11] However, it might be thought that we can uphold essentialism without postulating any social or cultural characteristics common to all women, if we instead identify women's essential properties with their biologically female characteristics. Yet anti-essentialists reply that biology, too, is always culturally mediated: we only experience and inhabit our bodies through cultural representations, which entails that bodies in fact partake of the same diversity as the socio-cultural field mediating them.[12] So, anti-essentialists conclude, any claims concerning a purportedly generic female biology are mere false generalisations from certain, culturally specific, constructions of female embodiment.

In *This Sex*, Irigaray seems to assert that women are constituted as women by their unique anatomy (their labia). Furthermore, she apparently thinks that this anatomy gives rise to other characteristics

---

[9] Naomi Schor cautions against 'essentialising' essentialism, which itself has not 'one' but multiple forms; see her 'This Essentialism Which Is Not One', p. 60. Ultimately, I agree with Schor, but I think a provisional definition of essentialism is indispensable for approaching and understanding debates around Irigaray.

[10] Prominent second-wave feminists to endorse forms of essentialism are Nancy Chodorow in *The Reproduction of Mothering* (Berkeley, CA: University of California Press, 1978), Catherine MacKinnon in 'Feminism, Marxism, Method and the State: An Agenda for Theory', in *Signs* 7 (1982), pp. 515–44, and Gilligan in *In a Different Voice*.

[11] For a critique of this feature of essentialism, see Elizabeth Spelman, *Inessential Woman: Problems of Exclusion in Feminist Thought* (London: The Women's Press, 1988).

[12] On bodies as socio-cultural and hence diverse, see Moira Gatens, *Imaginary Bodies*, esp. ch. 5; Elizabeth Grosz, *Volatile Bodies: Toward a Corporeal Feminism* (Bloomington: Indiana University Press, 1994), x–xi.

essential to all women (albeit currently repressed): a special mode of autoeroticism and a propensity to a special speaking style. For Irigaray, these other characteristics, although essential to women, derive ultimately from their bodies. As Monique Plaza says, it seems that, for Irigaray, the 'feminine essence . . . can only be discovered outside of the oppressive social framework, . . . *in the body of the woman*'.[13] Thus, Irigaray's apparent biological essentialism in *This Sex* seems closely linked to biological determinism – the view that bodily properties, not social arrangements, generate central features of women's condition such as their sexuality and speaking style.

Critics took issue, above all, with the *realism* implicit in Irigaray's apparent essentialism ('realism', to recall, denotes the view that we can know the world as it is independently of us and of our modes of representation). Irigaray seems to claim knowledge about female bodies as they really are, independent of their cultural representation. This includes knowledge of how the female body really operates, causally, to produce women's other essential characteristics. As Jane Gallop complains, 'Irigaray seems to propose the possibility of a language that can reflect women's natural specificity . . . transparently expressing the real'.[14] Irigaray's critics objected that we only ever approach and experience our bodies through a web of cultural representations: 'we never have access to anatomy *per se*, only anatomy as shaped/formed by *discourse*'.[15] These critics argued, as well, that in her misguided attempt to ignore this fact, Irigaray ended up naïvely reproducing traditional conceptions of women. As Gallop claims more generally: 'Belief in simple referentiality is . . . ultimately politically conservative, because it cannot recognise that the reality to which it

---

[13] Plaza, ' "Phallomorphic Power" ', p. 7.

[14] Gallop, '*Quand nos lèvres s'écrivent*: Irigaray's body politic', in *Romanic Review* 74: 1 (1983), p. 78. Others agree that essentialism is realist: according to Drucilla Cornell, essentialism propounds 'theories of who we truly are as women', 'a mere descriptive account of the way women are' (*Transformations: Recollective Imagination and Sexual Difference* (London: Routledge, 1993), pp. 5, 59). Likewise, according to Diana Fuss, essentialists see the body as ' "real", accessible, and transparent' (*Essentially Speaking: Feminism, Nature and Difference* (London: Routledge, 1989), p. 5). Fuss and Gallop defend (what I call) 'political essentialist' readings of Irigaray to avoid these problems – as does Cornell, although she declares herself an *anti*-essentialist, believing essentialism by definition realist. Indeed, several authors whom I classify as political essentialists are professed anti-essentialists (for example, see also note 33 below). I nonetheless believe that thinkers can legitimately be classified as political essentialists when their theoretical positions are identifiable as forms of political essentialism, even if they themselves do not use this label.

[15] Armour, *Deconstruction, Theology and the Problem of Difference*, p. 217.

appeals is a traditional ideological construction'.[16] For these critics, Irigaray's allegedly realistic description of women ended up simply reproducing the traditional idea that the female body grounds certain specially female characteristics: diffuse, uncontainable, sexuality and incessant, barely coherent, speech. Her pretended 'description' of women was, in fact, a dismayingly familiar artefact of patriarchal culture. From these critics' point of view, then, the enhanced cultural 'expression' of femaleness which Irigaray championed would be wholly undesirable, predicated on the acceptance of traditional stereotypical representations and serving only to consolidate their constricting power. So, the central criticism of Irigaray's 'essentialism' was that it rests on a misplaced faith in the possibility of describing the female body realistically, a faith which was thought to condemn Irigaray to regurgitate demeaning stereotypes about women uncritically.

II. Reading Irigaray as a Political Essentialist

By the early 1990s, these rather acerbic readings of Irigaray came to be widely viewed as inadequate. They had focused, highly selectively, on certain passages from *This Sex*, overlooking their background in Irigaray's complex reading of the history of western philosophy. Readers of Irigaray in the later 1980s and 1990s insisted on the necessity of attending to her work as a whole, especially its pervasive concern to criticise the symbolic structures which organise culture and regulate the formation of identities. Following the many feminist thinkers who employ the concept of the symbolic, I understand by 'symbolic structures' patterns of meaning, symbolism, and association which play an organising role in dominant areas of culture such as religion, philosophy, myth, art, and literature, and which bind these areas into an interlocking 'symbolic order'.[17] Such feminist understandings of the symbolic order, which largely derive from

---

[16] Gallop, '*Quand nos lèvres s'écrivent*', p. 83. Likewise, for Cornell, essentialism overlooks the linguistic constitution of reality and so necessarily ends up 'reinstating the vision of what is proper to us in patriarchal society' (*Transformations*, p. 71). Sayers agrees: because Irigaray (and others) 'mistake the historical genesis of the construction of woman . . . as depicting an eternal given, they not only fail to challenge that construction – they positively wallow in it' (*Sexual Contradictions*, p. 47). See also Plaza, ' "Phallomorphic Power" ', pp. 7, 31.

[17] Michelle Boulous Walker, for example, defines the 'symbolic law' as 'the mythologies, philosophies and literatures that combine to create cultural life' (*Philosophy and the Maternal Body: Reading Silence* (London: Routledge, 1998), p. 52).

Irigaray, broaden the more technical concept of the symbolic found in Lacanian psychoanalysis. For Lacan, the symbolic means language as a publicly given social structure.[18] While broadening the reach of the symbolic beyond the narrowly linguistic, feminists accept Lacan's view that symbolic structures form us as individual subjects and agents, where participation in these structures requires our prior repression of incommensurable desires and aspects of our experience. Feminist theorists of the symbolic also share Lacan's view that symbolic structures are fundamentally articulated around concepts of sexual difference.

Irigaray believes, more specifically, that the symbolic patterns which organise western culture are articulated through an understanding of the sexes which has been defined and redefined within the philosophical tradition: 'philosophical discourse . . . sets forth the law for all others, . . . it constitutes the discourse on discourse' (TS, 74/72). For Irigaray, philosophy legislates over other cultural and intellectual forms (for example, by defining what counts as a rational argument or a work of art), but philosophical texts also display particularly entrenched patterns of sexual symbolism which they communicate to the discourses over which they legislate. Irigaray's critique of western symbolic structures thus presents itself, primarily, as a critique of the philosophical tradition. Once this is acknowledged, it becomes apparent that we can only assess whether, and in what way, Irigaray is an essentialist after first understanding her analysis of the symbolic patterns embodied in western philosophical texts. We should therefore review the main features of her critical reading of the philosophical tradition in *Speculum*, then look at how increased awareness of this reading led to revised assessments of Irigaray's essentialism in the 1990s.

In *Speculum*, Irigaray criticises a series of canonical philosophers, starting with Freud and moving through Plato, Aristotle, Plotinus, Descartes, Kant, and Hegel before returning to Plato. Irigaray's basic claim is that this tradition insistently defines the female only in contrast to the male – as its absence, complement, inversion, or inadequate approximation. 'The "female" is always described as deficiency, atrophy, lack of the sex that has a monopoly on value: the male sex [*le sexe masculin*]' (TS, 69/68). For Irigaray, this traditional definition of the female has three interwoven aspects. Firstly, it devalues the female relative to the male: the contrast

---

[18] Feminist thinkers, such as Irigaray, define the symbolic more broadly than Lacan because they regard it as intertwined with the further dimension of the 'imaginary': see Section III.

between these terms is always hierarchical. Even when this hierarchy is not explicit, it is sustained through hierarchical contrasts between other, ostensibly neutral, concepts (such as mind and body) which have tacit sexual connotations. Secondly, the female is traditionally defined only in *relation* to the male, not as an independently intelligible term. Summarising her view on this, Irigaray remarks that in *Speculum* she 'showed how a single subject, traditionally the masculine subject, had constructed the world and interpreted the world according to a single perspective' (JLI, 97). Thirdly, for Irigaray, the definition of the female only in relation to the male amounts to a refusal of female identity. For this reason, she claims that our culture is 'monosexuate' – that sexual *difference* has never existed at the symbolic level, despite superficially abundant representations of women.

The claim that western culture has always denied sexual difference seems to contradict Irigaray's claim that this culture is centrally organised by understandings of sexual difference. This apparent contradiction finds dramatic expression when she declares that: 'Women's exploitation is based upon sexual difference; its solution will only come about through sexual difference' (JTN, 12/12). Her point, though, is that western culture interprets sexual difference as a hierarchical difference in which one sex (the female) is modelled on the other (the male), rather than as a difference within which each sex is *sui generis*. The hierarchical interpretation of sexual difference can therefore be said to 'deny' difference insofar as it denies that each sex has a *sui generis* identity. This hierarchical view is responsible for women's exploitation, in Irigaray's view, while the idea that each sex has its own identity – which would be an idea of 'sexual difference without hierarchy' – would, if institutionalised, terminate that exploitation.[19] Hereafter, whenever I refer to western culture's 'denial' or repression of sexual difference, I follow Irigaray in understanding this denial as coextensive with western culture's insistence on interpreting sexual difference in hierarchical terms.

Irigaray goes on to identify history's 'denial' of female identity with a suppression of the possibility of female subjectivity: 'All theories of the "subject" will have always been appropriated by the "masculine"' (S, 133/165). Philosophical tradition has disallowed women the autonomy and responsibility to interpret and define the meaning of being female in its own terms – irrespective of how femaleness relates to or

---

[19] Irigaray, interview with Elaine Hoffman Baruch and Lucienne J. Serrano in *Women Analyze Women*, ed. Baruch and Serrano (New York: New York University Press, 1988), p. 154.

compares with maleness. Notably, here, Irigaray is criticising the tradition, not for misrepresenting or failing to express women's real nature but rather for closing off from women any possibility of defining their female identity in a self-directed manner.

At this point one might wonder why, if Irigaray criticises the negative impact of cultural understandings on women's subjectivity, I have persistently referred to these as understandings of the *female* and not the feminine. Within English-speaking feminism, it is common to describe elements of biological sex as female and elements of social gender as feminine (for example, 'female anatomy' and 'feminine roles'). Since Irigaray criticises cultural understandings, it appears that she must be criticising conceptions which are constituents of gender (although she herself does not use any sex/gender distinction, simply referring to that which philosophical tradition devalues as the *sexe féminin*). However, Irigaray distinguishes the realm of culture and symbolism from that of social roles and relationships; she complains, for instance, that most feminists pay

insufficient attention to the fact that 'women's liberation' requires an exacting cultural effort, and not just strategies for social emancipation . . . We need to . . . understand that the human subject, woman or man, is not a mere social effect . . . And whoever renounces the specificity of both female subjectivity and identity, reducing them to simple social determinations, sacrifices even more women to patriarchy. (WD, 11)

For Irigaray, the cultural or symbolic realm – where injustice to women principally occurs – is distinguished from the social realm in several respects. The cultural realm fundamentally shapes our subjectivity, outlining identities which we must take up to become individual agents in the first place. As such, the assumption of these identities has pronounced psychical effects, necessitating a complete reorganisation of psychical life. Moreover, the patterns of sexual symbolism which structure the symbolic order are long-lasting; their content does not automatically change in response to social upheavals. Finally, these patterns consistently understand women as pre-eminently bodily beings, who are peculiarly immersed in and constrained by their bodies. Our cultural understandings thus concern women *as a sex*, and are best described as understandings of not the feminine but the female.

We see, then, that Irigaray's concern in her early work is to criticise the pejorative understandings of the female which she finds in the philosophical tradition. From the later 1980s onwards, her readers began to insist that a full appreciation of her apparently essentialist passages must situate them in the context of this ambitious critique of western philosophy.[20] This insistence on reading Irigaray in relation to philosophy converged with a broader trend in feminist theory questioning its now-widespread rejection of essentialism. This rejection was problematic because it appeared to undercut the possibility of feminist politics: if women share no common characteristics, they cannot readily be expected to mobilise in response to a common plight, or around any shared political identity or sense of allegiance. Confronted by this problem, several theorists began to advocate a new, 'strategic', form of essentialism.[21] According to this, we should acknowledge that essentialism is false: women have no shared social location or unitary female biology. Nonetheless, we should continue to act, strategically, as if essentialism were true, where this furthers political purposes. Such action is strategic because, as Denise Riley explains: 'it is compatible to suggest that "women" don't exist – while maintaining a politics of "as if they existed" – since the world behaves as if they unambiguously did'.[22] That is, essentialist preconceptions are deeply embedded in dominant symbolic structures, so much so that they can be overcome only when confronted and – paradoxically as it may seem – repeated and redoubled. Crucially, this strategic form of essentialism is *non-realist*. It does not hold that women really have essential characteristics independently of cultural practices but, rather, claims that many traditions and practices (falsely) insist that women have such characteristics, traditions which can be challenged only through the strategic reaffirmation of precisely those essential characteristics on which they insist.

The emergence of strategic essentialism suggested to those reading Irigaray in the late 1980s and early 1990s that her detractors had relied on an oversimplified view of essentialism and its political potential. There could, it had emerged, be different '*kinds* of essentialisms', with varying political consequences.[23] In particular, it seemed, a non-realist brand of essentialism could be politically transformative, and this opened up possibilities for reading Irigaray as essentialist in a non-realist

---

[20] See, for example, Fuss, *Essentially Speaking*, p. 71; Whitford, *Luce Irigaray*, pp. 2–3.

[21] 'Strategic' essentialism is associated with Gayatri Chakravorty Spivak, who coined the term (apropos of subaltern studies) in 'Feminism, Criticism and the Institution', in *Thesis Eleven* 10/11 (1984/5), pp. 175–87.

[22] Riley, *'Am I That Name?': Feminism and the Category of 'Women' in History* (London: Macmillan, 1988), p. 112.

[23] Fuss, *Essentially Speaking*, p. 4.

sense. As Margaret Whitford summed up this new mood, 'the binary pair essentialism/antiessentialism has been put into question. This enables essentialism to be interpreted as a *position* rather than as an ontology, and Irigaray to be interpreted as a strategist . . . rather than as an obscurantist prophet of essential biological or psychic difference'.[24] On the emerging non-realist interpretations, Irigaray's form of essentialism functions primarily to contest the entrenched devaluation of the female within philosophical orthodoxy. She does not intend her essentialism to describe the female body realistically but to reaffirm traditional representations of the female (through sustained mimicry and paraphrase of philosophical texts) in a way which operates, politically, to subvert their meaning. Accordingly, some commentators, such as Whitford, designate Irigaray's reconceived essentialism strategic.[25] This adjective, though, misleadingly suggests a merely temporary, and deliberate, adoption of essentialism in precisely delimited situations. Yet Irigaray is opposing a denigration of the female which is deeply enshrined in fundamental symbolic structures: she must therefore uphold essentialism on a longer-term basis, as not a transitory tactic but an ongoing 'stage' in feminist activism.[26] Irigaray's reconceived essentialism is better described as *political*, rather than narrowly strategic. *Qua* political, this essentialism is espoused as a means to change, not a descriptive truth: it makes no ontological commitment to the real existence of natural female qualities. Instead of describing women's nature, Irigaray aims to challenge traditional philosophical essentialism through its counter-affirmation.

But how can such reaffirmation oppose, and not simply duplicate, philosophical tradition? On (what I will call) the political reading of Irigaray, she repeats traditional conceptions of the female in a way which subtly transforms them – in two closely interwoven respects. Firstly, Irigaray revalues the female, lending it a worth and importance traditionally denied it. Secondly, she effects a shift in the content of the female, redefining it as intelligible independently of masculinity, as an identity in its own right. As a whole, then, Irigaray endeavours to redefine and

---

[24] Whitford, 'Reading Irigaray in the Nineties' in *Engaging with Irigaray*, ed. Burke et al., p. 16. Spivak agrees that: 'It is only if Irigaray is read as the pure theoretical prose of truth . . . that she may seem essentialist'; see *Outside in the Teaching Machine* (London: Routledge, 1993), p. 17.

[25] As does, for instance, Elizabeth Grosz, *Sexual Subversions: Three French Feminists* (Sydney: Allen and Unwin, 1989), p. 110.

[26] Naomi Schor, 'Previous Engagements: The Receptions of Irigaray', in *Engaging with Irigaray*, ed. Burke et al., p. 11.

revalue the female as symbolised in philosophical history. The 'essential' femaleness that Irigaray reaffirms thus differs subtly, though decisively, from that originally affirmed in traditional texts.

Typically, Irigaray's reconceptions of female identity effect a simultaneous reconception of matter and the body. This is no coincidence: as we have seen, she thinks that femaleness has traditionally been equated with matter, and women positioned as pre-eminently corporeal, immersed and ensnared in their bodies. Given this, Irigaray's essentialist project necessarily involves what Gallop calls the 're-metaphorisation' of the body together with women.[27] Irigaray's evocations of women's lips and their diffuse autoeroticism belong within this project: these evocations reiterate women's traditional connection with corporeality, but in a way which redefines this connection positively, as the source of an independent identity with its own specific worth. The lips, as Nicola Lacey explains, furnish a 'metaphor' or 'image' for a new 'form of feminine and relational human subjectivity', positively valorised for its fidelity to its corporeal roots.[28] So the point of this image is by no means to describe female anatomy and its causal effects realistically (as Irigaray's earlier detractors maintained). As Elizabeth Grosz maintains, the lips image is 'in no way a "true" or accurate description of women. Its function is not referential but combatative'.[29] Specifically, the image combats the historically intertwined denigration of the female and the corporeal.

Readings of Irigaray as a merely political essentialist quickly became favoured over the earlier realist readings, partly on textual grounds – because the newer readings better accommodated the full range of her early work – but also because they seemed, more charitably, to attribute to Irigaray a philosophically cogent position. Surely, it was thought, she could not be so epistemologically naïve as to believe it possible to describe reality and the body as they are independent of our modes of representation. Irigaray must be aware that there has been sustained 'philosophical critique of attempts to "objectively" describe women's "nature"'.[30] On charitable grounds, then, it was thought that Irigaray's evocations of the female body must be construed as political interventions aimed

---

[27] Gallop, '*Quand nos lèvres s'écrivent*', p. 83.

[28] Lacey, *Unspeakable Subjects: Feminist Essays in Legal and Social Theory* (Oxford: Hart, 1998), p. 110. Boulous Walker concurs that this image conveys that self and other are interrelated, faithfully reflecting 'the complex relationality of mother and girl-child' (*Philosophy and the Maternal Body*, p. 157).

[29] Grosz, *Sexual Subversions*, p. 116; see also Whitford, *Luce Irigaray*, pp. 171–3.

[30] Cornell, *Transformations*, p. 5; see also Chanter, *Ethics of Eros*, pp. 2–3.

at changing the symbolic order. Notably, here, political essentialist readers of Irigaray shared one key philosophical assumption with her earlier critics: namely, the assumption that realist essentialism is unacceptably naïve epistemologically, and in its naïvety it can only end up replicating traditional conceptions of women, reinforcing patriarchal oppression. Political essentialists differed from Irigaray's earlier critics in that they *also* believed a merely political form of essentialism to be possible, and, indeed, to be strategically necessary and to define Irigaray's project.

Certainly, the political essentialist reading is textually well supported by Irigaray's critique of philosophy in *Speculum* and her methodological reflections in *This Sex*. After all, she herself contends that

women . . . should not [ask] 'What is woman?' but rather, repeating-interpreting the way in which, within discourse, the female finds itself defined as lack, deficiency, or as imitation and inverted image of the subject, they should signify that with respect to this logic a *disruptive excess* is possible from the female side. (TS, 78/76)[31]

But Irigaray's later writings support the political essentialist reading significantly less well: they insistently describe sexual difference as 'real' (*réel*) and as 'natural reality' (TD, xi/11; ILTY, 39/70, 50/89, 54/96). For instance, she claims that: 'The natural is at least two: male and female . . . we should make reality the point of departure: it is *two* . . . The universal has been thought as *one*, thought on the basis of *one*. But this *one* does not exist' (ILTY, 35/65). On this basis, Irigaray criticises western symbolic structures and institutions for their estrangement from the reality of sexual difference:

I start from reality, from a universal reality, sexual difference. . . . [T]his reality of the *two* has always existed. But it was submitted to the imperatives of a logic of the *one*. . . . My procedure consists therefore in substituting, for a universal constructed out of only one part of reality, a universal which respects the totality of the real. . . . This forces us to refound our culture, our societies in order to reach a civilization at the same time more real, more just, and more universal. (WD, 146–7)

According to Irigaray's later works, the denial of real sexual difference leads to a myriad of other social problems: ecological degradation, alienation, war, racism, and nationalism.[32] One possible response is to reject

---

[31] In *This Sex*, Irigaray repeatedly distances herself from any realist essentialist project of stating 'what woman is' (TS, 122/121) or of producing a theory 'of which woman would be the object' (135/133).

[32] See Pheng Cheah and Elizabeth Grosz, 'Of Being-Two', in *Diacritics* 28: 1 (1998), pp. 3–18.

Irigaray's later work for sliding back to an epistemologically naïve (realist) position already surpassed by her earlier work.[33] But I wish to challenge that conclusion, by arguing against its presupposition that no cogent form of realist essentialism is possible. This will provide a vantage point from which to develop a realist interpretation of Irigaray's later writings.

III. Going Beyond Political Essentialism: Irigaray's Conception of Self-Expressive Bodies

As I have traced, the controversies surrounding Irigaray's work have given rise to a standard assumption that realist essentialism is philosophically implausible, whereas political essentialism is deemed both epistemologically cogent and politically radical. In this section, I shall argue, in contrast, that political essentialism is inherently unstable and can be made cogent only if developed into a full-blown realist essentialism. Political essentialism is unstable in that it contests the devaluation only of bodies as symbolised and imagined culturally, reinforcing the very privileging of the cultural over the corporeal which it purports to undermine. This instability can be surmounted only through a form of essentialism which seeks to revalue and enhance natural bodies by pursuing their cultural expression and development.

At first, my objection to political essentialism may seem misplaced. After all, political essentialists do not conceive the symbolic realm as narrowly opposed to the corporeal but rather as mediating corporeal experience, with which cultural structures always remain interwoven. Thus, Penelope Deutscher notes that 'the exclusion of sexual difference is not

---

[33] Another alternative is to reinterpret Irigaray's later work as merely politically essentialist, as does Deutscher in *A Politics of Impossible Difference*. (Admittedly, Deutscher claims to offer an *anti*-essentialist reading of Irigaray because she considers all essentialism realist [*Politics*, p. 111], but see note 14). Deutscher argues, for instance, that Irigaray defends 'sexuate rights' not because they would recognise the naturally existing identities of the two sexes but because they would *institute* an independently defined female identity whose possibility is presently foreclosed (p. 70). I think that Deutscher jettisons too much of Irigaray's later emphasis on the (currently denied and repressed) reality of sexual difference, and on the need for cultural structures which recognise this reality. Consider, for example, Irigaray's entirely typical statement that 'it is important to elaborate a still nonexistent culture of the sexual which respects the two *genres*. It is quite simply a matter of social justice to balance out the power one sex or *genre* has over the other by giving ... rights to women, rights *appropriate to* their sexed bodies [*corps sexués*]' (JTN, 80/98; emphasis added). Or, as she also states, we should create 'rights appropriate to the two sexes in place of abstract rights appropriate to *non-existent* neutral individuals' (TD, xv/15; emphasis added). A plausible interpretation of Irigaray's later work must accommodate its realist orientation.

just the exclusion of an idea. This is a lived corporeal, not just a conceptual, exclusion'.[34] Consequently, each woman 'lives an inhibited embodiment marked by one's sense that a . . . diverse range of possibilities is prohibited in advance'.[35] Because the way we inhabit our bodies is always culturally mediated, the cultural devaluation of the female, and of corporeality which is construed as female, adversely affects women's ways of inhabiting their bodies and practically engaging with the world. In view of these effects, Rosi Braidotti denies that the symbolic can be clearly distinguished from the material.[36] Political essentialists anticipate that symbolic change would simultaneously transform lived corporeal existence, by transforming the culture which mediates it.

Central to political essentialists' understanding of the interconnection between symbolic structures and lived embodiment is the concept of the *imaginary*. For political essentialist readers of Irigaray, the symbolic realm is simultaneously an 'imaginary' order, in the sense that its organising understandings of sexual difference are embodied in webs of imagery. To clarify, we can consider Patricia Huntingdon's claim (which is informed by Irigaray) that

variations in metaphysical conceptualisations of Being are . . . modelled after the morphological marks of the male body. Metaphysical depictions that reify Being as transcendent principle, first cause, absolute spirit, or powerful God evince a consistent privileging of phallic attributes.[37]

Huntingdon's point is that philosophical concepts are symbolised as male or female, where male and female, in turn, are defined in terms of their respective types of body as these are imagined – tacitly – within the philosophical and cultural tradition. Hence, the 'first cause' is symbolised as male in that it is assumed to share the form of the male body imagined as solid, phallic, erect, and unified.[38] Political essentialists believe, then,

---

[34] Deutscher, *Politics*, p. 119.

[35] Ibid., p. 119.

[36] Braidotti, *Metamorphoses: Towards a Materialist Theory of Becoming* (Cambridge, U.K.: Polity Press, 2002), p. 114–15.

[37] Huntingdon, *Ecstatic Subjects, Utopia, and Recognition* (Albany: SUNY Press, 1998), p. 48.

[38] The claim that concepts of male identity are embedded in imagery of the male body may seem to contradict Irigaray's view that concepts of the female and the corporeal are uniquely linked. However, according to feminist historians of philosophy, male bodies are traditionally imagined to be uniquely so formed that their inhabitants can transcend them; see Lloyd, *The Man of Reason* (second edition; London: Routledge, 1993), pp. 86–102.

that traditional understandings of sexual difference are supported by webs of imagery concerning sexed bodies, imagery which becomes embedded and articulated in the symbolic order. Through their incorporation in culture, these webs of imagery come to organise our entire corporeal life: as one assumes a cultural identity, one necessarily also acquires a particular image of one's body, an image through which one comes to experience and practically inhabit that body. As is conveyed by Freud's famous statement that 'the ego is first and foremost a bodily ego', one's sense of self becomes indissolubly linked to an 'imaginary' sense of one's body.[39]

On political essentialist readings of Irigaray, the symbolic is not narrowly opposed to the corporeal; rather, the symbolic incorporates an imaginary dimension which filters into how we live our bodies. In view of this intertwining of symbolic and imaginary registers, I must complicate my account of political essentialism, which I presented earlier as centring on the epistemological claim that we can only know bodies via cultural representations. We can now see that this apparently epistemological claim is, in fact, ultimately *ontological*: it reflects a determinate view about the real relationship between cultural representations and bodies – a view about what that relationship is really like. According to this view, cultural mediations shape how we inhabit our bodies and so shape how those bodies develop and act. Ultimately, bodies just *are* something shaped, mediated, and inhabited via cultural representations. Elizabeth Grosz, for instance, speaks (while explicating Irigaray) of a 'body that exists as such only through its socio-linguistic construction . . . Power relations

---

[39] See Freud, 'The Ego and the Id', in *On Metapsychology: The Theory of Psychoanalysis*, trans. James Strachey (Harmondsworth: Penguin, 1984), p. 364. Theorists call this web of culturally articulated imagery an 'imaginary' to capture the fact that it is publicly shared and preconditions individual agency, including individual powers of imagination (see Kathleen Lennon, 'Imaginary Bodies and Worlds', in *Inquiry* 47 (2004), pp. 107–22; Gail Weiss, *Body Images: Embodiment as Intercorporeality* (London: Routledge, 1999), p. 37). The concept of the imaginary descends from Lacan, who considers it an enduring stage of psychic development, beginning when the child identifies with its unified image as reflected by a 'mirror', which may consist of other people (especially the mother) who convey to the child their image of it; see Lacan, 'The Mirror Stage as Formative of the Function of the I', in *Écrits*, trans. Alan Sheridan (London: Tavistock, 1977), pp. 1–7. Whereas for Lacan the symbolic opposes the imaginary, breaking down fixed self-images by embroiling us in endless processes of linguistic signification, Irigaray and subsequent feminist thinkers think that the imaginary structures, and is embedded in, the symbolic. Consequently, unlike Lacan, they see the content of the imaginary as open to rearticulation and change (while, also, broadening the compass of the symbolic); see Whitford, *Luce Irigaray*, pp. 62–70.

and systems of representations . . . actively constitute the body's very sensations, pleasures'.[40] Braidotti, too, maintains that bodies are continuously 'built up' within the social field.[41] So the key point for political essentialists is not, after all, that representations veil our access to bodies as they might be 'in themselves'. Rather, their key point is that bodies are items which only ever take shape under the influence of cultural representations. Prior to this representational shaping, there *are* no bodies properly speaking but only what we might call (rather cumbersomely) a proto-bodily matter, which is naturally indeterminate. This (proto-)bodily matter is elevated into determinate, bodily form only by being acculturated. This view entails, though, that matter cannot shape the process whereby it is acculturated and made corporeal. Having no determinate natural character, there is nothing in matter which could work as an internal principle of activity, impelling it to respond to, react upon, or redirect the representations which engage it. Nothing inheres in (proto-)bodily matter which could galvanise it to shape or inflect the process of its own acculturation.

However, in maintaining that matter is indeterminate and passive in the face of cultural representations, political essentialism inadvertently reinstates a cluster of established conceptual hierarchies: between form and matter, culture and nature, and between the realm of meaning and symbolism and that of brute facticity and givenness. As Irigaray has maintained, each of these hierarchies identifies its second term as dependent and passive relative to the first – claiming, for example, that indeterminate matter first receives shape from form. Moreover, each hierarchy also valorises its first term over its second, interpreting these terms, respectively, as male and female. In terms of its implicit ontological assumptions, political essentialism paradoxically repeats the very devaluation of female matter which it aspires to expose and undermine at the symbolic level.[42]

To surmount this problem, we need a revised ontology according to which matter shapes the process whereby it becomes acculturated and, in this sense, exerts agency with respect to cultural processes. Several feminist thinkers have recognised this: Karen Barad, for example, has claimed

---

[40] Grosz, *Sexual Subversions*, p. 111.
[41] Braidotti, *Metamorphoses*, p. 99. At other times, however, Braidotti postulates really existing bodily forces; see Chapter 3, Section VI.
[42] For a similar criticism, see Vicki Kirby, *Telling Flesh: The Substance of the Corporeal* (London: Routledge, 1997), pp. 73–6.

that we must 'take account of how the body's materiality – for example, its anatomy and physiology – ... actively matter[s] to the processes of materialization'.[43] We need, firstly, to reconceive bodily matter as actively impelled to inflect and modify inherited cultural forms. But this requires, secondly, that we reconceive matter as having inherent shape and character, which it strives to realise. Only if matter has such a tendency to develop in accordance with its inherent character will it be impelled to adapt the content of cultural forms so that they give some expression and realisation to that character. Now, this second step might be challenged.[44] Elizabeth Grosz, for instance, thinks that matter endeavours to realise itself by adapting the content of representations, but she denies that this requires matter to have naturally determinate character(s). She insists that matter lacks determinate character prior to cultural inscription, defining it as 'malleable materiality', marked by 'plasticity and openness' and 'fundamentally open to history, to transformation'.[45] Nevertheless, for Grosz, formless matter actively endeavours to represent itself through cultural forms, and so matter is a 'locus of impetus and force' which carries out 'subversions of cultural life'. The problem is, though, that this notion of material activity is redundant unless matter is active in some *determinate* way, endeavouring to alter the content of cultural representations in some particular direction. Yet any determinate mode of material activity must have its ground in some determinate character which impels matter to exert this activity, a character which must exist pre-culturally, as matter's inherent nature. Because Grosz denies matter any such character, she can only attribute to it an impetus to a generalised 'becoming', 'evolution', and 'mutation', modes of activity which

---

[43] Barad, 'Posthumanist Performativity: Toward an Understanding of How Matter Comes to Matter', in *Signs* 28: 3 (2003), p. 809.

[44] One might object (appealing to the distinction between weaker and stronger forms of philosophical essentialism – see Introduction, this volume) that bodies can have inherent characters but need not strive to realise these. My argument here, though, is only that *if* we want to identify bodies as inherently active, then we must suppose that they are impelled to act from within themselves and that this impulse must derive from some inherent features of bodies (which they strive to realise). In addition, it could be argued that if something has an inherent character, then its existence will go well insofar as it realises or fulfils this character, and that it will therefore strive (not necessarily intentionally) for this self-realisation. Irigaray often seems to presuppose such a view, as we will see.

[45] Grosz, *Architecture from the Outside: Essays on Virtual and Real Space* (London: MIT Press, 2001), p. 97.

are sufficiently indeterminate that matter's contribution to the process of its acculturation becomes empty.[46]

These problems with Grosz's position confirm that we cannot conceive of matter as active without also thinking of matter as having inherent shape and character which call for self-realisation. We must therefore reinstate the belief that matter is naturally differentiated into bodies, each defined by an inherent, determinate character which motivates it to activity. To oppose the traditional devaluation of matter consistently, we need an ontology according to which bodies, having natural characters, strive for the enhanced expression or realisation of those characters (through cultural and social forms). Such an ontology accords bodily matter a value and importance which political essentialism implicitly denies it: for, on this revised ontology, bodily matter has inherent shape and character independently of symbolism and evinces creativity and dynamism in its own right.[47] Political essentialists may fear that this return to ontology attempts the impossible goal of knowing about reality as it is independently of our modes of representation. However, political essentialists themselves (more or less implicitly) espouse an ontology – a theory about the real character of the body/culture relation. Ontological assumptions are inescapable, yet political essentialism's implicit ontology conflicts with its central goal of revaluing matter and the female. A revised ontology on which bodily matter is active, and so, too, naturally determinate, coheres

---

[46] Ibid., pp. 100, 104. In her recent work, Grosz has moved beyond the views that I have considered and criticised. See her *The Nick of Time: Politics, Evolution, and the Untimely* (Durham: Duke University Press, 2004) and *Time Travels: Feminism, Nature, Power* (Durham: Duke University Press, 2005). In this more recent work, Grosz stresses that, if we regard bodies as culturally shaped, then this devalues biology and materiality (*Time Travels*, pp. 173–4). She also acknowledges that her own earlier work, because of its emphasis on cultural inscription, did not give a wholly satisfactory account of the material and the biological. She says that 'without some reconfigured concept of the biological body, models of subject-inscription, production, or constitution lack material force; . . . they lack corporeality' (*The Nick of Time*, p. 4). Grosz thus sets out in her latest work to think about 'how the biological induces the cultural rather than inhibits it, how biological complexity impels the complications and variability of culture itself'. This brings Grosz much closer to the late-Irigarayan philosophical position that I am (partly) defending in this book. Unfortunately, though, Grosz's recent work became available to me too late for me to discuss it in any depth.

[47] Similarly, Caroline New argues that the realist belief that bodies have natural capacities and powers sees bodies not as 'blank slates' for cultural inscription, but, on the contrary, as things which are 'not passive . . . [and] will not conform to whatever categories and attributions we may arbitrarily assign' ('Realism, Deconstruction, and the Feminist Standpoint', in *Journal for the Theory of Social Behaviour* 28: 4 (1998), p. 363).

significantly better with the project of revaluing corporeality, matter, and the female.

Having recognised political essentialism's limitations, we can re-engage with Irigaray's intellectual development. As we have seen, in her earlier writings, especially *Speculum* and *This Sex*, she commits herself fairly clearly to essentialism merely as a politics of reimagining and resymbolising the female and the corporeal. But, as her thought develops, she moves away from political essentialism – initially, towards the project of elaborating an ontology of active and naturally determinate bodies. This shift, I suggest, reflects Irigaray's recognition of the problems internal to any merely political essentialism and her attempt to overcome these problems – an attempt which leads her, in the first instance, to sketch a realist philosophy of the body.[48] This transition occurs in *An Ethics of Sexual Difference*.

When she discusses how her work has evolved over time, Irigaray notes that *Ethics* inaugurates a second phase in her work. *Ethics*, she notes, sheds the preponderantly critical orientation of her early texts for the more positive task of constructing 'mediations that could permit the existence of a feminine subjectivity' (JLI, 97). Irigaray does not, however, note that *Ethics* simultaneously marks a shift towards realism. Rather, at the beginning of *Ethics* she argues that we need to 'reinterpret... the relations between the subject and... the world, the subject and the cosmic, the microcosm and the macrocosm' (E, 6/14) just because traditional conceptions of these relations devalue the perceived female terms within them. This task of reinterpretation centrally involves reconceiving body, flesh, and matter, insofar as these have always carried tacit female connotations. The novelty of *Ethics* with respect to Irigaray's earlier writings, though, is that she now begins to understand this task of conceptual reinterpretation in realist terms – as the task of elaborating a picture of what material bodies are really like and of how those bodies really relate to the world around them.

---

[48] It may be objected that Irigaray cannot simply jump outside of traditional patriarchal representations to describe bodies as they really are. That is, her descriptions must remain culturally situated and informed, so must replicate patriarchal imagery. She indeed draws on Christian imagery of the incarnation, and on the pre-Socratic notion of the four elements, in describing how bodies really strive for self-expression. However, as I suggested in the Introduction, the fact that our cognitive access to reality is mediated by the cultural traditions amidst which we belong does not mean that we can never access reality as it is. Cultural resources can enable, not impede, cognition (for an expansion of this argument, see Haslanger, 'Feminism in Metaphysics', pp. 119–24).

We can see this shift towards realism when Irigaray states that we need 'a change in our perception and conception of *space-time*, ... *places*, and of *envelopes*' (E, 7/15). She immediately adds that this change would 'presuppose and entail an evolution or transformation of forms, [and] of the relations between matter and form [*rapports matière-forme*]'. That is, by changing the content of our conceptions of body and world, we would also be changing how the matter of our bodies can relate to these cultural forms. Because our changed conceptions would come closer to characterising bodies as they really are, bodies could express and realise themselves through these conceptions rather than being stymied by them. But the project of characterising bodies as they are also 'presupposes' all along that cultural forms should give bodies expression and should therefore describe them as faithfully as possible. Why should cultural forms do this?

Irigaray begins *Ethics* by criticising contemporary philosophers for 'wanting to break with ontology' in favour of mere 'literature or rhetoric' (6/13). Underlying her turn to ontology in *Ethics* is her recognition that it is insufficient to revalue and reconceive bodily matter only as it features in symbolism and imagery because this perpetuates the traditional hierarchy of culture over body, 'the dissociation of body and soul, of sexuality and spirituality ... and ... their distribution between the sexes' (15/21). We need to go beyond this hierarchy, and this means that we must remember that culture is rooted in and dependent upon matter – 'meaning ... [l]anguage ... feed on blood, on flesh, on material elements' (127/122). Rather than disavowing their material roots, cultural forms should recall us to 'our condition as living beings' – our condition of being embodied, inhabiting bodies which are material, living, growing, entities (127–8/122), and which exhibit these tendencies to grow and develop independently of how they become acculturated. Irigaray believes, then, that we need to revalue bodily matter fully and must therefore supersede the idea that bodies are wholly constituted through culture. *Ethics* sketches an alternative ontology – an 'affirmative ontology', as Irigaray calls it (147/139) – according to which bodies inherently seek 'alliance' with culture, straining for 'another incarnation, another *parousia*', to be attained through their self-expression and participation in the realm of culture or 'spirit' (15–16/21–2). Thus, although Irigaray does not explicitly state that she moves towards realism (in *Ethics*) and that she does so to overcome the shortcomings of political essentialism, we can see that *Ethics* does, implicitly, justify her move towards realism on these very grounds. *Ethics* implicitly argues that we can only consistently revalue matter – and the female – if we elaborate an ontology which describes bodies as actively needing, and pursuing, their own cultural transfiguration.[49]

This approach to bodies is already prepared in Irigaray's 1982 book *Elemental Passions*. Here, she describes bodies as composed of variable proportions of the four elements. Following the pre-Socratic philosopher Empedocles, she thinks that the elements display both mutual attraction (or love) and hostility (or strife).[50] By describing bodies as composed of the elements, Irigaray can conceive them as possessing internal principles of activity, which galvanise them to seek change and development. In this, she moves towards the recognition – crystallised in *Ethics* – that bodies must act *from* certain internal principles of change, principles which must be rooted in bodies' inherent (perhaps elemental) characters. Accordingly, in subsequent works, Irigaray refers to material bodies as having inherent 'forms' which call for spiritualisation or cultivation. For example, in *I Love to You* (1992), she praises

cultures where the body is cultivated as body ... cultivated [*cultivé*] to become both more spiritual and more carnal at the same time. ... There is no question, then, of renouncing the sensible, of sacrificing it to the universal, but rather it is cultivated to the point where it becomes spiritual ... spirit [should be] ... the means for matter [*matière*] to open out and blossom in its proper form [*sa forme propre*], its proper forms. (ILTY, 24–5/48–50)

As we can appreciate, Irigaray progresses intellectually from political essentialism towards an account of active and therefore naturally determinate bodies. But does this account necessarily support the view that bodies are naturally differentiated by *sex*? By addressing this question,

---

49 We might still wonder why Irigaray does not more explicitly address this shift when she periodises her work into three phases (see the Introduction to this book, note 8). But the fact is that this periodisation omits many of the most salient features of Irigaray's intellectual development, such as her shift towards concrete legal and political issues, her increasing attention to Hegel, her stylistic change, and her growing focus on the religious and the spiritual. Since Irigaray's self-periodisation is so far from all-inclusive, then, the fact that it includes no reference to her move towards realism is no evidence against that move. Indeed, it seems that Irigaray can only have intended this periodisation to be indicative, not exhaustive.

50 See 'Empedocles', in *Early Greek Philosophy*, ed. Jonathan Barnes (Harmondsworth: Penguin, 1987), pp. 165–71.

I hope to show why Irigaray's political essentialism ultimately develops into the realist essentialism defended in her subsequent works.

IV. Realism and Sexual Difference in Irigaray's Later Work

Even if bodies naturally have determinate characters, it does not automatically follow that these characters must be sexually dimorphic. In itself, the view that bodies have real characters is quite compatible with those characters being indefinitely diverse and carved into sexual dimorphism only through cultural operations. However, the idea that bodies are actively self-expressive does support the belief in natural duality when conjoined to Irigaray's critique of western culture, as becomes clear from her later work.

Irigaray's idea of active bodies obliges her to recast her earlier analysis of cultural structures. She must now regard these structures as always bearing the imprint and orientation of bodies which strive for self-cultivation and self-expression. This enables Irigaray to claim knowledge about natural bodies – including, crucially, their sexual duality – derived from her analysis of symbolic structures. Since these structures are always shaped and directed by bodies which actively pursue self-expression, identifying how these structures are organised allows her to draw inferences about bodies' natural characters and requirements. For Irigaray, traditional cultural structures suppress the possibility of a female identity defined independently of the male. Insofar, then, as some bodies come to self-affirmation within this tradition, Irigaray concludes that these must be bodies of a distinctively male type. Moreover, inasmuch as these male bodies express themselves in this tradition, they must be partially constituted by a visceral urge to suppress the possibility of different types of bodies coming to self-expression through autonomous representations of female identity: namely, female bodies. Hence, from her analysis of the asymmetry between cultural representations of sexed identities, Irigaray infers that males have a natural, bodily rooted, difficulty in accommodating female bodies, as she explains in a 1995 interview:

The little boy, in order to situate himself vis-à-vis the mother, must have a strategy . . . because he finds himself in an extremely difficult situation. He's a little boy. He has come out of a woman who's different from him. He himself will never be able to engender, to give birth. He is therefore in a space of unfathomable mystery. He must invent a strategy to keep himself from being submerged, engulfed. (JLI, 107–8)

The boy's continuously renewed 'strategy' is the construction of patriarchal culture, through which male bodies affirm themselves against female bodies.[51]

Irigaray's controversial claim is to extrapolate from the patriarchal character of western culture to knowledge of a natural difference between males and females which underpins its partiality and exclusions. She claims to know that there are male bodies, constituted (at least in part) by their inability to give birth and their attendant difficulty in accepting sexual difference. She also claims to know that there are female bodies, able to give birth and lacking men's psychical difficulties. A question arises here: if western culture bears the imprint only of male bodies, then how can Irigaray infer from this culture that another, distinctively female, type of body also exists? Her answer is that the structure of western culture testifies to men's fear of female bodies, a fear which – as she has argued – must be grounded in males' real relationships to female (especially maternal) bodies, so that these female (and potentially maternal) bodies must therefore exist, as bodies of a different kind.

However, Irigaray cannot rightly infer from patriarchal culture that there are naturally *only* two kinds of human body, male and female, and not also intersexed bodies (intersexed bodies, to recall, are ambiguous with respect to dualistic sex classifications). Presumably, her reasoning for that conclusion is that patriarchal culture privileges only the male body and denies self-affirmation only to the female body, on which it puts an unfailingly negative construal. Yet the very fact (if such it is) that western traditions only explicitly attend to male and female identities may evidence a still deeper repression of kinds of body which do not conform to sex categories. Still, although Irigaray's inference from western culture does not allow her to affirm that all bodies are either male or female, it entitles her to conclude, more weakly, that male and female bodies exist with distinct characters and, perhaps, that most humans are either male or female. Based on this inference, then, she asserts increasingly bluntly that sexual difference is natural and real – 'There is a physiological and morphological complementarity between the sexes. Why deny it?' (SG, 107/121) – and, illegitimately, that sexual difference is universal (that is, that all bodies are either male or female) – 'Sexual difference

---

[51] Irigaray's account of the development of infant males has been criticised; see Mary Beth Mader, 'All Too Familiar: Luce Irigaray's Recent Thoughts on Sexuation and Generation', in *Continental Philosophy Review* 36: 4 (2003), pp. 367–90. I defend Irigaray's account in Chapter 4.

is...both real and universal...[it is] an immediate natural given' (ILTY, 47/84).

Insofar as Irigaray can conclude that women have naturally different characters to men, she can argue that cultural transformation is necessary to bring women's bodies a level of expression and 'spiritualisation' equivalent to that available to men. Overcoming its current exclusiveness, western culture must start providing forms through which each woman can 'open out [her] female body, give it forms, words, knowledge of itself' (JTN, 116/141). Irigaray stresses, for example, that work is presently organised exclusively around the distinctive temporal rhythms characteristic of male bodies, a situation which inflicts distress and discomfort upon women, and which must be remedied (TD, 26/43). 'Women need a culture compatible with their nature [*adaptée à leur nature*]', she therefore declares (ILTY, 44/79). The proposals for social and institutional reform which occupy much of her later work rest on her overarching conviction that culture must give expression to bodies which are really, naturally, sexually different, and which therefore can achieve adequate expression only in a culture of sexual difference.

Irigaray has advanced towards this realist essentialist position starting from her recognition of the internal instability within the merely political essentialism she had endorsed initially. That initial project of revaluing corporeality proves to require a revised conception of bodies as intrinsically active by virtue of their natural characters, a conception which generates, in turn, a revised analysis of cultural structures as expressing, to different degrees, the inherent characters of male and female bodies. This revised analysis underpins Irigaray's later condemnation of modern social institutions for denying expression to specifically female characteristics. Far from being untenable, Irigaray's later realist essentialism has a careful grounding in her thinking through of the limitations of merely political essentialism. Her work opens up the possibility of a complex realist essentialism which recognises the need for consistency between ontological and ethical commitments and which also provides a basis for social criticism and transformation. Irigaray's realist essentialism also has considerable problems, though, to which we should now turn.

V. Problems with Irigaray's Later Philosophy

By reconsidering Irigaray's intellectual trajectory, I have argued against the view, now standard among her readers, that realist essentialism is philosophically naïve and doomed to reproduce traditional imagery uncritically. I have also questioned the concomitant assumption that merely political essentialism is philosophically preferable, capable of effecting a positive transformation and re-evaluation of traditional imagery. In contrast, I have argued that political essentialism is crucially inconsistent: its implicit ontology contradicts its re-evaluative project, a project which coheres better with a revised ontology according to which bodies display activity and striving, by virtue of their inherent natural characters. In conjunction with Irigaray's critique of patriarchal symbolic formations, this ontology implies that sexual difference exists naturally: that is, it supports a realist form of essentialism. According to this realist essentialism, articulated in Irigaray's later texts, women and men have essential corporeal characters which need self-expression and enhancement through a culture of sexual difference. However, Irigaray's later philosophy also faces four main problems.

Before looking at these problems, I should note a residual textual difficulty for my interpretation of the later Irigaray as a realist essentialist: namely, her consistent hostility to any 'magical' ontology which, as she puts it, postulates 'intangible essences' (WL, 10). In part, she denies that essential properties can exist because she believes that, if such properties were to exist, they would have to endure over time; but, she believes, reality is fluid and everchanging, and therefore has no room for such properties. Moreover, she believes that women's bodies have traditionally been understood as having no stable form (S, 165/206), so that the notion of essential properties threatens to reproduce imagery which privileges the male body. Despite her hostility to belief in essences, Irigaray's substantive view that men and women differ naturally in respect of determinate characters or 'forms' appears to entail that men and women are constituted as men and women by these different features, features which are, therefore, essential to their sex. The later Irigaray seems to be an essentialist who denies her own essentialism. I will return to this puzzle, assessing how far it undermines the otherwise strong textual evidence for the later Irigaray's essentialism, in Chapter 3.

Continuing, for now, to assume that the later Irigaray does espouse realist essentialism, four main criticisms can immediately be made of this position. Let me note that these criticisms may seem superficial and to fail to appreciate the philosophical depth and the complex, qualified character of Irigaray's apparently stark claims about nature, sexual duality, and western culture's denial of this duality. Ultimately, I accept this, but we should recall that many readers have found the problems with her later philosophy overwhelming. For this reason especially, it is important to set out the most pressing of these problems at the start, letting our awareness of them guide us in exploring Irigaray's thought and in tracing how far its philosophical complexity permits her to overcome these problems. This is particularly necessary because, it will transpire, refined versions of some of these problems continue to plague her thought even once its depth and complexity are acknowledged.

The first problem with Irigaray's later thought is its proximity to biological determinism. Recall that her reconception of sexual difference as really existing, independently of culture, is simultaneously a reconception of sexual difference as *natural*. Irigaray's move from political to realist essentialism, then, may equally be described as a move from the belief that sexual difference primarily exists symbolically to the belief that it primarily exists naturally. But, in holding that sexual difference is primarily natural, she appears to resurrect the belief that men and women are constituted as members of different sexes by their biology. In holding, too, that bodies direct and express themselves in culture, she seems to think that biological sex differences shape our culture and our experiences as men and women. As she says: 'Men and women are corporeally different. This biological difference leads to others: in constructing subjectivity, in connecting to the world, in relating' (WD, 96). But if cultural formations are inescapably shaped by biological realities which obtain independently of culture, then how can cultural formations be changed? If men are constituted as men by a biological urge to suppress female subjectivity, and if this urge has determined the content of western culture, then how can any other culture ever emerge? Although Irigaray asserts that cultural transformation is necessary to secure equivalent self-expression for female bodies, her own conceptual framework seems to imply that such transformation is impossible. Rather than being politically transformative as I have suggested, Irigaray's later philosophy comes disturbingly close to the conservative view that patriarchy is immutably grounded in biology.

Irigaray's second problem is that her argument for natural sexual difference relies on her claim that western culture, as a whole, denies and devalues female identity – a pattern which she traces to philosophy. But this claim is falsely overgeneralised, with respect not only to western art, myth, and literature but even to the philosophical tradition. As Deutscher objects, Irigaray 'universalize[s] a collective disavowal throughout the ages related to sexual difference . . . she is essentializing its absence throughout the ages, as when . . . she interprets all of the texts of the history of philosophy as evidencing a collective repression'.[52] Feminist historians of philosophy, however, have increasingly emphasised that even the most ostensibly patriarchal philosophical texts harbour ambiguities and open unsuspected conceptual linkages which imply a positive redefinition of the female. For example, although Descartes's *Meditations* defends mind/body dualism, his *Passions of the Soul* explores the mind's intertwining with and dependence upon the body in a way which resonates with Irigaray's own evocations of embodied female identity.[53] This and other similar examples suggest that Irigaray's monolithic view of philosophical history is untenable.

However, this accusation that Irigaray overgeneralises about the history of philosophy may seem to misfire. This is because, ironically, her own work is one of the most significant influences on those feminist scholars who have unearthed the ambiguities in historical texts. To generate positive images of the female, Irigaray 'mimetically' quotes and paraphrases traditional texts rather than speaking in her own voice. As such, her work implies that traditional texts already, potentially, contain non-hierarchical ideas of sexual difference, in the form of ambiguities and hesitations which female readers can draw out and build upon. Nonetheless, Irigaray remains convinced that, within the traditional texts themselves, these ambiguities feed back into an overarching denial of sexual difference. For example, she maintains that Hegel's idea that families are based on 'blood relationships' (an idea which he introduces in the *Phenomenology of Spirit*) could provoke a rethinking of our embodied nature. However, she argues, Hegel himself closes down this possibility by building this idea of blood relationships into his account of families as units which function in the service of disembodied political life (S, 214–26/266–81). As this illustrates, Irigaray takes ambiguities to contribute to, not disrupt, philosophy's enduring denial of sexual difference.[54] The

---

[52] Deutscher, *Politics*, p. 111. For this criticism, see also Allison Weir, *Sacrificial Logics: Feminist Theory and the Critique of Identity* (London: Routledge, 1996), p. 106.

[53] See Descartes, *Meditations on First Philosophy*, in *The Philosophical Writings of Descartes*, trans. John Cottingham, Robert Stoothoff, and Dugald Murdoch (2 vols.; Cambridge: Cambridge University Press, 1985), vol. 2, pp. 325–404; Descartes, *The Passions of the Soul*, in *The Philosophical Writings of Descartes*, vol. 1, pp. 1–62. On feminist explorations of ambiguities in the history of philosophy, including Descartes, see Lloyd, ed., *Feminism and History of Philosophy*.

[54] Deutscher agrees that for Irigaray: 'Masculine and feminine identity are...always...destabilised, but these identities function *on the strength of* this destabilisation', so that ambiguities prop up, rather than undermine, traditional ideas of sexual

work of other feminist historians of philosophy, though, plausibly suggests that these ambiguities introduce greater internal diversity and fracturing into philosophical ideas of sexual difference than Irigaray allows. This undermines her inference that, because the tradition consistently denies sexual difference, one particular type of body must be affirming itself through these traditions, and that this must be a male type of body which naturally tends to affirm itself through suppressing the female. Irigaray's monolithic view of philosophy, and, with it, her belief in natural sexual difference, is insufficiently substantiated.

The third problem with the later Irigaray's thought is her insistence that sexual difference is the most fundamental difference – she regards 'the problem of race' and 'other cultural diversities' as 'secondary' (ILTY, 47/84–5). She therefore contends that the political recognition and expression of sexual difference will precipitate the resolution of all other social injustices (DBT, 11–12). Furthermore, she asserts that natural sexual difference entails a natural attraction between the two sexes (see, for example, ILTY, 146/227), which means that, for her, heterosexual relations are natural and, indeed, are ethically superior to homosexual relations. Since heterosexual relationships, on her view, demand openness to someone who is other at the most fundamental level, such relationships are the most complex and challenging, conferring greater moral worth upon those who negotiate them.[55] Both Irigaray's heterosexism and her privileging of sexual over other differences stem from her belief that differences within each sex are relatively superficial compared with those between individuals of different sexes. As she glosses it, differences

---

difference. See Deutscher, *Yielding Gender: Feminism, Deconstruction and the History of Philosophy* (London: Routledge, 1997), p. 79.

[55] Irigaray's readers have offered (at least) three defences of her position here. (1) Cheah and Grosz claim that she is not lauding heterosexuality as currently practiced, which rests on a denial of sexual difference ('Of Being-Two', p. 12). However, the sexuality Irigaray lauds remains, although modified, a form of *hetero*sexuality. (2) Ofelia Schutte claims that the alternative heterosexual relations Irigaray envisages blur the fixed identities of their participants, so that by implication this 'heterosexuality' is not clearly distinguished from bi- or homosexuality anyway (Schutte, 'A Critique of Normative Heterosexuality: Identity, Embodiment, and Sexual Difference in Beauvoir and Irigaray', in *Hypatia* 12: 1 (1997), pp. 55–6). This implication does not follow, however, if, as Irigaray indeed holds, heterosexuality has *unique* power to confound identities, due to the uniquely fundamental nature of the difference it involves. (3) Cheah and Grosz allege that Irigaray is not praising certain sexual practices or 'life-styles' but a political culture which is 'heterosexual' in that it respects sexual difference ('Of Being-Two', pp. 12–13). But since, for Irigaray, this political culture of respect must infiltrate the family, and should be manifested between men and women in their intra-familial relations, her politics becomes inseparable from a privileging of heterosexuality as a practice.

within each sex are merely 'empirical', whereas differences between the sexes are differences in kind (JLI, 110). Yet, *prima facie*, there is little justification for considering sexual difference more fundamental than other differences which play equally significant roles in organising our experience and social life. Irigaray's stance is likely to be politically divisive, marginalising or antagonising those who experience other differences as equally, or more, fundamental. We need, then, to clarify why and in what sense Irigaray believes sexual difference to be most fundamental, and whether this *prima facie* unhelpful belief is an inevitable corollary of her view that sexual difference is natural.

Irigaray's fourth problem is that she affirms that all individuals are naturally either male or female. As I argued earlier, her inference from western culture (which, anyway, has since transpired to rest on a falsely overgeneralised view of that culture) does not allow her to conclude that sexual difference is universal as well as natural and real. But this is exactly what she does, continually, conclude: 'The fact remains that we are men and women. . . . This universal [humanity] has the particularity of being divided into two' (ILTY, 50/89). Such claims conflict with the growing body of evidence that intersexed conditions are much more widespread than has previously been admitted. Since intersexed individuals are not obviously either male or female, their existence poses a challenge to Irigaray's thought: 'intersexuals quite literally embody both sexes, [and so] they weaken claims about sexual difference'.[56] Irigaray needs, at least, to explain how her position is compatible with the existence of intersexed bodies, without simply categorising intersexed bodies as defective or aberrant. This categorisation has traditionally served to justify surgery to 'correct' intersexed infants, surgery which is still often routine. Since Irigaray's philosophy is premised on the belief that bodies need cultural expression in their natural forms, she cannot consistently adopt a view of intersexed bodies which implies that they need surgical adjustment. She therefore needs to show how her philosophy can accommodate intersexed bodies as a normal, non-aberrant, manifestation of nature.

Offsetting these problems, Irigaray's later thought has the attraction of intertwining feminism with environmentalism. Since she seeks to revalue natural bodies as active and self-expressive, her politics of sexual difference becomes inextricably linked to a politics which aims to revalue nature and create a culture which expresses, and so remains continuous

---

[56] Anne Fausto-Sterling, *Sexing the Body: Gender Politics and the Construction of Sexuality* (New York: Basic Books, 2000), p. 8.

with, nature. Indeed, she sees 'destroying nature itself as the source of life for each and every man and woman' as an unforgivable 'infamy' (ILTY, 147/229). The later Irigaray may therefore be seen as a contributor to, and interlocutor of, ecofeminism. In particular, her thought converges with that strand of ecofeminism which challenges traditionally interlinked, and derogatory, conceptions of women and nature, not by simply revaluing women and nature as traditionally conceived, but by redefining nature (and female identity) as active, 'no longer a repository of stasis' vis-à-vis culture.[57] However, whereas some ecofeminists attribute nature's agency to its being always already infused with and modelled by technologies (a view crystallised in Donna Haraway's image of the cyborg), others regard nature as independently active, shaping and imprinting culture of its own accord, prior to any subsequent technological remodelling. These latter thinkers object that in the former, technologistic, current:

Nature is . . . reduced to a cultural idea . . . and our incarnate, natural-cultural situation to purely cultural discursive products. [This] perpetuate[s] the deep modern alienation of our human being from nature [and] reinforce[s] the current anthropocentric . . . worldview that sees everything only in the light of humans' cultural use.[58]

Irigaray shares comparable suspicions, as is shown by her turn away from political essentialism with its belief in the cultural construction of bodies. She insists that we need to '*respect the cosmos as having an existence other than ours*' (KW, 178–9). To this end, her later work elaborates a form of ecofeminism according to which nature is inherently active; by engaging further with her work, we can explore the viability of such an ecofeminism.

Despite the ecological affinities of Irigaray's philosophy of natural sexual difference, its problems, taken in conjunction, seriously diminish its appeal. They suggest that, rather than being politically transformative, Irigaray's philosophy may actually be politically conservative and divisive.

---

57 Stacy Alaimo, *Undomesticated Ground: Recasting Nature as Feminist Space* (Ithaca: Cornell University Press, 2000), p. 10. My allusions to different ecofeminist positions draw on Alaimo's overview of these (pp. 2–13). Disappointingly, Alaimo herself reiterates the view that the later Irigaray, for whom ' "woman" and "the earth" have shifted ontologically from discursive constructions to "the real" ' (p. 7), is doomed only to restate traditional conceptions of woman and nature. In fact, Irigaray seeks to *re*define nature as active and growing, a redefinition which, she believes, captures nature's real character.

58 Carol Bigwood, *Earth Muse: Feminism, Nature, and Art* (Philadelphia: Temple University Press, 1993), p. 44. For the cyborg image, see Haraway, 'A Cyborg Manifesto: Science, Technology, and Socialist-Feminism in the Late Twentieth Century', in Haraway, *Simians, Cyborgs and Women: The Reinvention of Nature* (London: Routledge, 1991).

The problems also suggest that, even if Irigaray is right that we should rethink natural, material bodies as active and self-expressive, her claim that we should see these bodies as naturally sexed is much harder to substantiate. Given these problems, is Irigaray's later philosophy perhaps best discounted? This conclusion would be too hasty. Her later philosophy is deceptively complex, especially since she elaborates it, in its many ramifications, with reference to the traditions of German Romanticism, German Idealism, and phenomenology. As part of this elaboration, Irigaray addresses, and attempts to resolve, all the problems I have surveyed, albeit not always directly or explicitly. Inasmuch as she can resolve these problems, her philosophy can fulfil its political and ecological promise, as well as its promise to present a coherent improvement upon political essentialism by reconciling its conflicting ontological and ethical commitments. The promise of Irigaray's later philosophy of sexual difference, in these respects, is sufficiently great that it is worth exploring this philosophy in greater depth, so as to assess how far it can overcome the problems which face it.

2

Judith Butler's Challenge to Irigaray

In Chapter 1, I traced how Irigaray turns away from her early project of redefining and revaluing the symbolically female. I suggested that we can see, in *An Ethics of Sexual Difference* in particular, that Irigaray comes to believe that this earlier project presupposes a conceptual hierarchy which privileges (tacitly male) culture over (tacitly female) matter and nature, a presupposition which conflicts with the project's aim of revaluing matter and the female. Irigaray therefore reconceives sexual difference as primarily natural rather than symbolic, urging that social and political institutions be transformed to give expression and recognition to this natural difference. Her philosophy of natural sexual difference is fruitful in that it consistently undermines the culture/nature conceptual hierarchy and justifies a politics which aims, simultaneously, to end women's exploitation and the degradation of the natural environment. In view of this fruitfulness, I have suggested, Irigaray's philosophy of natural sexual difference merits further examination, despite its problems. Yet Irigaray's later philosophy would, after all, be undeserving of further examination should there exist an alternative feminist theory with the same conceptual and political attractions but no comparable problems. Arguably, this alternative exists in the guise of Judith Butler's theory of gender, which offers the most fully and coherently developed alternative to Irigaray's philosophy of sexual difference.[1] No defence of Irigaray's philosophy can carry conviction, then, unless it

---

[1] For Butler's account of the contrast between her theory of gender and Irigaray's philosophy of sexual difference, see 'Feminism by Any Other Name', her interview with Rosi Braidotti in *differences: A Journal of Feminist Cultural Studies* 6: 2 and 3 (1994), pp. 38–42.

proceeds by way of a reconstruction and assessment of Butler's theory of gender.

Reconstructing Butler's theory of gender is complicated by the fact that her thought has undergone a series of shifts since *Gender Trouble*'s initial publication in 1990. Consequently, no single, definitive statement of Butler's theory exists. Several of the shifts in Butler's thinking are especially noteworthy here. Whereas *Gender Trouble* stresses the need to subvert dualistic gender norms, Butler recently puts greater emphasis on our need to expose and recognise the instabilities which already exist within those norms (UG, 42). Moreover, whereas *Gender Trouble* criticises any belief in social groups with shared interests as exclusive, Butler more recently affirms that it can be politically valuable for marginalised groups to take up and adopt 'universalist' ideas. In part, she has revised her thinking in response to criticisms from others; for example, in *Bodies That Matter* (1993) she revises the conception of bodies outlined in *Gender Trouble*, and in *Precarious Life* (2004) she reformulates her political position in response to the accusation (made by critics such as Seyla Benhabib and Nancy Fraser) that her politics lacks sufficient normative foundations. In part, too, Butler's focus of attention has simply changed; compared with *Gender Trouble*, her recent collection *Undoing Gender* (2004) engages more with the 'new gender politics' of the transgender, intersex, and transsexual movements and not only with power imbalances between men and women.

Nonetheless, all these changes in Butler's thinking must be understood in relation to *Gender Trouble*. These changes invariably arise because Butler is reformulating the approach to gender which *Gender Trouble* presented so as to make this approach more plausible and defensible, or so as to extend its applicability to other social and political phenomena beyond that of gender *per se*. To grasp the distinctiveness of Butler's approach to gender, then, we must primarily focus on its main elements as presented in *Gender Trouble*. As I see it, these are three: the idea that bodies are formed socially by norms concerning gender, the idea that women (and men) are non-unified groups, and a politics which aims for the subversion of dualistic gender norms. This subdivision of Butler's theory may seem artificial, but it is guided by the fact that these are three areas in which Butler's thinking arguably advances on that of the later Irigaray.

Firstly – as Section I will examine – Butler offers a theory of how bodies are socially formed which endeavours to avoid presupposing belief in inert matter. Instead, she considers bodies as lived vehicles of action which only take on determinate contours as habitual, and culturally mandated, patterns of activity become ingrained within them. Potentially, then, Butler succeeds in conceiving of bodies both as inherently active and as culturally formed, bypassing the need to postulate inherent bodily forms and undermining the motivation for Irigaray's turn to natural sexual difference. Secondly, as Section II explores, Butler believes that individuals who assume the feminine (or masculine) gender always reinterpret pre-existing norms concerning that gender. These reinterpretations, over time, make up a historical chain of overlapping interpretations; hence, without sharing any common understanding or experience of femininity, women remain identifiable as members of a single gender in virtue of participating in this historical chain. This conception of gender can acknowledge deep differences between women, avoiding Irigaray's implication that sexual difference, as a fundamental difference in kind, confers certain common patterns of experience on all women. Butler's idea that cultural norms undergo constant reinterpretation also seems to escape the overgeneralisation of Irigaray's view of western culture. Thirdly, Butler urges, politically, that we subvert and introduce greater internal diversity into received gender norms; I examine this in Section III.[2] Her politics avoids the potential conservatism of Irigaray's view that symbolic formations express nature, while also recognising and opposing the restrictiveness of dualistic gender norms, which Irigaray's politics of sexual difference threatens to reinforce. At first sight, the comparative sophistication and radicalism of Butler's theory of gender may suggest that Irigaray's later philosophy has little merit.

Since my exposition of the elements of Butler's theory must be somewhat complicated, an anticipatory summary of my conclusions may help. I will argue that, in each area, Butler does not in fact improve upon Irigaray so decisively as to supersede her later thought. Firstly, Butler ultimately still believes that bodies acquire agency only through being moulded by cultural norms; this view that bodily agency derives from that of culture reproduces the hierarchical privileging of the cultural over the bodily. (Although Butler revises her account of bodies in *Bodies That Matter* to try to solve this problem, the same problem reappears in her revised account.) Secondly, her idea that elements of culture undergo constant

---

[2] As I noted, Butler recently places more emphasis on the fact that the meanings of gender norms already contain greater diversity than we tend to assume. But this is, precisely, a shift in emphasis, not in substance. From the start, she construes subversive activities as ones which make manifest the already existing instabilities which beset all gender norms because of their need for constant reinterpretation. This conception of subversion follows directly from her idea that norms are subject to this constant reinterpretation.

reinterpretation and change denies the tenacity and unconscious rooted-ness of ideas of sexual difference, which Irigaray's account of patriarchal culture, despite its overgeneralisation, highlights. Thirdly, Butler's pol-itics of subversion falls prey to a dilemma: either (as in *Gender Trouble*) she provides insufficient normative grounds to consider subversion desir-able, or (as in recent work such as *Precarious Life*) she justifies subversion with reference to her theory that bodies are socially formed – but this joins her politics inseparably to her ultimately hierarchical conception of the relation between culture and bodies. I will conclude, in Sections IV and V, that we can revise Butler's theory of sex and gender to relieve it of these problems, by basing it on a conception of active and multiple bodily forces. This realist revision of Butler's theory, though, raises a fresh ques-tion: why should we affirm the existence of natural bodily multiplicity, rather than duality, as Irigaray holds? Finally, Butler's theory of gender not only fails to surpass Irigaray's later philosophy, but it also forces our attention back to Irigaray's later philosophy and onto her deeper reasons for postulating natural sexual duality.

Given my inconclusive assessment of Butler's challenge to Irigaray, the space which this chapter devotes to Butler may look dispropor-tionate. Yet, although the strengths of Butler's approach do not deci-sively outweigh those of Irigaray's later thought, careful study of Butler's approach remains necessary because of its several advantages, such as its acknowledgement of fundamental differences between women. These advantages throw the weaknesses of Irigaray's later thought into clearer relief, indicating places where her philosophy needs rethinking to make it tenable. Since any such rethinking must be guided by appreciation of the advantages of Butler's approach, it must amount to a synthesis of the positive elements in both Butler and Irigaray. This makes thorough acquaintance with Butler's approach indispensable to the critical evalua-tion and rethinking of Irigaray's philosophy which I will undertake in later chapters.

I. Butler on the Cultural Formation of Bodies

As I have remarked, Butler develops her theory of sex and gender across a series of writings for which *Gender Trouble* (1990) provides the foundation. As the book's later (1999) preface clarifies, Butler explicitly conceives it to outline a feminist approach opposed to that of Irigaray.[3] *Gender Trouble*

---

[3] *Anniversary Edition of Gender Trouble* (London: Routledge, 1999), p. viii.

criticises Irigaray for falsely minimising differences between women (GT, 13), for her more or less overt heterosexism, and for viewing western culture as more homogeneous than it really is (13, 29). In another essay on Irigaray, also written in 1990, Butler criticises her on similar grounds – for seeing sexual difference as the primary difference; for tending to assimilate the feminine and the maternal; and for taking an overly negative view of the history of philosophy, neglecting the instabilities in philosophical writing – and in language generally – and their openness to reappropriation.[4] These problems which Butler detects in Irigaray's philosophy inspire her to try to develop an alternative perspective which sees sex difference as an effect of social norms but which does not lapse back into privileging culture and meaning over matter.[5] First, then, we should see how Butler thinks that social norms concerning gender form differently sexed bodies.

Butler maintains that gender always involves both language and bodily activity, activity which has a public, theatrical quality.[6] Thus, she conceives gender to arise at the intersection of two elements: a non-discursive element, consisting of practices of bodily behaviour, gesture, and ritual; and a discursive element, consisting of linguistically articulated norms concerning the meaning of those bodily activities. Gender exists insofar as bodily activity is organised and carried out following normative ideas concerning its meaning, purpose, and proper direction. As Butler stresses, corporeal activity has long been regulated by the particular constellation of norms which she terms the 'heterosexual matrix' (or, in more recent writings, 'heterosexual hegemony'), according to which bodily behaviour should fall into inversely symmetrical masculine and feminine forms which support heterosexuality.

---

[4] 'Sexual Difference as a Question of Ethics: Alterities of the Flesh in Irigaray and Merleau-Ponty', in *Bodies of Resistance: New Phenomenologies of Politics, Agency, and Culture*, ed. Laura Doyle (Evanston, Il.: Northwestern University Press, 2001), pp. 72–3, 75–6. This article addresses Irigaray's essay on Merleau-Ponty in *An Ethics of Sexual Difference*, specifically arguing that Irigaray takes an excessively negative view of Merleau-Ponty's descriptions of our experience of embodiment.

[5] Butler's views on Irigaray have changed over time too, and have generally become more nuanced. For example, in *Antigone's Claim* (New York: Columbia University Press, 2000), she is sympathetic to Irigaray's use of the figure of Antigone to explore the limitations of politics as predominantly conceived in the west (pp. 2–3). And *Undoing Gender* praises Irigaray's thorough engagement with the history of philosophy (UG, 245) and her invitation that we ask questions about sexual difference and think about how culture always depends on what is material and bodily (pp. 177–8).

[6] *Anniversary Edition*, p. xxv.

For Butler, norms regarding gender only subsist through being enacted: 'Norms are not static entities, but incorporated and interpreted features of existence'.[7] Because norms obtain only insofar as they are practised, Butler claims that gender is 'performative': 'Gender reality is performative which means, quite simply, that it is real only to the extent that it is performed'.[8] This requirement that norms be performed makes them ever vulnerable to reinterpretation, for corporeal activity always enacts norms in varied ways which alter their meanings. As Butler says, we always 'interpret received gender norms in a way that organises them anew' (VSG, 131). This ongoing reinterpretation of gender norms occurs at the level of bodily behaviour, as a corporeal process inevitably carried out by bodies as they take up inherited meanings. This might suggest that Butler presupposes some inherent 'volatility' or energy in bodies, such that they always enact norms in unprecedented ways.[9] Actually, though, Butler firmly rejects any idea that natural bodily energies direct reinterpretations of gender norms. This is apparent from her discussions of Foucault's views on the body.

In his methodological essay 'Nietzsche, Genealogy, History' (1971), Foucault develops the idea that power relations act directly on bodies, so as to reconstitute them, physically, in the image of power. Famously, he calls the body 'the inscribed surface of events ... totally imprinted by history'.[10] Changing power relations thoroughly infuse the body, instilling it with particular habits and capacities, and reshaping its physiology and rhythms. Bodies are, Foucault writes, 'moulded by a great many distinct regimes; ... broken down by the rhythms of work, rest, and holidays ... poisoned by food or values, through eating habits or moral laws'.[11] Foucault stresses that even the various bodily drives (for food or sex, for instance) are culturally shaped by shifting power relations and do not exist independently of (varying) cultural

---

[7] Butler, *Contingency, Hegemony, Universality: Contemporary Dialogues on the Left* (with Ernesto Laclau and Slavoj Žižek; London: Verso, 2000), p. 152.

[8] 'Performative Acts and Gender Constitution: An Essay in Phenomenology and Feminist Theory' (1988), in *Writing on the Body: Female Embodiment and Feminist Theory*, ed. Katie Conboy, Nadia Medina, and Sarah Stanbury (New York: Columbia University Press, 1997), p. 411.

[9] Lois McNay asks whether Butler presupposes some 'bodily volatility ... that renders strategies of domination vulnerable to displacement' (*Gender and Agency: Reconfiguring the Subject in Feminist and Social Theory* (Oxford: Blackwell, 2000), p. 50).

[10] Foucault, 'Nietzsche, Genealogy, History', in *Nietzsche*, ed. John Richardson and Brian Leiter (Oxford: Oxford University Press, 2001), p. 347.

[11] Ibid., p. 351.

practices.[12] Following Foucault, Butler insists that bodies are thoroughly historical artefacts, but she criticises him for not opposing the belief in inherent bodily forces consistently enough. At points in his work Foucault urges resistance to the prevailing régimes of power in the name of 'bodies and pleasures' – suggesting that bodies inherently consist of a plurality of distinct powers and characteristics – 'forces, energies, sensations, and pleasures'.[13] Butler takes such comments to reveal that Foucault fails to treat bodies as completely historical, a failing which, for her, is also manifested when he describes bodies as passively 'imprinted' or virtually destroyed by power, with the implication that bodies are inherently exterior to power.[14] Butler criticises Foucault's occasional belief in natural bodily forces for being 'ontological': that is, for being realist, attributing to bodies an inherent, pre-cultural, character, which we can know about and describe (GT, 96, 101–6).[15] She rejects realism, as I will now explain, because she thinks that what realists presume to be mere descriptions of reality are never simply descriptive but always normative as well.

Butler sets out her central argument to this effect in *Bodies That Matter*: 'The body posited as prior to the sign, is always *posited* or *signified* as *prior*. This signification produces as an *effect* of its own procedure the very body that it nevertheless and simultaneously claims to discover as that which *precedes* its own action' (BTM, 30). To explain: bodies are normally held to exist, pre-culturally, with particular characteristics. Yet viewing bodies in this way is itself a cultural activity, which positions the relevant characteristics of bodies as unalterable necessities. This view of bodies then affects how people act, corporeally – which in turn affects the shape which their bodies assume over time. Thus, beliefs that certain features of bodies are natural function, normatively, to constrain action – yet, precisely through the efficacy of these beliefs in constraining action, they come to appear as descriptive truths. For instance, Butler suggests that the claim that women are constituted by their reproductive capacities is not false but is 'the imposition of a norm, not a neutral description

---

[12] Butler also remarks that Foucault 'disavows any appeal to a desire that has a natural or metaphysical structure said to exist either prior or posterior to linguistic and cultural laws' (SD, 215).

[13] Foucault, *The History of Sexuality: Volume One* (1976), trans. Robert Hurley (London: Allen Lane, 1979), pp. 157, 155.

[14] Butler, *The Psychic Life of Power: Theories in Subjection* (Stanford: Stanford University Press, 1997), pp. 91–2.

[15] In another context, Butler criticises the 'postulation of a natural multiplicity' as 'an insupportable metaphysical speculation' (SD, 214). Yet she herself, on occasion, comes close to endorsing this idea, as we will see.

of biological constraints'.[16] Every supposed description of bodies' inherent characteristics arises internally to a complex of normative processes which effectively shapes bodies and *makes* them be as they are described. Any philosophical attempt to describe the inherent character of bodies therefore mistakes the epistemic status of its own claims.

For Butler's argument to work, our actions – or, more precisely, our habitually repeated activities – must shape our bodies physically. This seemingly rather debatable claim becomes more plausible given a phenomenological conception of bodies, which Butler generally presupposes (as is especially evident in her earlier articles preceding and leading up to *Gender Trouble*, articles which adapt ideas from de Beauvoir, Sartre, and Merleau-Ponty).[17] The phenomenological tradition considers bodies first and foremost not as the objects studied by the biological sciences but as lived, our vehicles of action and engagement with the world.[18] 'The body is not a static or self-identical phenomenon ... [but] is lived and experienced as the context and medium for all human strivings' (VSG, 130). Within this picture, we repeatedly carry out activities – physically – over time, in the process acquiring habitual dispositions to do those activities. These dispositions become ingrained in bodies physically, like a set of channels or contours cut into it by the activities which repeatedly pass through it. Bodies therefore take shape as precipitates of their past actions, 'legac[ies] of sedimented acts'.[19] Consequently, bodies are always in the process of 'materialisation', never achieving final, finished shape. Now, for Butler, the activities which we do and which mould our bodies are guided by social norms. Her point is not that people internalise these norms consciously and then voluntarily follow them, with secondary effects on people's bodies; rather, according to Butler, individuals take up and enact norms through a pre-conscious process which they carry out

---

[16] 'Gender as Performance: An Interview with Judith Butler', interview with Peter Osborne and Lynne Segal, *Radical Philosophy* 67 (1994), p. 33.

[17] See, especially, 'Sex and Gender in Simone de Beauvoir's *Second Sex*', in *Yale French Studies* 72 (1986), pp. 35–49, and 'Sexual Ideology and Phenomenological Description: A Feminist Critique of Merleau-Ponty's *Phenomenology of Perception*', in *The Thinking Muse: Feminism and Modern French Philosophy*, ed. Jeffner Allen and Iris Marion Young (Bloomington: Indiana University Press, 1989). On the phenomenological influence on Butler, see Sara Heinämaa, 'What Is a Woman? Butler and Beauvoir on the Foundations of the Sexual Difference', in *Hypatia* 12: 1 (1997), pp. 20–39.

[18] For a classic feminist exploration of the body as lived, see Iris Marion Young, *Throwing Like a Girl and Other Essays in Feminist Philosophy and Social Theory* (Bloomington: Indiana University Press, 1990).

[19] 'Performative Acts and Gender Constitution', p. 406.

directly at a bodily level.[20] This is why she insists that gender is 'performative', pre-consciously enacted, not consciously and voluntarily performed (BTM, x).

This conception of how norms shape bodies underlies Butler's well-known rejection of the distinction between biological sex and social gender. As she declares, 'this construct called "sex" is as culturally constructed as gender; . . . it was always already gender, with the consequence that the distinction between sex and gender turns out to be no distinction at all' (GT, 7). Biological sex classifications are made against the background of a set of social norms – the heterosexual matrix – which governs corporeal activity and actually shapes bodies into dyadic form (110). Purportedly merely descriptive claims about sex are made within a normative order which effectively produces sexually dimorphic bodies. Against this background, dyadic classifications cease to be merely descriptive: in being silent about the fact that sexual dimorphism is socially produced, they naturalise and reproduce prevailing gender norms. Hence, these claims about sex contribute to the production of dyadic bodies, becoming prescriptive and productive as well as descriptive (and acquiring descriptive truth only because of this productivity).

Epistemologically, Butler does not believe bodies to have real, independent characters to which we lack cognitive access. Instead, she thinks that the real characters and forces of bodies only exist as a result of our cultural activities. Moreover, since any descriptions of the characters of bodies take place against the setting of this array of cultural activities, these descriptions cannot but contribute to the further formation of bodies. For Butler, we cannot know about bodies as they are independently of our cultural activities, firstly because independently of us bodies have no character anyway, and secondly because any description of bodies itself exerts a further effect on their character.

If Butler's account of the cultural formation of bodies is to improve on Irigaray's philosophy of natural sexual difference, she must avoid the culture/nature, meaning/matter hierarchies which Irigaray rightly rejects. Butler therefore needs to avoid seeing bodily matter as passively moulded and imprinted by cultural forms. Yet since, for her, bodies acquire shape only through ongoing absorption of cultural norms, her account might

---

[20] As McNay says, 'The acquisition of gender identity does not pass through consciousness; it is not memorized but enacted at a pre-reflexive level' (*Gender and Agency*, p. 39). Butler leans here on Jean-Paul Sartre's concept of 'pre-reflexive' – spontaneous, tacit, and pre-deliberate – choice, a kind of choice which is directly embodied in one's actions (VSG, 130).

seem to reproduce this idea that bodily matter is passive stuff.[21] In *Gender Trouble* (and her early, phenomenologically informed, articles), Butler distances herself from that idea by conceiving bodies as *lived*, not bundles of malleable stuff but thresholds of activity. While Irigaray, too, emphasises that bodies are lived and experienced, she believes that a body's inherent character – its elemental composition or its sexuate 'form' – constrains how it becomes lived and experienced.[22] By contrast, for Butler, bodies only acquire definite contours through the sedimentation within them of (normatively inculcated) dispositions. By implication, though, Butler denies that there are any inherent contours of bodies which could affect how embodied individuals enact and absorb particular norms. So, without adhering to the familiar view that bodily matter is passive stuff, Butler does retain a picture of bodies as originally indeterminate. Being originally indeterminate, bodies have no grounds to redirect, inflect, or resist the cultural norms which they take up. In this way, although Butler regards bodies as thresholds of activity, she also sees them as necessarily labile in the face of cultural norms, and in this way she restates the conceptual hierarchy which pits passive matter against active culture.

In *Bodies That Matter* (1993), Butler reformulates her account of bodies to distance it more firmly from the view that bodily matter passively receives cultural forms. Ultimately, though, her modified account still privileges the cultural over the bodily, in a slightly different form. In the opening chapter of *Bodies That Matter*, Butler fuses Aristotle and Foucault to claim that bodily matter is both inherently active and socially produced. She approves of Aristotle's idea that matter (*hylē*) contains an inherent tendency or impetus to develop, 'an originating and formative principle which inaugurates and informs a development of some organism or object' (BTM, 31). A 'material' body, then, is one which tends to develop and actively to assume a definite form. This might suggest that Butler, like Irigaray, is reinterpreting bodily matter as having inherent

---

[21] Several critics have made this claim: see, for example, Claire Colebrook, 'From Radical Representations to Corporeal Becomings: The Feminist Philosophy of Lloyd, Grosz, and Gatens', in *Hypatia* 15: 2 (2000), pp. 76–93; Kirby, *Telling Flesh*, p. 107. Others believe that Butler's reformulation of her position in *Bodies That Matter* avoids this idea of bodily passivity; see Dorothea Olkowski, 'Materiality and Language: Butler's Interrogation of the History of Philosophy', in *Philosophy and Social Criticism* 23: 3 (1997), pp. 37–53. My own view is that Butler endeavours to distance herself from the belief in bodily passivity in both *Gender Trouble* and *Bodies That Matter* (in different ways), but that she fully succeeds in neither.

[22] On Irigaray's view that 'the body is always already a "lived body"', see Chanter, *Ethics of Eros*, p. 129.

character such that it actively pursues cultural self-expression. Actually, Butler rejects such a view:

> To install the principle of intelligibility in the very development of a body is precisely the strategy of a natural teleology that accounts for female development through the rationale of biology. On this basis, it has been argued that women ought to perform certain social functions and not others, indeed, that women ought to be fully restricted to the reproductive domain. (BTM, 33)

Butler believes that seeing bodies as naturally determinate and active (as Irigaray does) entails thinking that culture is shaped by biology and hence that women's presently unequal position is biologically rooted and immutable. To avoid this, Butler maintains (still following Aristotle) that matter only develops because it contains a form (*schēma*) which it is compelled to actualise, where (now following Foucault) the 'principles of formativity and intelligibility' (33) – the forms which infuse material bodies – do not naturally inhere in bodies but first enter them as normative ideals which are propagated socially. These ideals 'form and frame the body, stamp it, and in stamping it, bring it into being' (34). Normative ideals 'stamp' bodies by compelling them to enact these ideals, which thereby become ingrained into bodies as channels for habitual patterns of activity. These channels, by which the body becomes 'contoured', comprise its form.[23] On Butler's definition, then, bodies are neither material nor, properly speaking, do they even exist *as* bodies until they are moulded (and concomitantly 'brought into being') by norms.

Bodies That Matter continues to reject the idea that bodily matter is inert stuff, concurring with Irigaray that material bodies are intrinsically active, acting from indwelling forms. Butler thus reformulates her phenomenologically inspired view that the body is the inherent vehicle of action using Aristotle's form/matter terminology. Yet, unlike Irigaray, she thinks that material bodies only acquire their forms – the contours which bear habitual dispositions and give bodies capacities for, and impulses towards, action – through cultural operations. So, although these forms bring bodies into being as such and so render bodies intrinsically active, bodies acquire their intrinsic agency only derivatively, from cultural norms which Butler imagines to exercise agency prior to, and independently of, bodies. Of course, since cultural norms exert agency by moulding bodies, they can do this only if something proto-bodily pre-exists them, but their moulding activity is independent of the *agency* of bodies, which it

---

[23] Butler, 'Gender as Performance: An Interview with Judith Butler', p. 32.

bestows upon them in the first place. *Bodies That Matter*, then, reiterates that bodies are inherently active and are not passive stuff, but since Butler defines their agency as secondary to, and derivative of, that of culture, she again effectively reproduces the hierarchy of culture and meaning over matter and the body.

Later in *Bodies That Matter*, Butler concedes that she needs to better accommodate what she calls 'the "materiality" of the body' (BTM, 67) – its possession of some inherent character and resilience prior to cultural modelling. To try to meet this need, she claims that what social norms 'stamp' is

> *a demand in and for language*. . . To insist upon this demand . . . is to begin to cir-
> cumscribe that which is invariably and persistently the psyche's site of operation;
> not the blank slate or passive medium upon which the psyche [that is, the form]
> acts, but, rather, the constitutive demand that mobilizes psychic action from the
> start (BTM, 67).

Here Butler emphasises that even the proto-bodily matter which precedes social formation is not inert but demands to encounter and enact cultural norms and so relates actively to them. But this form of 'activity' is indistinguishable from the empty waiting or yearning which, traditionally, is symbolically female. As Vicki Kirby comments: 'Matter for Butler may not be a blank or passive surface, but it . . . still . . . demands to be interpreted or written upon, by something other than itself. It seems that matter is . . . incapable of calling upon itself to interpret itself'.[24]

Butler's continuing inability to distance her account of the body from traditional conceptual hierarchies weakens her claim to improve on Irigaray's later philosophy. A quite different objection might be that Butler's account of bodies is absurd: can she seriously maintain that we are wholly physically indeterminate at birth?[25] To be sure, Butler never says this in so many words. Rather, she claims that, when an infant is born, the announcement that (say) 'It's a girl!' is not neutrally descriptive but initiates a process of 'girling' – of moulding the infant's embodied life in line with normative expectations about femininity. Yet Butler's idea that this moulding process actually creates the contours of girls' bodies

---

[24] Kirby, *Telling Flesh*, pp. 114–5.
[25] One might reply that this objection to Butler is misguided because she is claiming that bodies are initially *lived* as indeterminate, not that they are initially indeterminate from the viewpoint of biological science. This reply is inadequate because Butler explicitly claims that the habitual shaping of the body generates its *materiality*, which implies that bodies must be materially – physically – indeterminate prior to such shaping.

implies that they have no inherent physical features in acknowledgement of which the announcement 'It's a girl!' is made in the first place. This is implausible: usually, when an infant is categorised as a girl, this categorisation tracks certain physical features of that infant.

At times, Butler herself admits that natural physical features exist; what she insists is that these features do not suffice to make individuals naturally sexed. In 'Variations on Sex and Gender' (1987), she claims that 'when we name sexual difference, we create it; we restrict our understanding of relevant sexual parts to those that aid in the process of reproduction . . . why don't we name as sexual features our mouths, hands, backs?' (VSG, 135). By implication, bodies inherently have various physical features, but, when classifying bodies as male or female, we focus on only a few of these features, which we treat as a group and take to constitute the body as sexed. In part, Butler makes these claims in 'Variations on Sex and Gender' because she has not yet fully developed her view that physical features are products of social norms.[26] Yet similar claims recur in *Gender Trouble* when she discusses intersexed people, in whose cases:

> The component parts of sex do not add up to the recognizable coherence or unity that is usually designated by the category of sex . . . sex, as a category that comprises a variety of elements, functions, and chromosomal and hormonal dimensions, no longer operates within the binary framework that we take for granted. (GT, 108–10)

This passage, again, suggests that bodies naturally have diverse features, some of which (for example, uterus, XX chromosomes, relatively high levels of estrogen) we perceive, when they co-occur, to constitute a natural group which defines the body as sexed. Intersexed bodies exhibit unusual combinations of features, which exposes that these features need not group together but are inherently diverse, capable of entering into varied combinations with other features. These features are not inherently the 'component parts of sex'; it is only we who perceive them as a natural and sex-defining group.

This claim that bodies are naturally not sexed, but have inherently diverse features, might be challenged. After all, perhaps we do not merely arbitrarily perceive certain features as constituting a natural, sex-defining group, but, rather, we recognise that these features are appropriately grouped together because, when they co-occur, they jointly exert

---

[26] Indeed, Butler adds here that sex 'differences do exist which are binary, material and distinct' (VSG, 135): she seems undecided even on whether sex difference naturally exists.

singularly important effects on people's lives. Butler would reply that these features only exert such important effects because social arrangements grant them this importance, based on the (politically motivated) assumption that they constitute a natural group: 'we assume that those traits will . . . determine [a person's] social destiny, and that destiny . . . is structured by a gender system predicated upon the alleged naturalness of binary oppositions' (VSG, 135).[27] Although Butler needs to explain more fully her claim that sex is not natural at all, then, this claim – and her attendant claim that bodies naturally consist of inherently diverse features – is less obviously untenable than her idea that bodies (or that which exists proto-corporeally) are naturally fully indeterminate. Later, therefore, I will return to this idea of natural bodily diversity as a basis for revising and strengthening Butler's approach to gender.

II. Butler's Historical Understanding of Gender

For Butler, norms concerning gender prevail only insofar as individuals practically enact them in their bodily behaviour. She also maintains that each enactment of a norm modifies its meaning, so that norms undergo incessant reinterpretation. Yet Butler denies that there are any inherent contours or impulses within bodies which could impel them to take up norms in ways which alter their meanings. How, then, does she explain the reinterpretation of norms? She appeals to the instability of language; the resulting conception of reinterpretation leads her to rethink women (and men, although here I shall focus on women) as non-unified groups defined by their histories.

To explain how norms undergo continual reinterpretation, Butler draws on post-Saussurean accounts of language. Whereas Saussure held that signs have meaning through their differences from all the other signs within a linguistic system, post-Saussureans – principally, Derrida – have argued that the meanings of signs become differentially defined

---

[27] One might object that these social arrangements simply track the importance which these features, as a group, naturally have. This importance presumably consists in the fact that all these features have a functional relation to reproduction. Butler would reply that the idea that the reproductive function of these features is primary is, again, politically motivated and reflects the fact that the heterosexual matrix of social institutions makes reproduction central to human life. After all, the breasts, vagina, etc., are sources of sexual pleasure outside of any context of reproduction; the supposedly 'female' hormone estrogen has many effects on the growth of bodies, including that of 'male' bodies (see Anne Fausto-Sterling, *Sexing the Body: Gender Politics and the Construction of Sexuality* (New York: Basic Books, 2000), ch. 7).

through a process which necessarily occurs over time. What Saussure saw as a fixed 'system' of language is always in process of composition. Consequently, the meanings of linguistic terms are never fixed but undergo modification with every event of speech. Each use of a term places it in new differential relations to other terms, redefining its meaning. This alters the meanings of those other terms too, by changing their place in the network of differential relations. So, as Butler puts it, all linguistic terms continuously undergo 'resignification'.[28] The resignification of a term alters and redirects the meaning which was sedimented within that term through its pre-existing relationships.

Butler especially emphasises the unstable meanings of linguistically articulated norms concerning gender. This does not mean that she treats gender as narrowly symbolic and linguistic (as Seyla Benhabib charges).[29] For Butler, linguistic norms concerning gender organise and constrain our corporeal life – which means, moreover, that the resignification of gender norms invariably occurs at a bodily level. Each act of re-using a normative term redefines its meaning, but each such act is inevitably a *bodily* re-enactment of the norm.[30] For instance, in acting according to norms concerning femininity, each woman subtly alters the meaning of femininity, an alteration registered in how she enacts these norms physically. Butler thus explains the corporeal reinterpretation of norms solely from the instability of linguistic meaning.

We should note an apparent ambiguity in Butler's conception of linguistic instability and resignification. On the one hand, she sees resignification as the inevitable effect of the instability of language, suggesting that resignification is something which linguistic terms do to themselves. On the other hand, she suggests that resignification is something which we, human individuals, bring about by re-enacting linguistically articulated norms.[31] This ambiguity can be readily resolved: it is *through* individuals' pre-volitional activities of re-enacting norms that linguistic terms undergo their inevitable changes in meaning. We should note, too, that, although Butler's account of instability and resignification is

---

[28] On the importance for Butler of the concept of resignification, see 'Gender as Performance', p. 32.

[29] Benhabib, 'Subjectivity, Historiography, and Politics: Reflections on the "Feminism/Postmodernism Exchange"', in Benhabib et al., *Feminist Contentions* (London: Routledge, 1995), p. 109.

[30] *Anniversary Edition*, p. xxv.

[31] Catherine Mills teases out this ambiguity in 'Efficacy and Vulnerability: Judith Butler on Reiteration and Resistance', in *Australian Feminist Studies* 32 (2000), pp. 265–79.

highly abstract, it implies that shifts in the meanings of norms will follow variations in social context. Concretely, any individual's re-use of a normative term places it in new differential relations to the other terms current within his or her surrounding contexts. Individuals thus re-enact and reinterpret terms in ways which reflect their particular social situations.

Butler's idea that norms are unstable enables her to deny that there are any characteristics necessary to, and shared by, all women (or men). According to Butler, norms concerning femininity (and masculinity) obtain insofar as individuals continually re-enact them in their bodily activities. One takes on a gender, over time, insofar as one acquires 'a contemporary way of organising past and future cultural norms, . . . an active style of living one's body in the world' (VSG, 131). Over time, these corporeal 'styles' or re-enactments shift the meaning of norms concerning gender. The meaning of gender norms is therefore considerably less unified than it might, superficially, appear.[32] Women may all identify themselves as feminine, but their ways of actually understanding and enacting femininity are indefinitely diverse. Butler therefore claims that ' "women" designates an undesignatable field of differences . . . [so that] the very term becomes a site of permanent openness and resignifiability' (FC, 50). Moreover, insofar as women's ways of enacting femininity shape the contours of their bodies, they cannot be said to share any physical characteristics either.

Butler's insistence on women's diversity appears to pose a problem: if women share no common features, experiences, or situations, then this seems to imply that there is nothing in virtue of which women form a distinct social group.[33] In turn, this would entail that women have no grounds for engaging in collective action. Avoiding these implications, Butler presupposes that women do remain identifiable as women: this is because, implicitly, she believes that women are constituted as a group not by sharing common features but by participating in the same history. For Butler, each woman can be identified as a woman because her corporeal activity reworks inherited norms regarding femininity: on this view, as she summarises, 'gender identity [is] . . . reconceived as a

---

[32] Fiona Webster clarifies that, for Butler, the 'meaning or content' of 'the gender identity category "woman" is shifting . . . it will mean different things at different times and in different contexts' ('The Politics of Sex and Gender: Benhabib and Butler Debate Subjectivity', in *Hypatia* 15: 1 (2000), pp. 15–16).

[33] As Iris Marion Young remarks, anti-essentialism seems to 'cast doubt on the project of conceptualising women as a group' ('Gender as Seriality: Thinking about Women as a Social Collective', in *Signs* 19: 3 (1994), p. 713).

personal/cultural history of received meanings subject to a set of imitative practices' (GT, 138). By 'imitating' – or re-enacting and reinterpreting – received norms, each woman becomes located within a historical chain composed of all those women who have effected successive reinterpretations of femininity. Moreover, through this relation to a pre-existing history, each woman's corporeal reinterpretation of femininity comes to overlap in content with reinterpretations which other women are simultaneously effecting: 'imitative practices . . . refer laterally to other imitations' (138). Although there is no unity among women (either within or across generations), their understandings and experiences of femininity nevertheless overlap to varying degrees with those of other women. These overlaps secure a continuous history within which all women are located; through their membership in this history, they can be identified as a distinctive group, despite the absence of any characteristics common to all women.

This historical view of gender can accommodate fundamental differences between women. On this view, successive modifications in the meaning of femininity necessarily build upon one another, which will predictably lead to the formation of distinct historical patterns of interpretation of femininity. These patterns branch apart in particular directions, a process which tracks the different social situations of different sets of women. As this branching occurs, the erosion of the earlier, still shared, layers of meaning concerning femininity ensures that quite separate understandings of femininity emerge in different social contexts. Women committed to these separate understandings will have ceased to share any experience as women, despite all identifying themselves as feminine. In these cases, women remain connected together only indirectly – via the chains of overlapping interpretation which span the gulf between them. So women differ not merely in how their behaviour exemplifies a common category of femininity; more strongly, their behaviour exemplifies *different* understandings of femininity, understandings which may be quite opposed in content (and in their place in power relations). Butler therefore refers to incessant 'rifts among women over the content of the term' (that is, 'woman'; FC, 50). This 'rifting' remains compatible with women's existing as a distinctive social group because they all have self-understandings and experiences which they reach by reinterpreting previous understandings of femininity.

Butler's idea of women as a historical group has two main advantages over Irigaray's idea that all women are members of the same sex. Firstly, Butler can identify women as a distinct social group without falsely postulating situations or experiences which are common to all women. In contrast, the later Irigaray cannot readily avoid postulating forms of experience common to all women. Since she believes that all women, *qua* women, have a certain bodily character, and that this character shapes women's experience, she seems obliged to conclude that all women's experiences will exhibit certain shared patterns – a conclusion, though, which is falsely overgeneralised. Secondly, Butler denies that differences between women and men must be more fundamental than those which regularly arise between different women. In contrast, Irigaray asserts, without sufficient justification, that sexual difference is invariably the most fundamental.

Furthermore, on Butler's historical view of gender, western culture cannot be said to oppress women in any uniform way: the way in which inherited gender norms are oppressive must vary relative to their shifting content. Eschewing Irigaray's generalised picture of western culture and philosophy, Butler's approach to gender recognises ambiguities and continual change in ideas of masculinity and femininity. Arguably, though, Butler *over*estimates this cultural diversity: for her, cultural ideas continually change meaning in track with social relations – femininity, for instance, endlessly shifts meaning in different social contexts. Butler therefore rejects Irigaray's distinction between the social and symbolic/ imaginary realms, which, she thinks, artificially isolates cultural formations from their social background, wrongly picturing the former as fixed and static.[34] Braidotti, defending Irigaray's distinction, objects that, on Butler's opposing view, 'the symbolic automatically register[s] the kind of social changes and ... transformations brought about by movements such as feminism'.[35] For Braidotti, this is naïve: conceptions of sexual difference structure our conscious and unconscious psychical lives and are heavily sedimented historically, which makes them peculiarly resistant to change. So Irigaray's view of cultural history, despite its overgeneralisation, does at least allow her – as Butler cannot – to recognise the deep-rootedness and intransigence of the symbolic structures through which sexual difference is defined.

To illustrate the dispute between Irigaray's and Butler's positions here, consider again the history of philosophy. The symbolic equation of the bodily with the female, and the attendant imagery of women as peculiarly ensnared in their bodies, can be found – to varying degrees of

[34] Butler, 'Feminism by Any Other Name', p. 55.
[35] Braidotti, 'Feminism by Any Other Name', p. 56.

explicitness – in authors as diverse as Plato, Descartes, and Hegel.[36] This is despite the enormous difference in the social contexts within which they wrote, from the ancient Athenian city-state to early nineteenth-century Germany in the throes of modernisation. Although these contextual variations affect the significance, and some of the detailed content, of these philosophers' symbolisations of sexual difference, the basic lineaments of this symbolism – the equation of women with a relatively benighted realm where mind remains enmeshed in body – are surprisingly enduring and resilient. It is true that Irigaray falsely downplays the extent to which philosophical traditions of symbolism contain ambiguities which tell against her claim that sexual difference has never existed symbolically in the west. But Butler's philosophy has the equally false implication that changing social circumstances should bring about so many successive revisions to patterns of sexual symbolism that nothing common can endure across the patterns found in Plato's, Descartes's, and Hegel's works.

On the whole, we can conclude that the strength of Butler's approach to gender is that it escapes Irigaray's untenable assumptions that women share common forms of experience and that women's differences are necessarily superficial compared with their differences from men. Irigaray's philosophy remains preferable to Butler's in regarding bodies as inherently active in their relation to culture, and as impelled into self-expressive activity by their natural characters. Irigaray's philosophy also better recognises the tenacity of symbolic structures. Thus, Butler's theory of gender is not unequivocally superior to Irigaray's later thought. Still, since Butler's historical conception of gender circumvents problems which Irigaray faces, Butler's work confirms that Irigaray's philosophy needs rethinking to render it acceptable. But before drawing final conclusions regarding

---

[36] For example, in the *Timaeus* Plato claims that bad men's souls are reincarnated in women, that is, in the inferior position of being more encumbered by corporeal matter (*Timaeus and Critias*, trans. Desmond Lee (Harmondsworth: Penguin, 1977), pp. 58–9). Sexual symbolism is relatively concealed in Descartes's texts, but Susan Bordo, for instance, has argued that he wrote in the context of a wider cultural collapse of the belief that the self is essentially situated in an animate female cosmos. Descartes wanted to defensively reaffirm the self's independence of the cosmos, by establishing a dualistic separation between mind and (extended, inanimate) body. He thereby tacitly symbolises separate mind as male, and extended body as female; see Bordo, *The Flight to Objectivity: Essays on Cartesianism and Culture* (Albany: SUNY Press, 1987), pp. 105–8. As for Hegel, he implicitly equates women with immersion in corporeal life when he structures the contrast between the family and the state in parallel to the contrast between slaves and masters; see Lloyd, *The Man of Reason*, pp. 80–5.

the respective merits of Butler's and Irigaray's approaches, we should assess Butler's politics of gender subversion.

III. Butler's Politics of Subversion

According to Butler, feminist politics should aim to subvert dualistic gender categories – not to recognise and express sexual difference, as Irigaray advocates.[37] Butler's proposal for a politics of subversion arises, I shall explain, from her account of linguistic instability. The problem is that Butler fails to explain why the subversion of dualistic gender norms is desirable. Recently, she has filled in the normative basis for her politics by deriving it from her theory that bodies are culturally formed; yet this joins her politics inseparably to the conceptual hierarchy of culture over matter.

Butler understands subversion, more precisely, as 'subversive resignification' (GT, 147) – a concept importantly different from that of resignification *per se*.[38] For Butler, resignification *per se* occurs, incessantly, through linguistic instability. Subversive resignification is a specific form of resignification, in which people re-enact norms in ways which undermine the meanings traditionally entrenched within them. A re-enactment achieves this subversive result if it *explicitly displays* its status as the re-enactment of a norm, revealing that the norm only exists insofar as it is perpetually re-enacted, and hence that this norm is unstable in meaning. By exposing entrenched meanings as unstable and mutable, subversive resignifications strip them of their authority. Butler adduces drag to illustrate this process: drag re-enacts established gender norms, but openly displays that it re-enacts those norms, exposing their instability. She stresses: '*In imitating gender, drag implicitly reveals the imitative structure of gender itself – as well as its contingency*' (137).

Butler emphasises that resignifications (or 'reiterations') need not take a subversive form: 'The reiterative speech act . . . offers the possibility – though not the necessity – of depriving the past of the established

---

[37] Butler's politics is not exclusively feminist: its subversive aim makes it equally apposite for all those who might seek to oppose gender norms, or for a 'coalition of sexual minorities that will transcend . . . restrictive norms' (*Anniversary Edition*, p. xxvi).

[38] See Sara Salih, *Judith Butler* (London: Routledge, 2002), p. 66. As Salih notes (p. 95), Butler does not always uphold this distinction clearly, sometimes speaking simply of 'resignification' when she means specifically subversive resignification. This unclarity arises because, for Butler, subversive resignification makes explicit the real character of resignification per se, whereas what she sees as 'conservative' resignification conceals it.

discourse of its exclusive control over defining the parameters' of action.[39] Resignifications can also be conservative. Butler explains conservative resignifications as follows: they '*accumulate the force of authority through the repetition ... of a prior and authoritative set of practices.... [A resignification of this kind] draws on and covers over* the constitutive conventions by which it is mobilized'.[40] Although these acts of resignification inevitably modify the traditional meaning of some norm, they conceal this, portraying the new meaning they propose as identical to the norm's received meaning. This strengthens the authority of that traditional meaning. Butler's perhaps surprising example is lesbian and gay marriage, which, she thinks, pretends that the new meaning which it gives to the institution of marriage is already part of its traditional meaning, thereby strengthening that traditional meaning.[41] Butler, then, distinguishes resignifications which are explicit about what they do (and hence achieve subversive results) from conservative resignifications which project their novelty back into accepted meanings to cement their authority.[42]

In debate with Butler in *Feminist Contentions* (1995), Nancy Fraser has challenged Butler to explain *why* the subversion of dualistic gender norms is desirable, or ought to be practised. Fraser complains that Butler is 'incapable of providing satisfactory answers to the normative questions [that her framework] unfailingly solicits'.[43] Butler replies that her philosophy attempts to explain how subversion is possible (in terms of linguistic instability), not to provide a general account of whether, or why, it is good (FC, 138). She denies that philosophers can properly furnish general answers to those normative questions. Rather, she implies, for those specific individuals who need to subvert gender norms to improve their lives or to make survival possible (because those norms deem their bodies unacceptable in some way), subversion is good, insofar as it helps those individuals to achieve that end (on the value of survival, see UG, 29). This suggests, though, that for those whose lives are improved by activities which perpetuate oppressive norms in their traditional meaning, this conservative behaviour will be equally good. But Butler denies

---

[39] *Contingency, Hegemony, Solidarity*, p. 41.

[40] Butler, *Excitable Speech: A Politics of the Performative* (London: Routledge, 1997), p. 51.

[41] For this example see *Contingency, Hegemony, Solidarity*, pp. 176–7.

[42] On this distinction see, Lisa Disch, 'Judith Butler and the Politics of the Performative', in *Political Theory* 27: 4 (1999), p. 550; Veronica Vasterling, 'Butler's Sophisticated Constructionism', in *Hypatia* 14: 3 (1999), p. 30.

[43] Fraser, 'False Antitheses', in *Feminist Contentions*, p. 68.

that conservative and subversive practices have equal worth; she supports 'practices, institutions, and forms of life in which the empowerment of some does not entail the disempowerment of others' (139). This commitment, as she states, depends on her normative judgement that some ways of identifying and differentiating oneself are worse than others: 'there are better and worse forms of [self-]differentiation' (140). Identities which depend on others' exclusion and oppression, and can be sustained only by perpetuating oppressive meanings, are worse than identities and ways of behaving which 'lead to ... more capacious, generous, and "unthreatened" bearings of the self'.

At this point, Fraser would surely press Butler to explain why it is better to act and identify oneself in ways which subvert and contest, rather than perpetuate, oppressive meanings. Butler replies to this hypothetical question: 'whatever ground one might offer would have to be communicated and, hence, become subject to ... [a] labour of cultural translation' (FC, 140). In other words, for Butler, there can be no transhistorical reasons to judge subversion better – only culturally specific reasons which, qua specific, can always be contested with respect to their own location within particular clusters of power relations. More broadly, she holds that the grounds or foundations for any normative judgements are always culturally situated, and so liable to challenge. Given this, Butler believes it best that the theorist or philosopher always acknowledge his or her specificity. Yet Butler's very antipathy to offering transhistorical grounds *presupposes* a normative judgement that it is best to make explicit that any normative claims one makes are open to contestation and subversion. Presumably, though, this explicitness is best because it solicits subversive, rather than conservative, responses. Thus, Butler cannot oppose making transhistorical normative claims without first presupposing that subversion is desirable; as such, she continues to need a general explanation of why this is so. This explanation must itself be cast in a culturally specific lexicon, and will be fallible and contestable, but Butler still needs some such (fallible, specific) account to justify her normative claims.

Butler gives a more developed account of the normative basis for her political claims in her recent book *Precarious Life*, which justifies subversion of gender norms on the basis of an ethic which Butler derives, in turn, from her theory of how bodies are culturally formed.[44] The structure

---

[44] Butler similarly derives an ethic from her account of bodies in *Kritik der ethischen Gewalt* (Frankfurt: Suhrkamp, 2003), esp. pp. 99–101.

of this justification becomes particularly clear in the chapter 'Violence, Mourning, Politics'. Butler stresses that bodies are *vulnerable* – not simply in that, as physical organisms, they can be harmed, but in that each body is 'socially constituted' – inherently 'attached to others [and so] at risk of losing those attachments' – and also inherently 'exposed to others [and] at risk of violence by virtue of that exposure' (PL, 20). Butler does not merely mean that our bodies are vulnerable due to their physical dependency on others or public accessibility. Above all, bodies are vulnerable because their physical features are socially formed: as Butler's earlier writings have claimed, they only arise and persist *as* bodies, with their distinguishing contours, through the operation of social norms. 'Constituted as a social phenomenon . . . my body is and is not mine. Given over from the start to the world of others, it bears their imprint, is formed within the crucible of social life' (26). Primarily, bodies are vulnerable to the social norms which shape them, and which may mould them into inherently contorted and painful shapes which are difficult to inhabit (recalling, for instance, Deutscher's remark that each woman is constrained to 'live an inhibited embodiment marked by the sense that a . . . diverse range of possibilities is prohibited in advance').[45]

Butler suggests that although we may respond to our bodily vulnerability by denying and disavowing it, we each have reason to acknowledge our vulnerability and to desire that it be protected rather than abused. However, others cannot protect my vulnerability unless they first recognise it (43). Each of us therefore has reason to desire recognition of our vulnerability; yet, just as my own vulnerability gives me a reason to desire its recognition and protection, so I have a reason to recognise and protect the same vulnerability when it occurs in others: 'each partner in the exchange [must] recognize . . . that the other needs and deserves recognition' (43–44). So, Butler derives an ethical imperative to recognise and care for others from her claim that 'the body [is] the site of a common human vulnerability' (44).

How might this ethic underpin a politics of subverting dualistic gender norms? Butler introduces the idea that recognition only takes place in accordance with norms which constrain whether, and in what way, people's bodies can be recognised as vulnerable. These norms can prevent us from obtaining recognition and protection (or from recognising and protecting others), and in such cases we have reason to subvert these norms.

[45] Deutscher, *A Politics of Impossible Difference*, p. 119.

Butler contends that dualistic gender norms are among those which constrain how far we recognise vulnerability: for example, these norms stipulate that each person must have a single coherent sex, hence that intersexed people need surgery, which cannot harm or violate them (33). For Butler, this case illustrates a more general pattern: established gender norms hold that some bodies are defective and so cannot be hurt or violated, since forcible interventions against these bodies – such as coercively imposed surgery – are presumed to benefit, or be merited by, them. She concludes that there is a 'profound affinity between movements centering on gender and sexuality and efforts to counter . . . normative human morphologies' and 'notion[s] of what the body of a human must be'. These normative notions preclude recognition of our common corporeal vulnerability, and their subversion is justified because it enables this recognition.

For Butler, then, bodies are vulnerable to the social norms which can mould them in hurtful ways. Such norms are hurtful not because they prevent bodies from existing in their inherent, natural, forms, but because they constitute bodies which can be lived and inhabited only in endemically contorted and painful ways. For example, traditional ways of treating the intersexed presume not only that certain bodies are intersexed but also that intersex is an aberration and that intersexed individuals must be forced to assume a sex, by being forced to perform the gender which will mould their body into an (at least approximately) male or female form.[46] Thus, the norms which shape intersexed bodies instil an inherent experience of physical unease, discomfort, and non-conformity. Through the idea that social norms produce modes of embodiment which they simultaneously denigrate, Butler identifies bodies as socially produced but vulnerable to harm precisely due to this social dependence, thereby deriving an ethic and a justification of subversion from her view that bodies are socially shaped. This ethic of recognising corporeal vulnerability remedies her earlier dearth of normative grounds for subversion, but this ethic has a problem in turn: it intrinsically links Butler's politics of subversion to her account of the social formation of bodies. This account, though, is problematic, I have argued: either (as in *Gender Trouble*) it denies that bodies have any inherent features or agency or (as in *Bodies That Matter*)

---

[46] For Butler, the non-intersexed are also forced to assume a sex in this way but without the accompanying interpretation of their bodies as belonging to the distinct, aberrant category of the intersexed.

it makes their inherent agency secondary to that of culture. Whichever way Butler takes this account, by deriving her ethical and political claims from it she ties them to the conceptual hierarchy which privileges culture and meaning over matter and bodies.

Opening this chapter, I asked whether Butler's approach to sex and gender might improve on Irigaray's later philosophy by underpinning a politics which avoids Irigaray's potential conservatism. Whereas Irigaray's understanding of sexual difference as natural and self-expressive risks entailing that existing, hierarchical conceptions of sexual difference are immune to change, Butler believes that gender norms constantly shift in meaning and are therefore changeable. Moreover, insofar as Irigaray does promote social change, she envisions an ideal society which expresses and recognises sexual difference in all spheres. This arrangement threatens to restrict us to ways of acting and living deemed compatible with our sexuate identity. Some readers, such as Toril Moi, 'shudder to think what it might be like to live in the fully "sexuate" culture which makes up the stuff of Irigaray's dreams'.[47] As a welcome antidote, Butler's politics aims to break down fixed and constricting norms surrounding gender and to expose their internal fragmentation. More negatively, though, this politics rests on an account of bodies as socially produced which remains continuous with the traditional culture/nature hierarchy. Furthermore, because Irigaray seeks expression for bodies qua natural, her feminism becomes simultaneously ecological, whereas Butler seeks to enhance the well-being only of the *human* bodies which, uniquely, are socially formed – as she admits, her ethics is a form of 'humanism' (PL, 42; UG, 13). Politically too, then, Butler's approach to sex and gender is still not straightforwardly preferable to that of Irigaray: despite opposing constricting gender norms and escaping Irigaray's potential conservatism, Butler abandons Irigaray's ecologically oriented revaluation of nature.

It has transpired that Butler's apparently more sophisticated theory of gender is not unequivocally superior to Irigaray's later philosophy in any respect. However, we can modify her theory to overcome its chief problems; the question then arises whether this modified version of Butler's theory improves more emphatically on Irigaray. Since Butler's theory's principal weaknesses stem from its idea that bodies are entirely formed by social norms, we can best revise this theory by basing it on

---

[47] Moi, *Simone de Beauvoir: The Making of an Intellectual Woman* (Oxford: Blackwell, 1994), p. 291.

the notion that bodies inherently have diverse physical capacities and forces. I will elaborate this notion with reference to Nietzsche's concept of multiple bodily forces, a concept which, since it informs Nietzsche's own understanding of how social practices undergo constant reinterpretation, already stands in proximity to Butler's thought. The next sections outline this revision of Butler and measure its renewed challenge to Irigaray.

IV. Revising Butler: The Multiplicity of Bodily Forces

The notions of resignification and instability in meaning which are central for Butler derive, ultimately, from Nietzsche.[48] Nietzsche introduces these notions in his *Genealogy of Morality* (1887), studying how the practises and beliefs which make up the institution of morality become subjected to repeated reinterpretations which impact upon their 'meaning [*Sinn*], purpose and expectation'.[49] Like the meanings of gender norms for Butler, the meanings of these practises undergo continual change, due to successive waves of reinterpretation. Unlike Butler, Nietzsche appeals to the multiple, active forces within human bodies to explain why they strive to reinterpret practises. '[E]verything that occurs in the organic world consists of *overpowering, dominating*'.[50] All organic bodies strain to dominate other entities, a straining which Nietzsche equates with will to power (*Wille zur Macht*): 'the essence of life [is] its will to power...the spontaneous, aggressive, expansive, re-interpreting, re-directing...powers'.[51] As this sentence indicates, Nietzsche thinks that the will to power is not a unitary drive. Rather, for him, organic bodies

---

48 On how Derrida's view of language and meaning is influenced by Nietzsche's view of reinterpretation, see Alan Schrift, *Nietzsche and the Question of Interpretation: Between Hermeneutics and Deconstruction* (London: Routledge, 1990), ch. 4. Foucault, too, theorises the instability of power relations and intellectual formations based on the 'genealogical' method which he derives from Nietzsche; see his 'Nietzsche, Genealogy, History'.

49 Nietzsche, *On the Genealogy of Morality*, trans. Carol Diethe (Cambridge: Cambridge University Press, 1994), p. 57.

50 Ibid., p. 55.

51 Ibid., p. 56. See also Nietzsche, *The Will to Power*, trans. Walter Kaufmann and R. J. Hollingdale (New York: Random House, 1967), p. 342. It might be objected that Nietzsche does not really endorse an ontology of will to power, which figures prominently only in his unpublished notebooks. But Nietzsche's published works can also be read as supporting this ontology, as they are by John Richardson in 'Nietzsche's Power Ontology', in *Nietzsche*, ed. Richardson and Leiter. Moreover, passages in the *Genealogy* clearly derive reinterpretations from the bodily forces which Nietzsche identifies with will to power (*Genealogy*, pp. 54–6).

are composed of a variety of powers – forces (*Kräfte*) or drives (*Triebe*). A drive, Nietzsche presumes, is a motivation or impulse to pursue a particular kind of activity, a motivation which exists at a bodily, pre-conscious and pre-volitional, level (and which is therefore a drive rather than, say, a desire or a preference). Drives are equally 'forces' in that each drive pursues its given pattern of activity with a certain degree of vigour or energy. Being pre-conscious and not deliberately willed, drives automatically – instinctively, we might say – pursue the kinds of activity at which they aim, immediately converting their motivation into action. Thus, drives are directly exhibited in bodies' physical patterns of activity.[52]

According to Nietzsche, each of these bodily drives seeks to dominate the others. Each drive seeks to extend its own typical mode of activity: for example, the sex-drive seeks to dominate other drives by extending the sphere of its sexual activity, harnessing other drives towards its own tendency to pursue sexual satisfaction.[53] Bodies themselves only take shape, as coherent entities, when some drives succeed in gaining a stable (but potentially reversible) dominion over others, thereby establishing a structured hierarchy of forces.[54] Within human bodies, these various drives also strain to reinterpret and redirect practises so as to extend their own characteristic modes of activity. 'The will to power *interprets*... interpretation is itself a means of becoming master of something'.[55] Bodily drives encounter existing practises as opportunities to extend their influence by harnessing these practises to their own ends. Nietzsche's understanding of historical reinterpretation is thus underpinned by his theory of bodily forces (as Butler herself stresses when she considers his account of morality: see SD, 207, 219, 222).

Nietzsche's theory of bodily forces allows criticism of existing institutions on the grounds that they constrict or diminish the level of power open to bodily forces (as, for example, the institutions of traditional

---

[52] Nietzsche's notion of drives – and so, too, the notion of multiple bodily drives which I partly derive from Nietzsche – deviates from the prevailing feminist view of drives. On the latter, which follows Freud, drives are psychical and cultural urges, which 'insinuate' themselves into the bodily behaviours and organs which infants at first use to gratify their – merely biological – instincts (see Grosz, entry on 'Drive' in *Feminism and Psychoanalysis: A Critical Dictionary*, ed. Elizabeth Wright (Oxford: Blackwell, 1992), pp. 71–3). I diverge from this view because of my broader rejection of the belief that bodies are culturally constructed. However, although I see bodily drives or forces as natural, I do not see them as biological; see Chapter 3, Section V.

[53] Richardson, 'Nietzsche's Power Ontology', pp. 165–6.

[54] *The Will to Power* speaks of 'the body as a political structure' (pp. 348–9).

[55] Ibid., p. 342.

Christianity inhibit the sex-drive). Conversely, the activity of reinterpreting institutions can be justified insofar as it enhances the power of hitherto constricted forces. Thus, Nietzsche measures the 'value' of the traditional institutions of morality by their capacity to enhance (*fördern*), rather than constrict (*hemmen*), the vitality and abundance – and, he says, the 'flourishing' (*Gedeihen*) – of bodily drives.[56] Now, Nietzsche understands any drive to gain in power and vitality insofar as it prevails over *other* drives, redirecting them to its own purposes. He therefore cannot coherently advocate expanded power for all bodily drives, and instead he advocates it only for those drives which he deems inherently suited for mastery – 'vital', 'courageous' drives.[57] This commits Nietzsche to an aristocratic model of the body, according to which vital, masterful drives are suited to dominate the others. In turn, he espouses an aristocratic politics, according to which those individuals with a predominance of masterful drives are suited to dominate and direct those in whom the 'weak' drives are ascendant.[58] He therefore condemns traditional institutions, and urges their reinterpretation, only when they diminish the power of masterful drives and individuals.

Nietzsche's aristocratic positions can hardly appeal to Butler, who supports radical democracy. In any case, she overtly rejects his belief in organic drives, which is (by implication) realist, insofar as Nietzsche takes these drives to objectively exist and really direct the procession of historical reinterpretations.[59] Implicitly, too, Nietzsche presumes that it is possible to describe the inherent, pre-cultural, character of bodies (as composed of determinate hierarchies of forces). In contrast, as we saw earlier, Butler sides with Foucault's view that power relations produce bodily habits and drives.[60] Building on Foucault, Butler regards any realist account of natural bodily forces as epistemically confused.

[56] *Genealogy*, p. 5; the German reference is in Nietzsche, *Kritische Gesamtausgabe*, ed. Giorgio Colli and Mazzino Montinari (Berlin: de Gruyter, 1967–), division 6, vol. 2, p. 262. The widespread fear that Nietzsche's philosophy has no normative content is misplaced: he retains an expanded ethical standpoint from which to criticise traditional morality.

[57] Nietzsche, *Genealogy*, p. 5.

[58] See Keith Ansell-Pearson, *An Introduction to Nietzsche as Political Thinker: The Perfect Nihilist* (Cambridge: Cambridge University Press, 1994).

[59] Nietzsche is often regarded as an anti-realist, a 'perspectivist' who denies that there is any univocal 'reality' to be known (see *Genealogy*, p. 92). Nevertheless, his theory of forces is – at least implicitly – realist, as Butler herself notes (SD, 207, 222).

[60] My claim that Foucault disagrees with Nietzsche on whether natural bodily forces exist may seem at odds with my statement earlier that Foucault derives his genealogical method from Nietzsche. But Foucault reads Nietzsche in 'Nietzsche, Genealogy, History' in a way which specifically minimises any role of given bodily forces in historical reinterpretation.

Despite Butler's overt hostility to Nietzsche's realist notion that bodies are composed of a plurality of natural drives, her theory of gender can fruitfully be reformulated on the basis of this notion. As Irigaray's intellectual trajectory implies, the adoption of the realist idea that bodies have determinate characters, existing independently of cultural practises and motivating bodies to give their characters expression, would allow Butler to avoid construing bodies as inherently indeterminate or active only derivatively of cultural norms. Instead, she could see bodies as consisting of inherently diverse forces all striving for self-expression. This view would provide a new basis for judging the subversion of entrenched gender norms to be desirable, on the grounds that it brings previously constricted forces greater power. To be sure, Butler herself would probably resist adopting such a view, especially given her anti-realism. A question therefore arises as to whether I can rightly call this feminist view of multiple bodily forces a 'revision' of Butler's approach to gender, rather than an alternative to her approach. I will be better placed to answer this question after I fill out what this feminist view of multiple bodily forces consists in. So let me first attempt to do this, drawing on elements of both Nietzsche's and Butler's thought.

An initial problem in elaborating such a view is that, as we have seen, Nietzsche's belief that only the 'vital', masterful – and symbolically male – drives deserve greater power conflicts with Butler's feminist and democratic political standpoint.[61] The ethical premise of a modified version of Butler's theory must be the desirability of flourishing for *all* bodily drives. But flourishing for all bodily drives can be consistently advocated only if drives are reconceived as gaining power not by dominating and harnessing other drives but by participating in a process of ongoing engagement, struggle, and contention with those other drives. Whereas, in the *Genealogy*, Nietzsche envisages drives as gaining power by channelling other forces into their own characteristic patterns of activity, a conception of bodily forces which is consistent with Butler's feminist politics must include a rethinking of drives as gaining power by contesting and battling with other drives, without definitively prevailing. On this

---

[61] That Nietzsche imagines the masterful drives as male is shown by his claim that feminism – or pursuit of rights for women – is a decadent outgrowth of the weak drives (*Genealogy*, pp. 121, 126). Still, such claims hardly exhaust Nietzsche's complex relationship to feminism; see Paul Patton, ed., *Nietzsche, Feminism, and Political Theory* (London: Routledge, 1993). Irigaray's own reading of Nietzsche is in *Marine Lover of Friedrich Nietzsche*, trans. Gillian C. Gill (New York: Columbia University Press, 1991).

conception, the process of ongoing conflict and competition invigorates all the contending drives, by stimulating each to pursue more vigorously its distinctive pattern of activity in contradistinction to those of the others.

Ironically, Nietzsche himself suggests that drives gain power through competition in his early essay 'Homer on Competition' (1872). He explores the ancient Greeks' 'agonistic' education and culture, which fostered individuals' powers by encouraging them to strive to excel in competition. This required that there always be '*several* geniuses to incite each other to action [and to] keep each other within certain limits'.[62] Consequently, anyone who established a position of domination had to be ostracised – Greek culture 'loathes a monopoly of predominance'. Although in this essay Nietzsche recognises the possibility of bodily forces growing through competition, he later discards this insight for an aristocratic ethics. However, his early insight strengthens the case for saying that bodily forces gain power just when they do not simply prevail over the others but remain challenged and provoked by them.

If bodies are made up of a plurality of discordant drives, then we have reason to break down any norms which suppress or restrict bodily drives (or, to be more precise, which exact more than the minimal level of suppression which, presumably, is necessary if individuals are to have moderately coherent identities at all). In particular, we have reason to subvert norms prescribing gender duality. These norms insist that our bodily life should give consistent expression to our gender, stipulating that our embodied lives should be as seamlessly masculine or feminine as possible. These norms illegitimately truncate and stultify the majority of our diverse bodily forces, allowing growth in power to only those few of our forces which can fulfil their purposes consistently with the satisfaction of gender norms.

It might be objected that we *can* realise our multiple forces consistently with assuming a stable gender and sex. On this view, we can give expression to our diverse forces just by enacting gender norms in an irreducibly particular and unique way – so that we do not crush most of our forces to realise our gender but adapt gender norms to fit with the realisation of these forces. This objection misrecognises what it means to ascribe to individuals a *multiplicity* of bodily forces. At this point, I should explain this concept more fully. Crucially, just insofar as bodies have multiple forces, bodies are not sexed. Individuals would naturally have a sex if they

[62] Nietzsche, 'Homer on Competition', in *Genealogy*, p. 192.

shared, with certain other individuals, an essential bodily character which differs from the character which another group of individuals (those of the other sex) share. However, Nietzsche's conception of the body states that *all* individuals have multiple forces, or that the natural character of every individual consists in his or her possessing a diversity of forces. Yet this need not automatically mean that all individuals are by nature non-sexed. Perhaps some of individuals' forces are themselves sexed? For a force to count as sexed, though, it would have to be one among a range of forces which are found only in certain individuals, but which certain other individuals lack. For example, perhaps some – female – bodies' forces include drives to bear children, breast-feed, and maintain relationships with others, drives which other (male) bodies lack. So forces could be sexed if they belonged within a range of forces which confers a sexually specific character on certain bodies. But this position falls foul of Butler's earlier argument against the naturalness of sex. To recapitulate (see Chapter 2, Section I), Butler believes that we only regard certain features (or forces) as constituting a natural, sex-defining group because social arrangements direct us to do so. Naturally, these features/forces are inherently diverse and need not co-occur; nor, therefore, do they form a natural group when they do happen to co-occur. On the resulting picture of bodies, their diverse forces are never inherently clustered but are inherently separate from one another and capable of entering into varied combinations and relations with other forces. Some of those whom we would conventionally see as 'women' may have some supposedly 'female' drives while lacking others, which might, on the other hand, be present in some 'men' (such as a drive to nurture young children or to maintain relationships). As a result, the differences between some 'women' may often be greater than those between some 'women' and some 'men'. The multiplicity within individual bodies therefore constitutes them as *non-*sexed, since it precludes the possibility that these bodies could have an essential character (defined by a range of naturally clustered properties) which they share with just some other bodies. Instead of having sexually specific characters, on this view, all bodies share the same character of internal diversity. Hereafter, then, when I refer to 'bodily multiplicity' (or just 'multiplicity'), I mean that bodies are composed of diverse forces and are, in that respect, *non-*sexuate.

The same argument which I have just sketched is outlined by Butler. Debating the merits of the concept of sexual difference with Braidotti, Butler argues for replacing our language of sexual difference with one of multiple forces. She points out, firstly, that 'there is masculinity at work in [say] butch desire . . . [and so] there may be ways that masculinity emerges in women, and . . . [that] femininity and masculinity do not belong to differently sexed bodies' (UG, 197). But here, as she goes on to argue, we find ourselves

> at an edge of sexual difference for which the language of sexual difference might not suffice, and . . . this follows . . . from an understanding of the body as constituted by . . . multiple forces . . . If this particular construction of desire exceeds the binary frame, or confounds its terms, why could it not be an instance of the multiple play of forces . . . ? (UG, 197–8)

To reconstruct her reasoning: we all have diverse components (affects, desires, or drives) and apparently some of the drives which women have are masculine/male. But since this means that those drives do not inseparably cluster with certain other drives to make up a character specific to the male sex, there remains no reason to regard these drives as male. Not being naturally clustered into sex-defining groups, drives/forces simply form a multiplicity, elements in a 'multiple play' of possible combinations and relations.

Given the diversity of forces in a body, at least some of these will inevitably conflict, pursuing incompatible aims. This is why, to acquire a coherent identity, any individual must curb some of these forces. The believer in bodily multiplicity might therefore advocate that individuals continually strive to undo any coherent identities they have achieved. More realistically, one might – following Butler – think that we should oppose unnecessarily restrictive forms of identity and replace these with forms which are as inclusive and open to change as possible. Now, dualistic gender norms unnecessarily constrict our non-sexuate multiplicity, by forcing us to develop only a limited set of features and capacities which we share with those of the same gender/sex and which are lacking in those of the other gender/sex. The subversion of gender norms is therefore desirable because it allows our non-sexuate multiplicity to increase in power and vitality.

A question arises here: does the revised version of Butler's approach which I am proposing – which, politically, advocates not the expression of the repressed female body but growth in multiple bodily forces – retain any specifically feminist dimension? I believe that this advocacy can in fact underpin a specifically subversive form of feminism. According to this, those who have been historically constituted as women should act together to subvert the norms of femininity which have curtailed their bodily plurality. Since these norms have already been reinterpreted in innumerable ways, different women will be constricted by these norms in diverse ways. Nonetheless, enough overlaps will remain between the patterns of their constriction to motivate women to act collectively, as women, notwithstanding that their aim is to break down the very norms which connect them.

Now, as I mentioned earlier, it is arguable that my realist revision of Butler actually constitutes an alternative to her framework rather than a mere revision of it. Certainly, my revision of Butler is significant, abandoning her anti-realism and her view that bodies are wholly shaped by culture. Nonetheless, it remains a revision, not a rejection, of Butler because it preserves her other core ideas: that gender norms exist only through constant reinterpretation; that women and men are non-unified, historical groups; and that subversion of dualistic gender norms is possible and desirable. Instead of abandoning these important ideas, my revision of Butler refounds them on the notion of active corporeal forces. This revision, moreover, converges with Butler's occasionally voiced idea that bodies have multiple, inherently diverse features, none of which inherently group together to constitute a sexed character. Despite its fidelity to important elements of Butler's thought, though, my revision of Butler is sufficiently significant that she would probably not endorse it. Whenever I speak of this revised version of Butler's theory, then, I do not intend that this revised theory should be attributed to Butler herself.

V. Butler or Irigaray?

The contrast between this revised version of Butler's philosophy and Irigaray's later philosophy can be redescribed as a contrast between (realist) anti-essentialism and (realist) essentialism. Irigaray's later philosophy, to recall, is essentialist because she believes that men and women naturally have different characters which constitute them as sexed. According to my revised version of Butler's philosophy, all bodies are naturally multiple – they share a common, not sexually specific, character of being composed of multiple forces. This position is anti-essentialist in two ways. Firstly, it denies that natural differences in sexed character exist. Secondly, this position holds that even the merely *artificial* sex differences resulting from social norms do not confer a common character on all those of a given sex/gender. The meaning of social norms is shifting, and so they exert only varied, albeit historically linked, effects upon bodies.

Unsurprisingly, Irigaray rejects the belief that multiplicity, not duality, is the natural character of humanity. For her, duality, not unity or multiplicity, is original: we must '*free the two from the one*, the two from the many' (DBT, 129). We can see why she links the beliefs in unity and multiplicity: to affirm multiplicity is to see it as the common, unitary, character of all bodies. Opposing any belief in unity as she does, she gloomily prophesises that 'multiplicity is likely to lead to death' (ILTY, 143/223). *Pace* Irigaray, though, we might well suppose that the revised version of Butler's theory – which postulates bodily multiplicity – must improve decisively on Irigaray's later philosophy, since it retains the attractions of Butler's approach while shedding her damaging idea that bodies are entirely socially formed. Thus revised, Butler's theory can not only recognise the self-expressive agency of bodies but also – unlike Irigaray – can acknowledge deep differences among women while opposing restrictive norms concerning gender. Yet, just because this revised version of Butler's theory rests on belief in natural bodily multiplicity, a fresh question arises. What reasons are there to assent to this conception of bodies – to believe that all bodies really do consist of multiple forces?

Perhaps the belief in multiplicity can be supported by Butler's view that western culture is diverse and ever-changing (just as Irigaray infers, from the alleged constancy of western culture's denial of sexual difference, to natural duality). So, we might surmise that this cultural diversity reveals the operation of a plethora of conflicting, diverse, bodily drives, all seeking to express themselves by reinterpreting cultural phenomena. The problem, though, is that Butler's view of culture, as presented, is itself untenable, underestimating the tenacity and deep-rootedness of cultural ideas of sexual difference. This view, therefore, does not provide a sound basis from which to infer natural multiplicity in bodies. As yet, then, we have no more reason to believe in bodily multiplicity than in natural duality. To decide whether to embrace the revised version of Butler's philosophy or Irigaray's later philosophy, we need to bracket out consideration of their respective advantages and disadvantages to ascertain which philosophy – if either – is supported by a view of bodies which we have grounds to endorse. We therefore need to return to Irigaray's conception of natural duality and assess her reasons for believing that bodies naturally have sexually different characters. Having done that, we can identify and evaluate the contrasting arguments which might recommend belief in bodily multiplicity and then decide which conception of bodies (if either) commands support. So, even now that Butler's theory of gender has been revised to remove its problems, it still fails

to displace the interest of Irigaray's philosophy of natural sexual difference. On the contrary, because this revision of Butler rests on a conception of bodies which is no more immediately credible than that of
Irigaray, it drives us back to explore Irigaray's deeper reasons for postulating natural sexual difference. This exploration is the task of the next
chapter.

3

Nature, Sexual Duality, and Bodily Multiplicity

Irigaray's philosophy of natural sexual difference is potentially fruitful in promising to revalue nature and bodies by attributing self-expressive agency to them, and in promoting social change to give nature and bodies expression and recognition. But this philosophy is challenged by Butler's theory of gender. According to the revised and strengthened version of this theory which I have proposed, bodies are composed of multiple forces which actively pursue self-enhancement, and which seek political change to encourage this pursuit, in the form of the subversion of gender categories. To decide which approach to embrace, we need, crucially, to ascertain which conception of bodies (if either) is true: Irigaray's conception of natural bodily duality or the competing conception of bodily multiplicity. We need to explore Irigaray's reasons for postulating natural sexual duality and ask what countervailing reasons might support an ontology of bodily multiplicity. This chapter will conclude that some considerations support each ontology, and that we therefore need to develop a theory on which human bodies are naturally both sexed and internally multiple.

In Section I, I examine how Irigaray supports her belief in natural sexual duality with a philosophy according to which nature, as a whole, obeys polar rhythms which find their fullest manifestation in human sexual dimorphism. As Sections II and III explore, this philosophy of nature leads Irigaray to a concomitant rethinking of sexual difference as consisting, ultimately, in a difference between basic *rhythms* which regulate the development of male and female bodies and forms of experience. She distinguishes this conception of sexual difference from scientific accounts by claiming that she sees this difference as (in a sense to be explained) ultimately a difference in *being*, not in biology. In this way, as Section IV explains, Irigaray positions sexual difference as natural without reproducing biological – or biological determinist – accounts of that difference. Her idea that sexual difference ultimately consists in a difference between not static forms or properties but rhythmic principles, which regulate development, growth, and change, also distinguishes her position from essentialism as usually understood. This explains Irigaray's reluctance to identify herself as an essentialist, despite holding the view – which remains identifiably essentialist – that men and women are constituted as such by their naturally different rhythms. Precisely because Irigaray's conceptions of nature and the body are unusual, though, the question arises as to why we should prefer them to more standard scientific conceptions. As I will show, Irigaray defends her conceptions phenomenologically, on the grounds that they remain close to lived, embodied, experience. However, this defence opens up the possibility that contrasting, yet equally phenomenologically rooted, conceptions of nature and the body may equally compel support.

Against the background of Irigaray's defence of her account of sexual duality and its supporting philosophy of nature, I turn in Section V to ask what contrary reasons exist for believing in the natural multiplicity of bodies. I begin by asking whether intersex supports this belief in bodies' natural multiplicity, as Butler and Georgia Warnke have maintained.[1] They argue that the medical treatment of the intersexed exposes how all ascriptions of sex are culturally laden impositions upon bodies which consist of inherently diverse features. On this argument, intersex does indirectly support the notion that bodies are made up of multiple forces, insofar as bodies' inherently diverse features can be construed as manifestations of those forces. This notion of multiple forces, moreover, has phenomenological grounding in aspects of our lived experience of embodiment. Since, therefore, there are considerations which favour belief in bodily multiplicity as well as duality, I conclude that we need an ontology which synthesises these two conceptions of the body. Section VI starts to outline the form which a synthesis of these conceptions could take.

I. Irigaray's Philosophy of Nature

We have seen previously how Irigaray attempts – unsuccessfully – to justify her belief in natural sexual duality by inferring it from her reading of

---

[1] See Warnke, 'Intersexuality and the Categories of Sex,' in *Hypatia* 16:3 (2001), pp. 126–37.

western culture. Ultimately, though, her deeper reasons for affirming natural duality stem from her philosophy of nature. Across various later writings, she sketches a novel theory of the natural world as the terrain in which human bodies are situated, 'which surrounds us, which constitutes us as bodies, sexed bodies, as woman and man' (DBT, 47). She argues that all natural phenomena contain a duality between two rhythms, and that nature realises this duality most fully in the case of the human species because humans are uniquely able to accentuate their duality by engaging in cultural activity. Humans must naturally be sexually dual, then, because nature's overall organisation requires this. (From Irigaray's perspective, one can consistently say that humans are necessarily sexually dual, that they have a unique potential for realising this duality by expressing it culturally, and that western symbolic structures have not in fact allowed this duality any cultural expression; that is, the human species has not yet realised its unique potential fully.)

Irigaray never sets out her account of nature systematically but offers several fragmentary discussions of nature, contained mainly in *Sexes and Genealogies*, *I Love to You*, and *Democracy Begins Between Two* (1994). Manifestly central to all these discussions is the idea that sexual dimorphism pervades every aspect of nature: '*Nature has a sex [La nature est sexuée]*, always and everywhere. All traditions that remain faithful to the cosmic have a sex and take account of natural powers (*puissances*) in sexuate terms' (SG, 108/122). One interpreter, Gail Schwab, surmises that Irigaray must be using the term 'nature' rather loosely here, strictly meaning only the higher plants and animals.[2] If not, Irigaray blatantly overlooks the fact that much of nature is non-organic and that many organisms reproduce asexually. Irigaray, though, insists that the 'natural powers' whose sexual difference she recognises include non-organic phenomena – referring, as examples, to the seasons and times of day: 'Spring is not autumn nor summer winter, night is not day' (108/122). 'Plants, animals, gods, the elements of the universe, all have a sex' (178/192). Elsewhere, she states that the 'movement' of sexual difference

is true of the entire universe, but can already be seen in the sap of the plant world, in the behavior of animals, just as in the movement of the sea, in the alternating of the seasons, in the respective intensities of the light and of the heat of the sun, in the cycles of humidity and dryness, of the winds, of cyclones. (DBT, 111–12)

[2] Schwab, 'Sexual Difference as Model: An Ethics for the Global Future', in *Diacritics* 28: 1 (1998), p. 79.

Sexual difference is found in not only higher organisms but also lower organisms and all non-organic phenomena – even the seasons, light, and climatic forces. This claim probably has more intuitive resonance in Romance languages, in which all these natural phenomena are grammatically gendered.[3] But this does not mitigate the problem that Irigaray's attribution of sexual dimorphism to the entire cosmos seems false.

Closer study of Irigaray's writings, though, reveals that she ascribes sexual difference to most natural processes only in an attenuated sense. As she explains, natural processes contain 'sexual' difference insofar as they all contain two 'poles' between which a continuous 'alternation' takes place (SG, 108/122). The climatic process, for example, contains cycles of humidity and dryness. The two poles of this process are interdependent, cyclically supplanting one another. They alternate not by turning into one another but by engaging in a kind of breathing – each pole, alternately, inhales and exhales air, so that the one expands while the other shrinks. Analogous processes occur elsewhere: for example, the different parts of plants emerge as they imbibe and circulate sap according to distinctive rhythms. The entire cosmos, then, can be said to 'exist between expansion and concentration' (DBT, 111): the cosmos is composed of phenomena and processes which contain poles, each of which regulates the fluids flowing through it according to a distinctive rhythm. As this indicates, the basic materials constituting the cosmos are various fluid substances, such as air and water (FA, 83–4/78–9), which circulate within the poles of natural phenomena. Irigaray sometimes alleges that air is the most basic of these fluid substances, the 'universal matter [*matière*] of the living' (ILTY, 148/232) or the 'arch-mediation . . . of the world' (FA, 12/18). Elsewhere, though, she counts air as just one among a number of fluid substances which make up natural things (FA, 33/35, 96/90).

For Irigaray, then, all natural phenomena have poles, which are placed in their polar relations to each other by the complementary rhythms at which they suck in fluids (expand) and expel fluids (contract). Insofar as this rhythmic bipolarity inherent in all natural processes and phenomena makes them 'sexuate', this is because this bipolarity approximates in structure to human sexual difference. The way each pole depends upon its other and yet follows its unique rhythm parallels the situation of the two human sexes, which differ fundamentally yet also depend upon one

---

[3] Irigaray sees these languages as closer to the natural reality of sexuation, against which grammatically ungendered languages such as English have reacted (SG, 173/187–8).

another within the overall process of human life, which regenerates itself through sexual reproduction (JTN, 37/12–13). Irigaray thinks of nature in terms of human sexual difference, then, depicting natural phenomena as containing a bipolarity which is analogous to human duality. It is more helpful, though, to simply say that natural phenomena are rhythmic and bipolar, and not that they are strictly sexuate. On this basis, it can also be said that organic phenomena follow bipolar rhythms but that only some plant and animal species manifest this bipolarity in the fuller guise of sexual dimorphism.

With the idea that all nature obeys bipolar rhythms, Irigaray aims to justify her belief that human duality is natural, by portraying human duality as one manifestation of the generalised bipolarity within nature. Indeed, she regards humanity as the exemplary manifestation of natural bipolarity: 'The natural, aside from the diversity of its incarnations or modes of appearing, is at least *two*: male and female [*masculin et féminin*]' (ILTY, 37/69). Rhythmical bipolarity appears in 'diverse modes', each less adequate than its most perfect manifestation, human dimorphism. 'The paradigm of two is to be found in sexual difference' between human beings (DBT, 129). Human duality realises – embodies in its most transparent form – the rhythmical bipolarity which the entire cosmos displays. Irigaray identifies human beings, in particular, as the site where natural duality comes to complete realisation because she thinks that humans are unique in their ability to express themselves – including their duality – through cultural activities. She always claims, traditionally enough, that culture elevates humans above 'animality' (see, for example, ILTY, 36/66), referring to humans as uniquely 'hybrid' creatures who can only develop in culturally mediated ways.[4] For Irigaray, though, non-human animals and plants also achieve greater dimorphism than non-organic things to the extent that, as organisms, they engage in self-realising activities that fully develop and manifest their inborn polarity (Irigaray defines the organic as what 'grows' and 'becomes'; see WD, 153). Since

---

4 'Being Two, How Many Eyes Have We?', in *Paragraph* 25: 3 (2002), p. 148. Irigaray's unqualified contrast between non-cultural animals and cultural humans is oversimplified. As David Wood points out, 'the use of the word "animal" or "the animal" to refer to any and all living creatures is a conceptual violence [to the immense variety of 'animal' species] that expeditiously legitimates our actual violence' to 'animals' ('Thinking with Cats', in *Animal Philosophy*, ed. Peter Atterton and Matthew Calarco (London: Continuum, 2004), p. 133). Ultimately, then, Irigaray's contrast must be complicated considerably; this is beyond my remit. Irigaray herself acknowledges the difficulty of 'talking about' animals in her 'Animal Compassion', in *Animal Philosophy*, pp. 195–201.

nonhuman animals and plants nevertheless lack culture, they lack an important domain in which to develop their polarity and can never do so as fully as human beings.

Irigaray's picture of nature is, broadly, hierarchical (E, 128/123), with non-organic phenomena realising their bipolarity least perfectly; then come organic, open-endedly active, beings which can manifest their polarity more fully; finally, we have human organisms, who can participate in culture and thereby express their duality still more fully, by evolving cultural manifestations of it. Thus, for Irigaray: 'Human becoming corresponds to stages of differentiation from other species' (KW, xi). Human sexual difference acquires massive metaphysical significance, realising most completely the polarity which structures the entire natural universe. It must be stressed that, for Irigaray, human beings do not realise the dimorphism pervading the cosmos by being born with particularly strongly dimorphic structures. Rather, they realise nature's dimorphism only because they have the potential to express themselves culturally.

Irigaray's philosophy of nature justifies her belief that humanity is naturally dual by implying that this duality manifests nature's general bipolarity and, moreover, must necessarily exist if natural bipolarity is to find full expression. This invites the further question: how does Irigaray justify this account of nature itself? This question is pressing because her account of nature appears somewhat fanciful. However, it has at least one significant antecedent, in Goethe's philosophy of nature (an antecedent which, as far as I know, Irigaray does not acknowledge). A brief review of Goethe's philosophy of nature may make Irigaray's account seem less far-fetched.

Goethe contends that there are 'two great driving forces in all nature: ... *polarity* [*Polarität*] and *intensification* [*Steigerung*] ... Polarity is a state of constant attraction and repulsion, while intensification is a state of ever-striving ascent'.[5] Polarity manifests itself in that all natural phenomena develop into two poles which then become attracted and reunite. Intensification propels natural phenomena to pass through successive stages of development, each of which sees the emergence of a fresh polarity. Goethe finds both forces exhibited in the growth of plants; in 'The Metamorphosis of Plants' (1789), he claims that plants grow by repeatedly expanding into different parts, which then contract back together. Moreover, he believes that these parts expand by ingesting fluids which

---

[5] Goethe, 'A Commentary on the Aphoristic Essay "Nature"' (1828), in *Scientific Studies*, ed. and trans. Douglas Miller (Princeton: Princeton University Press, 1995), p. 6.

become progressively more rarefied as the process of intensification proceeds.[6]

Anticipating Irigaray to a surprising degree, Goethe sees natural phenomena as hierarchically organised, bipolar, composed of fluids, and undergoing continual processes of expansion and contraction. Yet his account is not arbitrarily fanciful; he devised it to explain the various phenomena to which he devoted sustained empirical study – including geology, meteorology, the metamorphosis of animal skeletons, colours, and plant development. Goethe, though, always tries to give these phenomena a specific kind of explanation, one that articulates the structure of these phenomena *as experienced* and observed. Explanations of the type which Goethe seeks elicit unifying principles which are contained within concrete experience. Hence, he writes: 'The blue of the sky shows us the basic law of chromatics. Let us not seek for something behind the phenomena – they themselves are the theory'.[7] Idiosyncratic as Goethe's general picture of nature might look, he actually intends it to capture nature as we experience it – to describe structuring principles which we concretely experience to organise natural phenomena.

Unsurprisingly, given the affinities between her account of nature and that of Goethe, Irigaray also defends her account on the grounds of its continuity with perception and lived experience. Before considering this defence, though, we should examine more carefully how her philosophy of nature justifies her in postulating a natural human duality which she reconceives as, ultimately, a difference in rhythms. Having understood nature as bipolar and rhythmic, Irigaray reconceives human sexual duality on the model of nature so understood. Thus, her philosophy of nature justifies belief in natural human duality only insofar as that duality is rethought in an original, metaphysically complex, way. The next two sections gradually unpack the conception of sexual duality as rhythmic which arises from Irigaray's philosophy of nature.

II. The Ontological Status of Sexual Difference

Based on her philosophy of nature, Irigaray asserts that human duality is situated within the natural order. Seeing human sexual difference as natural, she writes: 'Between man and woman, there really is otherness: biological, . . . relational' (ILTY, 61 / 105). She is, apparently, resuscitating

---

[6] Goethe, 'The Metamorphosis of Plants', in *Scientific Studies*, pp. 95–6.
[7] Goethe, 'Selections from *Maxims and Reflections*', in *Scientific Studies*, p. 307.

the view that biological sex differences shape our experience as men and women. This belief in the determining power of biological sex would be problematic for several reasons. Firstly, it would neglect the irreducibility of gender and its (partial) independence of sex, assuming that social practises are shaped by biology. Secondly, this belief would neglect the irreducibility of the symbolic level of existence, treating cultural formations, too, as functions of biology. Thirdly, the belief that sex has determining power would seem to amount to biological determinism, suggesting that patriarchal culture is an inevitable effect of male biology, immune to change. Compared with Irigaray's early philosophy, her later thought appears premised on a belief in the determining power of sex which entails an unattractively simplistic and (from a feminist perspective) pessimistic analysis of social and cultural reality.

Fortunately, on closer inspection, Irigaray's mature conception of human sexual difference proves different from this belief in the determining power of biological sex. She generally distinguishes between *sexual* difference (*la différence sexuelle*) and biological *sex* difference (*la différence des sexes*). She draws this distinction because, as she repeatedly states, she sees sexual difference as an *ontological*, not a biological, phenomenon. 'Philosophy's task is to raise this difference [between the sexes] to a . . . somewhat ontological level; it's been left . . . to empiricism' (WD, 71). She also states that

between a man and a woman the negativity is . . . of an ontological, irreducible type. Between a woman and another woman it's of a much more empirical type, and, furthermore, can only be understood and can only live in the ontological difference between man and woman. (JLI, 110)

In expounding Irigaray (and Butler) so far, I have used 'ontology' simply to mean a theory of what exists – of what kinds of entities populate the world.[8] Accordingly, I have claimed that Irigaray espouses an 'ontology' of sexual difference and of bodily matter, that is, a theory of what sexual difference and bodily matter are really like. However, the later Irigaray uses the term 'ontological' in a much more specialised way, to designate the non-biological yet still natural manner in which sexual difference exists. Hereafter, when I refer to sexual difference as 'ontological', I will use this adjective in Irigaray's sense, although I shall also continue to

---

[8] Irigaray, too, sometimes uses 'ontology' in this broader way. For example: 'If the human is divided into two, . . . each of its parts and . . . their common world no longer belong to a traditional ontology' (WL, 11).

speak, more broadly, of 'ontologies' of sexual duality and multiplicity (that is, theories which say that bodies are naturally dual or multiple).

Unpacking Irigaray's more specialised understanding of the ontological is complicated, since her statements on the theme are allusive. At one point she remarks that she construes sexual difference, *qua* ontological, as a difference in men's and women's *being* (*être*): 'I often use the word "sex" for the sexed identity. This doesn't designate the sexual [that is, the erotic] per se, rather the woman being and the man being' (WD, 190). What does this mean? Irigaray sometimes equates the difference between men's and women's 'being' with a phenomenological difference between men's and women's 'worlds' (85) or between their 'subjectivity'.[9] This suggests that men and women experience and render the world intelligible in different ways. However, Irigaray clarifies that, for her, having a 'world' means having a particular way of relating to other people and to things: 'sexual difference corresponds first of all to a manner that human beings have of entering into relationship . . . the difference between the sexes [is] above all a difference in relational identity'.[10] These different ways of forming relationships (here, Irigaray repeatedly suggests that women prioritise relationships between people whereas men prioritise relationships with objects) inform correspondingly different ways in which men and women perceive and interact with things and people. Yet, although Irigaray claims that these differences in 'relational identity' fundamentally comprise sexual difference and, therefore, that this difference is not biological, she always traces differences in relational identity back to differences between men's and women's bodies. For example:

How can we explain the differences of subjectivity between male and female? We can say . . . [that it is] equivalent to being able, or not being able, to engender [like] the mother. Or . . . to engender in oneself or outside of oneself. [Or] . . . to make love in oneself or outside of oneself. These features determine two worlds that will be different.[11]

If differences of 'world' derive, ultimately, from different bodily features and capacities, then these bodily differences must constitute the ontological difference between the sexes. In what sense, though, are these bodily features non-biological? We seem no closer to comprehending what Irigaray means by the ontological.

---

[9] 'Why Cultivate Difference?' in *Paragraph* 25: 3 (2002), p. 82.
[10] Ibid., pp. 79–80.
[11] Ibid., p. 82.

Irigaray's notion of the ontological is best elucidated as a response
to Heidegger's well-known distinction between 'ontological' discourse,
which concerns being (*Sein*), and 'ontic' discourse concerning entities
(*Seiende*). The point of Heidegger's distinction between being and beings
is that being – the sheer fact that there is (*es gibt*) existence, that existence unfathomably surges up – is not itself an entity, although the philosophical tradition has often construed it ontically, as a highest entity or
first cause.[12] Heidegger's understanding of being evolves over time and
comes increasingly close to the Greek concept of *physis*. Thus, his thinking
of being intertwines more and more closely with reflection on 'nature'
(although he firmly distinguishes the Latin concept of *natura* from the
Greek *physis*, which he consistently refuses to translate). By his 1939 lecture course on Aristotle's *Physics* – 'On the Essence and Concept of *Physis*
in Aristotle's *Physics* B, I' – Heidegger is sympathetically exploring what
he identifies as the pre-Socratic view that being is *physis*. According to this
view, 'to be' means to emerge into appearance spontaneously through
an ongoing process, a process, however, which always occludes itself just
in coming to appearance.

According to Heidegger, Aristotle examines being-from-*physis* ('natural' being) as a specific mode of being, characteristic of, for instance, animals and plants, and distinct from the mode of being of that which is artificially produced, such as knives or tables. However, Heidegger discerns in
Aristotle's examination two significant residues of the older, pre-Socratic,
view, which equates *physis* with being *per se*. These residues make Aristotle's
examination helpful – indirectly – for thinking through the idea of
being as *physis*. Firstly, Aristotle thinks of natural beings as undergoing

---

[12] Irigaray regularly notes that she relies on Heidegger's distinction between being and
entities. In *The Way of Love* (2002), she says that she 'converses with Heidegger' by
employing the term *être* (being), where *être*, she says, 'is irreducible to the almost object-
like factuality of an "*étant*" – [a] being' (WL, xii–xiii). Yet Irigaray's ontology, on which
the two sexes really have different characters, looks like an example of the kind of metaphysical theorising which Heidegger criticises for neglecting the 'ontological difference'
between being and entities, by assuming that metaphysics has simply to give an exhaustive account of what types of being there are (on this discrepancy between Irigaray and
Heidegger, see Sandford, 'Feminism Against "The Feminine"', p. 12). As we will see,
though, Irigaray actually understands the sexes' different characters as rhythms which
regulate their growth into presence – their *being*, the movement by which they surge
up into existence. As such, her ontology is more consistent with Heidegger than it initially seems. On Irigaray's influence by Heidegger more generally, and for an overview
of literature on Heidegger and Irigaray, see Patricia Huntingdon's introduction to *Feminist Interpretations of Martin Heidegger*, ed. Nancy J. Holland and Patricia Huntingdon
(University Park, PA: Penn State Press, 2001), pp. 6–9, 15–18.

a process of genesis, spontaneous emergence into *morphē*, where the latter, according to Heidegger, does not straightforwardly mean 'form' but rather 'appearance' (*Aussehen*) – form as something perceptible and only temporarily enduring.[13] Whereas artefacts arise only when craftspeople actualise pre-existing blueprints or 'ideas', in nature forms emerge spontaneously as perceptible resting points within a process of genesis. Hence, whereas craft skill (*technē*) produces objects which differ from it (as, for example, medicine produces health), a plant in 'producing' buds is not putting forward anything different from itself, but just entering into another phase in its own process of coming-into-appearance. This process of natural coming-into-appearance therefore has no clear end point.[14]

Secondly, Heidegger contends, Aristotle also retains pre-Socratic thought when he suggests that, as any natural appearance becomes present, it makes an absence perceptible as well – the absence of its own preceding process of genesis and of the previously perceptible phases within that process. For Aristotle: 'The self-placing into the appearance always lets something be present in such a way that *in* the presencing an absencing simultaneously becomes present'; for example, when a blossom flowers, the leaves which prepared for the blossom's emergence die away.[15] The absence of these leaves is apparent in the newly emerged blossom, and is apparent *as* the perceptible absence of the process which has prepared and preceded the blossom's emergence. Aristotle's view here reflects the pre-Socratic idea that being, as *physis*, 'loves to hide', concealing itself just in its emergence.[16] Through his reading of Aristotle, then, Heidegger articulates two crucial aspects of the idea of being as *physis* – growth into presence which is (1) open-ended and (2) self-concealing.

---

[13] Heidegger, 'On the Essence and Concept of *Physis* in Aristotle's *Physics* B, I', in *Pathmarks*, ed. Will McNeill (Cambridge: Cambridge University Press, 1998), pp. 209–10; '*Vom Wesen und Begriff der* Physis *Aristoteles, Physik B, 1*', in *Wegmarken, Gesamtausgabe* division 1, vol. 9 (Frankfurt: Klostermann, 1996), p. 275.

[14] See Trish Glazebrook, 'From *Physis* to Nature, *Technē* to Technology: Heidegger on Aristotle, Galileo, and Newton', in *Southern Journal of Philosophy* 38 (2000), pp. 104–5. According to Heidegger, the pre-Socratic view holds that natural growth has no *telos* (no definite end-state), and so this view is not teleological. Heidegger indeed rejects teleological views, which, he claims, wrongly interpret organisms as artefacts which make themselves according to an internal blueprint (Heidegger, 'On the Essence and Concept of *Physis*', p. 195; '*Vom Wesen und Begriff der* Physis', pp. 254–5).

[15] 'On the Essence and Concept of *Physis*', p. 227; '*Vom Wesen und Begriff der* Physis', p. 297.

[16] Heraclitus's dictum, 'Nature [*physis*] loves to hide', is crucial for the later Heidegger; see Heraclitus, Fragment 10, in *The Art and Thought of Heraclitus*, ed. and trans. Charles Kahn (Cambridge: Cambridge University Press, 1979), p. 33.

Heidegger's idea of being as open-ended growth reappears in Irigaray, who also distinguishes the Latin concept of *natura* from the Greek *physis* as ' "coming to appear" – to be born in a concrete sense – growing' (WD, 95). Following Heidegger, she maintains that, insofar as they are natural, things – including human bodies – give themselves their own forms as phases in an indefinite process of becoming.[17] But she also amends Heidegger's idea of *physis* by claiming that *physis* is composed of fluid materials, referring, for example, to '*phuein* in its fluid medium' (FA, 83/78) and to 'the fluid matter that [has] made its [being's] constitution possible'.[18] Unlike Heidegger, she regards fluid materials (*le fluent*) as the ultimate constituents of reality, which enter into processes of growth. To understand this modification which she makes to Heidegger's conception of *physis* (and so of being), we need to examine her notion that material reality is basically fluid.

The notion of material fluidity emerges out of Irigaray's earlier analyses of the western philosophical tradition, which, she believes, consistently fails to think through the fluid – as, for her, does modern science, with its comparative difficulty in theorising fluids (TS, 106–7/105).[19] Her early writings suggest that the tradition has equated the fluid with female bodies and cast both – pejoratively – as boundless, troubling, and contaminating. Within traditional symbolic structures, the fluid figures as a mere lack of, and threat to, solidity imagined as male. 'The "subject"... finds everything flowing abhorrent'; fluids 'threaten to deform, propagate, evaporate, consume him, to flow out of him and into another who is difficult to hold on to' (S, 237/294–5). The early Irigaray therefore proposes a symbolic revaluation of the fluid and of the female body imagined as fluid. She advances a more

---

[17] 'Being Two, How Many Eyes Have We?', p. 145. Prior to this short text – which, Irigaray says, 'without referring directly to it... partially corresponds to a critical reading of' Heidegger's 1939 Aristotle course (p. 151) – she discusses Heidegger's concept of *physis* extensively in *The Forgetting of Air* (1983). Unsurprisingly, therefore, Heidegger's Aristotle course 'echoes... throughout *The Forgetting of Air*', although Irigaray does not overtly cite it; Helen Fielding notes this in 'Questioning Nature: Irigaray, Heidegger and the Potentiality of Matter', *Continental Philosophy Review* 36: 1 (2003), p. 3.

[18] 'From *The Forgetting of Air* to *To Be Two*', in *Feminist Interpretations of Martin Heidegger*, p. 310.

[19] Amplifying Irigaray's discussion of fluid mechanics, see N. Katherine Hayles, 'Gender Encoding in Fluid Mechanics: Masculine Channels and Feminine Flows', in *Differences: A Journal of Feminist Cultural Studies* 4: 2 (1992), pp. 16–44. On Irigaray's idea that reality is *au fond* fluid, see Schor, 'This Essentialism Which Is Not One', p. 69.

positive rendering of female fluidity, in which 'woman [has] a form that in(de)finitely transforms itself without closing . . . Metamorphoses which never make up a totality . . . Transmutations, always unexpected, since they do not . . . accomplish any telos' (233/289).

Irigaray's later work re-examines fluidity in the changed context of her conception of human bodies as active and self-expressive. As part of this conception, outlined in *An Ethics of Sexual Difference*, she describes human bodies as porous, composed of permeable membranes through which fluid substances from other, exterior, bodies continually seep so as to integrate themselves, by osmosis, into the body's interior (E, 69/71, 98/98, 109–11/107–8). These fluids – blood, water, air – permeate the body and coagulate into the more or less solid substances and membranes which make up the body, including the 'mucous' (*muqueux*) which Irigaray describes as 'in great measure the matter of which flesh is made' (SG, 180/194).

Irigaray's description of bodies as composed of fluid materials contributes to her thinking of how bodies naturally have determinate forms, for she understands forms as the configurations into which bodies' component fluids enter. From this perspective, Irigaray begins to understand the *forms* of bodies, as well as their material composition, as fluid. But whereas bodily matter is fluid in a relatively obvious sense, it is less clear how corporeal forms can be fluid. To complicate things further, Irigaray characterises the fluidity of bodily forms by associating them with rhythms. This returns us to her crucial concept of rhythm. Familiarised with her notion of fluidity, we can now at last examine her concept of rhythm and see how it integrates her thinking about form, fluidity, *physis*, and sexual difference. Thereafter, we can return to the question of what she means in identifying sexual difference as ontological.

III. Sexual Difference Between Rhythms

References to rhythm occur intermittently throughout Irigaray's work, but she nowhere gives a sustained exposition of this concept. We can start from one of her indirect passages on rhythm: 'Nature's noise is rhythmic . . . it respects the differences in rhythms. It informs [*informe*]. . . . It becomes continuously. . . . It grows, becomes, uniting its roots and its flowers. It endlessly informs' (SG, 108/122). *Informe* conveys a process whereby nature simultaneously assumes and sheds form, thereby rendering itself perceptible and intelligible. The passage, as a whole, implies that naturally occurring forms are 'rhythms', or exist rhythmically. The concepts of rhythm and form are, indeed, deeply connected both linguistically and philosophically, as Emile Benveniste shows in his 1951 article 'The Notion of "Rhythm" in its Linguistic Expression'. Irigaray does not explicitly cite this paper in discussing nature's rhythm, but she must be aware of it, since she draws elsewhere on Benveniste's work in linguistics (including his *Problems in General Linguistics*, which contains his paper on rhythm).[20]

Benveniste amasses many examples to show that the ancient Ionian philosophers, and, subsequently, Greek poets and writers in general, used the word *rhythmos* to mean *schēma* – form. The atomist Democritus, for example, held that the elements of water and air differ due to the different forms (rhythms) assumed by their component atoms – just as, for Democritus more broadly, objects only differ because of the different arrangements of their atoms. Thus, according to Benveniste, the ancient Greeks used *rhythmos* to mean 'distinctive form, proportioned figure, arrangement, disposition'.[21] Yet, he continues, the Greeks equated *schēma* and *rhythmos* because they understood *schēma* itself in a distinctive way: as something which exists only temporarily, fleetingly. This can be seen, Benveniste claims, from the fact that *rhythmos* derives etymologically from *rhein*, to flow. Moreover, Greek endings in *–mos* generally indicate 'the particular modality of [an] accomplishment as it is presented to the eyes', and as it presents itself temporarily. Benveniste concludes that *rhythmos*

designates the form in the instant that it is assumed by what is moving, mobile and fluid . . . it fits the pattern of a fluid element. It is the form as improvised, momentary, changeable. Now, *rhein* is the essential predication of nature and things in the Ionian philosophy . . . We can now understand how *rhythmos*, meaning literally 'the particular manner of flowing', could have been the most proper term for describing 'dispositions' or 'configurations' without fixity or natural necessity and arising from an arrangement which is always subject to change.[22]

---

[20] See, especially, 'Does Schizophrenic Discourse Exist?' in *To Speak is Never Neutral* (1985), trans. Gail Schwab (London: Continuum, 2002), p. 176, and, on Irigaray's use of Benveniste more generally, p. 173, and Marjorie Hass, 'The Style of the Speaking Subject: Irigaray's Empirical Studies of Language Production', in *Hypatia* 15: 1 (2000), p. 67.

[21] Benveniste, 'The Notion of "Rhythm" in its Linguistic Expression', in *Problems in General Linguistics* (1966), trans. Mary Elizabeth Meek (Coral Gables, Fla.: University of Miami Press, 1971), p. 285.

[22] Ibid., p. 286.

'Rhythm', then, appropriately characterises forms as understood by a worldview in which things only ever exist temporally, transiently.[23]

Benveniste's analysis shows that in pre-Socratic philosophy, a rhythm is the form assumed by something which fluctuates, flows, and therefore only ever assumes form ephemerally. Similarly, Irigaray understands natural bodies to acquire forms as their fluids circulate and enter into configurations which, as configurations of unstable, volatile, fluids, can only ever exist evanescently. Bodies only ever take on form provisionally, forms comprising transitory resting points amidst their flows. Because bodily forms are evanescent, then, Irigaray characterises them as fluid and rhythmic.

Against the background of this conception of rhythmic form, Irigaray identifies sexual difference as a difference between rhythms. She states in *Thinking the Difference*, for example, that

time in a woman's life is particularly irreversible, and compared to men's time, it agrees less with the repetitive, cumulative, entropic, and largely non-progressive, nullifying economy of our present environment. . . . Female sexuality does not correspond to the same economy [as male]. It is more related to becoming, more linked to the time of the universe. . . . A woman's life is marked by irreversible events that define the stages of her life. This is true for puberty, . . . the loss of virginity, . . . becoming pregnant, childbirth, breast-feeding. (JTN, 114–15/138–9)

In contrast, according to Irigaray, male temporality is relatively linear and unchanging. She distinguishes the more cyclical rhythm of female sexuality from the linear rhythm of male sexuality, which she regards as marked by ever-repeated processes of building up tension, releasing, and returning to homeostasis (TD, 25/42–3). Again, *I Love to You* states that women differ from men in that their bodies 'grow' (*croître*) in cycles, following a rhythm of slow but irreversible change (ILTY, 37/70–1).

With these claims, Irigaray employs the notion of rhythm in an altered way from the pre-Socratics (as Benveniste interprets them). She takes rhythm to denote not the varying forms (configurations of fluid materials) which male and female bodies assume but an overarching temporal pattern which regulates the process by which these successive forms

---

[23] According to Benveniste, Plato decisively changes the meaning of *rhythmos* to describe the form of movement of a dancing human body, the movement being broken down into steps and the intervals between them numerically measured. This generates the modern concept of rhythm as 'a configuration of movements organized in time' (ibid., p. 287).

emerge.[24] This notion of rhythm is a development from the notion of rhythm as temporary form. Insofar as forms only arise temporarily and fleetingly, there must be a process by which they emerge – a process which, although spontaneous, still results in these forms succeeding one another in a definite order and at a determined pace. The process discloses the operation of a regulating principle, which orchestrates the sequence of the forms which bodies assume over time.

Irigaray's further claim is that different principles regulate the emergence of female and male bodily forms. The forms of women's bodies change dramatically over time, most obviously with the onset of puberty and menstruation, changes following pregnancy or giving birth, and the arrival of menopause. In contrast, Irigaray believes, the forms of men's bodies remain relatively constant over the course of their lives. She therefore describes women's bodily development as regulated by a rhythm of irreversible change, as opposed to continuity in men's case. Women's rhythm can also be described as cyclical because, with the onset of each specific stage in women's lives, the possibility arises of passing through a whole cycle in the course of which the corresponding bodily forms and capacities are developed fully and then superseded. Because men's development is more continuous, this possibility of undergoing different, successive cycles does not arise for men. On the other hand, Irigaray suggests, men constantly pass through small cycles of tension and return to homoeostasis, cycles which take the same basic form throughout men's lives. She therefore characterises men's rhythm in terms of both linearity (or continuity) and punctuation by miniature cycles.

The idea that the sexes differ in respect to rhythms may seem puzzling and oblique. Would it not be more accurate to say that their differing biological makeup (in hormones and chromosomes) causes different patterns of physical change and therefore different rhythms? Irigaray opposes that view because she thinks that it misunderstands the organic body as a kind of self-making artefact, which actualises a blueprint built into it. Based on a deeper understanding of nature as *physis*, she believes, we see that patterns of bodily growth (*croissance*) cannot be programmed by chromosomes and hormones but must take shape openendedly, as does all growth which occurs within the realm of *physis*. Hence,

---

[24] Irigaray's idea that rhythms orchestrate the emergence of bodily forms seems similar to Plato's concept of rhythm (as Benveniste identifies it). Insofar as Irigaray's idea of rhythm naturally extends that of the pre-Socratics, this suggests that, *pace* Benveniste, the Platonic concept extends, and is not sharply differentiated from, the pre-Platonic.

Irigaray writes: 'The sameness of women, among women . . . takes place from within the *open* . . . Cosmic, creative, fermentation [that is, growth] that is always . . . free. Though this is not to say that it is . . . without rhythm' (E, 115/111). For Irigaray, the difference between the rhythms which regulate open-ended bodily growth cannot be derivative but must be the fundamental factor differentiating the sexes.

As we have found, for Irigaray, bodily matter is fluid, entering into derivatively fluid corporeal forms according to a rhythmic process. For Irigaray, the sexes differ in the rhythms which regulate their bodily development, and which – more precisely – regulate the circulation of the fluid bodily materials which coagulate into successive, transitory forms. Thus, she ultimately locates sexual difference in the difference between the more cyclical and irreversible rhythm which regulates the sequence of emergence of female bodily forms, and the more continuous, yet punctuated, rhythm regulating that of male forms. We can now, finally, see how Irigaray identifies sexual difference as an ontological difference, a difference at the level of *physis* or being.

The rhythmic difference which, for Irigaray, is most fully manifest in human beings also obtains throughout nature as a whole. She stresses, '*we are living and sensible, subject to the times and rhythms of the universe, a universe with which we share certain properties, different according to whether we are men or women*' (SG, 87/102). In that she believes polar rhythms to organise all of nature, her discussions of rhythm and fluidity constitute a two-fold revision of Heidegger's conception of *physis*. Firstly, while concurring with him that natural forms emerge through open-ended growth, she thinks that this growth occurs as forms crystallise out of circulating fluids (hence, she claims that *physis* basically consists of fluid materials). According to Irigaray, Heidegger overlooks the role of these fluid materials in natural growth because he follows the philosophical tradition in privileging form (*morphē*) over matter (*hylē*), and so he understands *physis* solely in terms of form (FA, 74/70, 154/137).[25] Heidegger indeed states that '*morphē* – not just more than *hylē* but in fact alone and completely – is *physis*'.[26] Irigaray deviates from Heidegger not only by emphasising the

---

[25] On this Irigarayan criticism of Heidegger, see Fielding, 'Questioning Nature', pp. 8–12.

[26] Heidegger, 'On the Essence and Concept of *Physis*', p. 222; '*Vom Wesen und Begriff der Physis*', p. 290. Irigaray suggests that Heidegger defines *physis* solely in terms of *morphē* – as the process by which forms spontaneously burst forth – because forms, as appearances, are inherently accessible and intelligible to the subject (FA, 103/95). Thus, Heidegger wants *physis* to exist in inherent relation to the human subject (to *Dasein*, he would say) (74/70, 87/81, 133/121). Irigaray rejoins that *physis* grows independently

material conditions of natural growth, but also, secondly, by maintaining that the growth of any phenomenon is always regulated by one of two different rhythms. These rhythms introduce difference into *physis* itself. In that human sexual difference is the fullest manifestation of this rhythmic difference, sexual difference, too, exists as a division within nature as *physis*. '[S]exual difference [is] ... the difference that attributes to each one a *physis* to take into consideration, a history and a relational world proper to each one'.[27] As a difference within nature as *physis*, sexual difference is also a difference in being – 'Being presents itself as two – man and woman'[28] – a difference which exists 'ontologically', between processes of growth, not merely 'ontically', between the entities which result from these processes.

Irigaray, we can now see, understands sexual difference as 'ontological' in a specialised sense: as a difference between the rhythms which govern the natural growth of men's and women's bodies. This rhythmic conception of sexual difference has arisen from Irigaray's philosophy of nature, which leads her to rethink human growth as structured by polar rhythms in the manner characteristic of all natural phenomena. Her complex and novel reconception of sexual duality poses two main questions. How does the metaphysical complexity of Irigaray's understanding of sexual difference bear on my interpretation of her later philosophy as realist essentialism? And how, exactly, does her conception of sexual difference as 'ontological' differ from a biological conception of it? The next section tries to clarify these issues and then addresses her justification for her novel account of nature.

IV. Nature, Biology, and Essence

Irigaray's idea that nature is in dynamic flux complicates my claim that her later philosophy endorses realist essentialism, that is, the view that men's and women's bodies have different natural characters, requiring expression. Specifically, Irigaray's idea that bodies constantly grow, passing

of human subjectivity; it must first exist and develop into human subjectivity before any relation of subjectivity to nature can be possible. An independently growing *physis*, which 'opens ... in an efflorescence that does not produce itself for the look' (116/106), is the condition of possibility *for* subjectivity. Heidegger, she believes, has forgotten that every subject has its conditions of possibility in a process of physical growth beginning in the womb.

[27] 'From *The Forgetting of Air* to *To Be Two*', p. 314.

[28] Ibid., p. 310.

through forms which only ever exist transiently, conflicts with the recognisably essentialist view that bodies have fixed, invariant forms which constitute them as belonging to a particular sex and which need to be expressed in culture. Because of this conflict, Irigaray persistently refuses to call herself an essentialist. As Whitford notes: 'When Irigaray is called essentialist by Anglo-American critics, she looks puzzled ... [because in] the French context, essence ... is the question of the proper (*propre*)'.[29] Irigaray assumes that essentialism means belief in properties which are essential, and so enduring, attributes of substances. Professing to reject any such ontology, she claims that her philosophy involves concepts of matter, reality, and of bodily 'unfolding' which are 'released from intangible essences and more or less magical ontologies' which posit substances and properties (WL, 10).[30] That Irigaray's dynamic view of nature conflicts with belief in enduring properties or forms has been noted by other readers: Olkowski, for example, notes that for Irigaray 'there are no metaphysically valid substances or universals, ... because fluid reality cannot be posited in terms of substances or universals'.[31] Likewise, Gail Weiss refers to Irigaray's 'non-substance-based ... metaphysics of fluidity'.[32]

But, although Irigaray does not believe in unchanging forms which constitute bodies as members of a sex, she does think that bodies are constituted as male or female by the *rhythms* which regulate their growth. Her conception of sexual difference remains identifiably essentialist insofar as she holds that cyclical or linear rhythms are necessary to make bodies female or male. These rhythms are the essential characters without which bodies (as collections of fluids) would not be sexed. As she says, there is a '*physis* ... proper to each' sex; although we should 'giv[e] up the appropriation of the other', we should not 'renounc[e] the proper [but] start ... from a proper' which is dual.[33] That is, we should recognise and seek to express what is proper to each sex: the rhythm of its growth.

Irigaray's essentialism is unusual in seeing rhythms as essential to sexuation, rather than bodily forms or the capacities to which these forms give

---

[29] Whitford, *Luce Irigaray*, p. 135.

[30] Already in *This Sex*, Irigaray refers to 'the birth that is never accomplished, the body that is never created once and for all, the form that is never definitively completed' (TS, 217/216).

[31] Olkowski, 'The End of Phenomenology: Bergson's Interval in Irigaray', in *Hypatia* 15: 3 (2000), p. 79.

[32] Weiss, *Body Images*, p. 67.

[33] 'From *The Forgetting of Air* to *To Be Two*', pp. 314, 313.

rise. For example, she denies that it is essential to being a woman that one menstruate or be able to give birth. Essential to being a woman is undergoing a certain sequence of transitory bodily forms, this sequence being regulated by a particular rhythm of irreversible and gradual change. If a woman's bodily forms are emerging in line with this sequence, then she remains female, for example, once she can no longer give birth.[34] Given this unusual character of Irigaray's essentialism, I must qualify my earlier claim that, for her, bodies have naturally different characters which require expression. For Irigaray, the naturally different characters of bodies are their rhythms, which need to realise themselves by presiding over the unimpeded unfolding of a sequence of bodily forms. *Qua* rhythmic, bodies actively engage with cultural representations in the effort to unfold the developmental pattern inherent within them.[35] More specifically, bodies strive to express their forms culturally, because these forms are stages in the growth at which bodies aim. For Irigaray, socio-cultural change (for instance, to work routines) is necessary to express men's and women's inherent rhythms, and to accommodate and express particular bodily forms and capacities (such as menstruation) inasmuch as these are stages in a rhythmic process of unfolding. Despite Irigaray's dynamic view of nature, then, she remains a realist essentialist for whom men and women have inherent characters which need cultural expression; but

---

[34] What can Irigaray make of women who never become able to give birth at all, for example, due to infertility? She sometimes suggests that the ability to give birth *is* essential to women: 'the little girl . . . [is] a little woman born of another woman. She is able to engender like her mother' (JLI, 108). However, elsewhere she clarifies that 'engendering' need not mean literally giving birth to a child: 'the two sexes regenerate one another aside from any question of reproduction' (JTN, 15/17), where procreation is one possible outcome of erotic 'fecundity' between the sexes (E, 26/32). Another possible outcome is cultural creation: 'We need to discover and declare that we are always mothers just by being women. We bring other things than children into the world: love, desire, language, art, the social, the political, the religious' (SG, 30/18). On the most charitable reading of Irigaray, then, her saying that all women (at a certain stage in their lives) have the same engendering ability means that they can create things in the same sort of way – a way expressive of their shared rhythm.

[35] In 'Flesh Colors', one of the essays in *Sexes and Genealogies*, Irigaray argues that western societies have disrupted individuals' (sexuate) rhythms and that individuals can restore these rhythms by learning to express them creatively through art and painting. 'If colors, sounds, were manifest, . . . [then] the sexuate would be organized according to rhythms of becoming' (SG, 161/175). Irigaray's idea that rhythms can be expressed creatively (and that this has a therapeutic role) builds on Nicolas Abraham's *Rhythms: On the Work, Translation, and Psychoanalysis*, trans. Benjamin Thigpen (Stanford: Stanford University Press, 1995). Abraham argues that lived consciousness has a rhythmic dimension, moving between expectations, surprises, and fulfilments (*Rhythms*, p. 76), and that this rhythmic dimension can be expressed by the rhythms of poetic literature (pp. 107–19).

her realist essentialism is itself dynamic, identifying men's and women's characters with the rhythms regulating their incessant growth.

An important problem resurfaces here. If bodies naturally strive to give themselves cultural expression, then how has it been possible that we have for centuries inhabited a culture which denies sexual difference, and so fails to express bodies *qua* sexually different? For example, if women's bodies strive to express themselves in their special rhythm, then how has it been possible for us to evolve work routines which (as Irigaray contends) conflict with women's rhythms and are suited only to the rhythms of men? Irigaray seems to face a dilemma: she can either insist that culture expresses nature, which suggests that western culture cannot really be monosexuate after all; or she can insist that western culture is monosexuate, but this suggests that bodies cannot really be engaged in striving to express themselves after all. Later, I will explain how Irigaray escapes this dilemma; to anticipate, Irigaray thinks that male bodies have satisfied their striving for self-expression at the expense of female bodies. More specifically, she believes, men have created an *anti*-natural culture which denies expression not only to female bodies but also to many aspects of men's own natures. The peculiarity of men is that they spontaneously – and self-defeatingly – express their natures by developing an anti-natural culture. Irigaray's detailed analysis of this peculiarity will be the topic of Chapter 4.

For now, I want to clarify how Irigaray's rhythmic conception of sexual difference deviates from a biological conception of it. After all, for her, being (say) female does not require having XX chromosomes, ovaries, and female genitalia but rather requires undergoing a particular process of growth guided by a relatively irreversible, gradual rhythm (a rhythm which is not itself the effect of chromosomal and hormonal makeup). Irigaray does not understand this female growth in terms derived from the biological sciences but, instead, via Heidegger and Aristotle, as an open-ended unfolding through which circulating fluids stabilise into successive forms. In the background to Irigaray's departure from scientific conceptions is Heidegger's belief that his thinking of *physis* offers an alternative to the view of being which is presupposed by modern science. Modern science, for Heidegger, is above all projective – it projects understandings of nature and then designs experiments to test these understandings in controlled conditions.[36] This

[36] Heidegger, 'Modern Science, Metaphysics, and Mathematics' (1962), in *Basic Writings*, ed. David Farrell Krell (second, revised, edition; London: Routledge, 1993).

reliance on experimentation reveals that science presupposes a deeper-level understanding of the world as a stock of resources available for human use, including for experimental control and manipulation. Science presumes that to be is to be available for use, whereas Heidegger thinks that to be is to emerge into appearance. The conception of *physis* that Irigaray inherits from Heidegger is therefore alien to modern science, including the biological sciences inasmuch as they share in science's projective, experimental orientation. Irigaray's alternative conception of *physis* is advantageous, as she sees it, firstly because it departs from the arrogant presumption that all that is consists of resources for human use, and secondly because it remains attuned to our lived experiences of growth and unfolding, as features of both our own embodied existence and that of the things, especially the living things, which surround us.

Moreover, Irigaray identifies the fluids which circulate within bodies as materials which are familiar from our embodied experience: air and water, blood, milk, and mucous. She also resists describing the forms into which these fluids stabilise in biological terms. Sometimes she describes them quite generally, as membranes, tissues, skins, and envelopes (E, 93–4/94, 105/103, 109–11/107–8); at other times, she equates these forms with specific physical features: lips, blood, the umbilical cord (18/18, 101/100, 145/137). In both cases, she identifies bodily 'forms' with familiar physical features as given in embodied experience. It is notable that, even when she states that 'the return to nature can be done by scientific means . . . [since science] state[s] certain obvious facts: woman makes love and engenders within herself, she can give milk, she has some specific illnesses related to her morphology, etc. These realities are self-evident' (ILTY, 38/70), the 'facts' that she lists are not specifically scientific at all, but are given in lived experience. Generally, then, Irigaray steers clear of understanding either rhythms or bodily materials and forms in terms specific to biological science.

Irigaray's concept of 'morphology' helps to clarify how her description of sexual difference is non-biological. From her earliest writings, she has stressed that sexual difference is a difference of 'morphology', where 'morphology' differs from biology. She writes in 1977 that 'we must go back to the question not of the anatomy but of the morphology of [the] female sex. . . . [A]ll western culture [has a] . . . morpho-logic [that] does not correspond to the female sex'.[37] Here the 'morphology' (*morphē*) of the female sex is its form as imagined culturally – or spoken about (in

[37] 'Women's Exile', p. 64.

logos) – that is, traditionally, as a defective and incomplete form. This cultural imagery shapes how women live their bodies and hence the shape which these bodies actually assume. So, in Irigaray's earlier work, 'morphology' denotes the form which a body assumes in culture.[38] But the later Irigaray believes that bodies *naturally* assume form (*morphē*) – indeed, successive forms, which unfold in a regular pattern governed by an inner ordering principle (*logos*), namely, a rhythm. The 'morphology' of a body now becomes identifiable as the rhythm which regulates its formation. This concurs with Irigaray's statements that the 'female has not yet developed its *morphology*' because 'woman has yet to find her own forms, yet to spread roots and bloom. She has yet to be born to her own growth' (SG, 180/194), and that women 'are in need of our... basic rhythm [*rythme de base*], our morphological identity' (71/83). Women will only develop their morphology when they live and grow by their own rhythm, instead of having that of men imposed upon them.

That Irigaray's conception of sexual difference is non-biological is important, to recall, because, if she were to collapse sexual difference into biological *sex* difference, then she would have slipped into biological determinism, overlooking the specificity of both social relations and symbolic formations. But, although she does believe that men's and women's ways of relating and experiencing are 'determined' by their bodily forms, her non-biological conception of bodily forms – which she understands in perceptually concrete terms – distinguishes her position from biological determinism.[39] Now, one might object that this distinction is inconsequential: Irigaray still holds that our natural characters – our rhythms and consequent bodily forms – condition our experience and cultural activities, and so she seems to endorse a form of 'natural' determinism which retains all the political conservatism of biological determinism. However, the originality of Irigaray's conception of nature

[38] Most scholars understand morphology in this way: Whitford, *Luce Irigaray*, pp. 58–9; Grosz, *Sexual Subversions*, pp. 111–12. Evidently, this construal of morphology aligns with the idea that sexual difference is symbolically, culturally, constituted.

[39] 'Why Cultivate Difference?', p. 82. Irigaray's view of biology may seem simplistic, given feminist efforts at a non-deterministic biology, which Lynda Birke proffers as an alternative to social constructionism in *Feminism and the Biological Body* (Edinburgh: Edinburgh University Press, 1999). Birke concedes, though, that another – distinct – alternative is phenomenological description of the lived body (p. 26; see also pp. 84, 90). Irigaray, moreover, suggests the possibility of new biological accounts of the body that take lived experience as a starting point: hence, her interest in biologist Hélène Rouch's phenomenologically inflected study of how placental mechanisms furnish 'a sort of negotiation between the mother's self and the other that is the embryo' (JTN, 41/49).

may give it unexpected non-deterministic implications – in other words, she may think that natural forms 'determine' experience and culture in some non-standard sense which loses the usual implication of cultural conservatism. Pending examination of this, we should for now remain open to her non-biological conception of sexual difference, which describes human bodies as made of rhythms, forms, and fluid materials, remaining close to our lived experience of our bodies. Even when this description becomes most philosophically abstract, discussing processes of growth which follow different rhythms, it continues to evoke the familiar processes of growing and unfolding which structure experienced bodily life.

Irigaray's description of sexual difference, too, remains evocative of lived, embodied experience. Firstly, her description articulates our sense that sexual difference is not superficially inscribed on us but deeply orchestrates our bodily being, infusing our physical desires and processes. Her philosophy articulates our lived sense that our actions are constrained by somatic processes which unfold at their own pace, and which seem to be located deeply within us. By relating the idea that there are principles regulating these processes to such lived phenomena as menstruation, pregnancy, and menopause – or, in men's case, to sexual impulses which follow a relatively constant pattern – Irigaray gives phenomenological resonance to her notion of sexed rhythms. But why should we prefer Irigaray's phenomenologically resonant account of human bodies and sexual difference to a biological account?

Irigaray deems her account of human bodies preferable because it sees these bodies as exemplifying broader natural processes of rhythmic growth, processes which, in turn, she thinks are best described in a phenomenologically resonant way. Passing, therefore, to her phenomenological justification for her account of nature, she suggests that this account is preferable to competing scientific theories because it remains connected to our perceptual, pre-scientific experience of nature. Whereas scientific theories of nature aspire to 'theoretical truth that forces us to abandon all subjective reference points', she wishes to include these subjective reference points 'as an element of knowledge' (TD, 30/47). She therefore claims that it is necessary to

recover an immediate perception of the real and . . . elaborate a symbolic universe which correspond[s] to it . . . A certain recourse . . . to the phenomenological method seems necessary in order to make enter into the universe of the rational some natural, corporeal, sensible realities which until now had been removed from it. (WD, 147–56)

An adequate theory of nature would 'elaborate' and defend, or treat as 'knowledge', the pre-theoretical way we perceive and experience nature – as post-Newtonian scientific theories typically do not, Irigaray believes: 'Matter . . . is not perceivable by the subject operating the experiment . . . the Newtonian break having led scientific inquiry into a "universe" in which perception by the senses has almost no validity' (E, 123/118). In contrast, for Irigaray, epistemic privilege must be assigned to a theory of nature which confirms, includes, and amplifies perception. She intends her conception of nature as *physis* – as growing through the circulation of fluids such as air, water, and sap – to incorporate perceptual experience in this way. She develops her account of nature through constant discussion of concretely experienced phenomena (the seasons, the tides, plants), describing the general principles which govern their growth as they are embodied in these phenomena. For example, her extended meditation on nature at the start of *To Be Two* (1994) is interspersed with passages describing her own perceptions: 'I perceive her [nature] through all of my skin, immersed in her, leaving every thought behind . . . I am impregnated with her colors, with her smells' (TBT, 6).

Why should consonance with perception be thought to render an account of nature more adequate than relatively detached scientific accounts? After all, perhaps perceptual experience is suffused with anthropomorphic projections, so that we can develop an accurate account only by distancing ourselves from immediate perception. A central argument of all Irigaray's writings on science, though, is that one *cannot* really distance oneself from perceptual experience; as embodied beings, we ineluctably have a pre-theoretical, perceptual mode of encountering the world (E, 125/120–1). Our lived manner of experiencing nature must surreptitiously infiltrate even an ostensibly detached account. For example, she suggests, the scientific quest to split the atom reflects a desire for the 'disintegration' of identity which has hidden perceptual roots in male sexual rhythms (TD, 31/48). Since lived experience inescapably influences our enquiries into nature, a preferable account of nature will make its basis in perception explicit and openly show how it has been elicited from perceptual experience.

Irigaray's discussions of science and perception might give the impression that she intends her accounts of nature only to articulate our experience of it but not to describe nature as it really is. This would challenge my interpretation that she offers a realist account of nature and of human bodies within it. Actually, though, her phenomenological defence of her account of nature is consistent with realism. Following other philosophers in the phenomenological tradition (WD, 156), Irigaray believes that perceptual experience does not constitute a self-contained realm of representations but directly gives us access to things in the world, so that the contours of perceptual experience simultaneously are the structure of the world.[40] To the extent that an account of nature builds on and articulates our perceptual experience, then, we have reason to believe this account, and to believe that natural things really *do* exhibit the general contours which this account elicits from our experience.

Let me review the argument of this chapter so far. I first asked what reasons Irigaray gives us to believe that humanity is naturally sexually dual, beyond her unsuccessful inference from the patriarchal content of western culture. We have seen that she supports the belief in human duality with her unusual philosophy of nature (which also leads her to reconceive sexual difference as rhythmic, and as an ontological difference, obtaining within nature as *physis*). Specifically, for Irigaray, we have reason to believe that human duality naturally exists because its existence is upheld by a philosophy of nature which, itself, is preferable to rival scientific accounts in being fully and openly grounded in embodied experience. Moreover, Irigaray believes, her account of sexual difference in terms of rhythms also has phenomenological support in our lived experience of being subject to constraining somatic processes and – in women's case – of passing through palpably different phases of life, demarcated by such events as childbirth and the start of menstruation. This, she believes, makes her account of sexual difference preferable to a biological account of it.

However, there is a problem with Irigaray's phenomenological defence of her philosophy of nature and sexual difference: namely, there are extensive areas of experience which this philosophy cannot readily accommodate. Often, our immediate experience seems to be that natural phenomena are chaotically, almost disturbingly, diverse (like the mass of blades of grass in a meadow, the profusion of roots on a plant); this chaotically energetic and plural dimension of nature is occluded by Irigaray's focus on regular development and polarity. Arguably, too, a sense of sexual specificity does not constantly pervade every aspect of our experience. We can often feel pleasingly liberated from our sexed identity, or be aware of having conflicting, complex motivations and impulses which prohibit or, at least, jar with any sense of a stable sexed identity. We can

---

[40] On this aspect of the phenomenological tradition, see Michael Hammond, Jane Howarth, and Russell Keat, *Understanding Phenomenology* (Oxford: Blackwell, 1991), pp. 2–3.

also be aware of having a range of future possibilities, or past experiences, which are too diverse to be adequately regarded as expressing the coherent unfolding of one single sexed character. Taking it, then, that there are significant areas of lived experience which Irigaray downplays, the question arises whether lived experience better supports an alternative, non-Irigarayan, view of bodies. This opens up the space to return to the idea that human bodies are naturally multiple and to explore the considerations which may support it.

V. Intersexed Bodies

When Butler occasionally suggests that human bodies naturally have diverse features, she refers to intersexed bodies as giving an unusually clear manifestation of this more general diversity within human bodies. But exactly how might intersex support belief in bodily multiplicity? Surveying recent discussions of intersex discloses some disagreement as to what it implies about the nature of human bodies. Within these discussions, two main positions can be identified: (1) that naturally there are more than two sexes or, perhaps, a plurality of components of sex; (2) that sex is entirely a cultural artefact, and bodies naturally consist of an inherently diverse set of features. Both positions imply criticisms of Irigaray, which I shall outline in turn.

Intersex (formerly called hermaphrodism) encompasses various physical conditions: individuals may have ambiguous genitalia, or their genetic makeup may conflict with their anatomy (for instance, those with Androgen Insensitivity Syndrome have a Y chromosome and testes, but their cells cannot detect testosterone, only estrogen, and so they develop an exterior female form). Although long recognised, intersex has traditionally been frowned upon: in late medieval Europe, the intersexed were legally compelled to choose a sex and abide to it, sometimes on pain of death. In the twentieth century, responsibility for regulating the intersexed shifted from the judiciary to the medical profession, whose standard practise until recently has been to operate on the intersexed shortly after birth so as to render them as close as possible to being consistently male or female, also providing supporting hormonal and psychological treatment. Despite its generally humanitarian motivation, this medical practise remained premised upon acceptance of the prevailing two-sex classification. In recent years, intersexed people have challenged their treatment by the medical profession, criticising the practise of performing unnecessary, often coercive, surgery, and demanding an end to the secrecy and shame long surrounding intersex. This secrecy is responsible for the widespread perception that intersexed conditions are less common than they in fact are – recent scholars' estimates range between 0.1%, 1.7%, and 2% of all births. Whatever the exact percentage: 'The significance of these figures lies not so much in the actual numbers of persons involved as in demonstrating that nature . . . is less absolute in creating sexual dimorphism than we humans are in thinking about it'.[41]

Intersexed bodies refute Irigaray's claims that all individuals are naturally either male or female: 'The whole human kind [*genre humain*] is composed of women and men and it is composed of nothing else' (ILTY, 47/84). Some have claimed that intersexed bodies reveal the existence of more than two sexes in nature: for example, some intersexed people identify themselves as belonging to a third sex category, neither male nor female.[42] Extending this point, Anne Fausto-Sterling, in her 1993 article 'How Many Sexes Are There?', postulated five biological sexes: males, females, 'herms' – those with an ovary and a testis (or a fused ovo-testis), 'merms' – those with testes and some elements of female genitalia, and 'ferms' – with ovaries and some elements of male genitalia.[43] If correct, such claims suggest that Irigaray's ontology must, at least, be extended to acknowledge the existence and specific rhythm of those other sexes.

Fausto-Sterling's claim that there are five sexes has been criticised, however, and in recent work she has acknowledged its limitations: it continues to classify individuals by their genitals rather than asking whether one can adequately classify individuals on this basis at all.[44] What intersex exposes, Fausto-Sterling now argues, is that the characteristics which we ordinarily see as 'sex' characteristics (for example, the 'male' hormone testosterone) can occur in various combinations with other such characteristics (such as 'female' genitalia), creating various possibilities for how individuals identify themselves. '[O]ne should acknowledge that people come [with] an even wider assortment of sexual identities and

---

[41] John Money, quoted in Alkeline Van Lenning, 'The Body as Crowbar: Transcending or Stretching Sex?' in *Feminist Theory* 5: 1 (2004), p. 33.

[42] Mairi MacDonald, 'Intersex and Gender Identity (2000)', at www.ukia.co.uk/voices/is_gi.htm

[43] In *New York Times*, March 12, 1993, p. A29.

[44] For some criticisms, see Cheryl Chase et al., 'Intersexual Rights', letters section, *The Sciences* July/August 1993, pp. 3–4. Fausto-Sterling outlines her amended stance in 'The Five Sexes, Revisited', in *The Sciences* July/August 2000, pp. 19–23, and *Sexing the Body*, pp. 95–114.

characteristics'.[45] Our ordinary view that sex is dual is oversimplified and, moreover, is pernicious insofar as it underwrites the practise of imposing sex duality coercively. We should instead recognise, Fausto-Sterling concludes, that the components of sex are plural, separable from one another, and capable of entering into varied combinations. It is not clear, though, that we can even identify these characteristics as components of sex if they do not belong to natural clusters which define individuals as male and female. It would be more accurate to say that these characteristics are not naturally sexed (or contributory to sex) at all, sex being something that is entirely socio-cultural. Indeed, Fausto-Sterling draws this conclusion in *Sexing the Body* (2000): 'There *are* hormones, genes, prostates, uteri and other body parts and physiologies...that become part of the ground from which varieties of sexual experience and desire emerge' – but these varieties emerge only because we attribute 'social meanings' concerning sex/gender to these parts.[46]

The most compelling conclusion from intersex, then, is that it implies that there is no natural sex difference at all. This challenges Irigaray more radically, not merely affirming more natural sexes than she countenances, but holding her entire belief in natural duality to be misguided. The argument from intersex to the denial of natural sex is presented by Butler in *Gender Trouble,* and further elaborated by Georgia Warnke in her article 'Intersexuality and the Categories of Sex'. Butler points out that in the case of intersexed people: 'The component parts of sex do not add up to the recognizable coherence or unity that is usually designated by the category of sex' (GT, 108); consequently, these individuals must be forcibly carved into maleness or femaleness. This, Butler claims, exposes that all ascriptions of sex are imposed and culturally constraining (110). Just as stated, Butler's argument may seem weak: it does not follow that because ascriptions of sex are coercive for intersexed people, they are universally coercive; plausibly, these ascriptions are coercive for the intersexed just because, *un*like most people, they lack one natural sex.

But the force of Butler's argument becomes visible once we resituate it within her broader approach to gender. The perception that an individual has a given sex never simply tracks any fact of this individual's possessing a sex-defining cluster of features. Our bodily features are inherently diverse, not inherently clustered, as is exposed when these features appear

---

[45] 'The Five Sexes, Revisited', p. 22.
[46] *Sexing the Body*, pp. 22–3.

outside of their presumed clusters, in different combinations, within the bodies of the intersexed. When we perceive an individual as sexed, we perceive some of their inherently diverse features as constituting a (sex-defining) group because social norms direct us so as to perceive these features. These are norms which prescribe heterosexuality and gender duality, and which force individuals to perform one or other gender and, consequently, to acquire the corresponding sex. The prevailing norms also presume that gender expresses sex (rather than sex resulting from gender), encouraging us to think that sex naturally occurs in bodies. In this way, Butler argues that the practise of compelling the intersexed to assume a sex exposes the ongoing occurrence of a process of compulsory sexing to which all bodies are subject.

Georgia Warnke elaborates on Butler's argument by stressing how operations on the intersexed reflect social assumptions: for example, an intersexed individual will typically be surgically reconstructed as male if 'his' genitalia are capable of performing certain functions deemed socially normal for a penis, such as penetrating vaginas and urinating while standing.[47] In contrast, if an intersexed person can perform (presumptively normal) female reproductive functions and/or be penetrated, 'she' will typically be reconstructed as female. Thus, operations reflect social assumptions about gender, about the appropriate reproductive and sexual roles for women and men.[48] Warnke concludes that

the relevant question is not whether cases of ambiguous or unacceptable genitalia occur often enough to undermine the biological basis for dividing populations into two sexes. The relevant question is rather what genital surgery says about the categories of sex themselves: are they written into nature or are they insisted on by cultural and historical conceptions of gendered forms and practices?[49]

For Warnke, the treatment of the intersexed exposes how ascriptions of sex generally rest on cultural assumptions about whether bodies can realise the gender norms of a given society. But, one might object, in most cases these ascriptions might still categorise bodies – accurately – in terms of capabilities which they biologically possess. Warnke claims,

---

[47] For evidence, see Suzanne Kessler, *Lessons from the Intersexed* (Brunswick, NJ: Rutgers University Press, 1998), pp. 19, 25.

[48] For further evidence, see Fausto-Sterling, *Sexing the Body*, pp. 56–60; she concludes: 'if labeling intersex children as boys is tightly linked to cultural conceptions of . . . maleness and "proper penile function", labeling such children as girls is a process even more tangled in social definitions of gender [and, above all, the medical] rule that reproductive function be preserved' (p. 59).

[49] Warnke, 'Intersexuality and the Categories of Sex', p. 129.

though, that these ascriptions do not neutrally pick out features or capabilities which inherently cluster together to give someone a sex; rather, the ascriptions reflect a cultural and political decision to treat as clustered an inherently diverse bunch of features.[50] That is, bodies are scrutinised as to whether they can realise social norms, and, of their diverse features, those that are relevant to the possibility of realising social norms are perceived to cluster together.[51] Shape of nose, height, and eye colour are irrelevant to gender norms and hence are not located among the cluster of properties which is taken to constitute sex.

One might still object that bodily features can naturally cluster together as well as being perceived, culturally, to cluster. Perhaps any features which jointly enable a body to realise gendered norms constitute a natural (as well as a culturally perceived) cluster and hence define their bearer as either male or female. Butler's/Warnke's reply must be that, even if certain properties sometimes cluster naturally, those clusters cannot be the same as those which are perceived to exist socio-culturally. Because certain features are perceived, socio-culturally, to cluster just insofar as they jointly permit the realisation of particular gender norms, these perceived clusters cannot also occur naturally where no question of realising social norms arises. Because, by definition, reference to socio-cultural norms cannot exist in nature as a non-cultural domain, clusters of features which inherently refer to cultural assumptions just are not the *kind* of thing which can be found in nature. From Butler's/Warnke's perspective, belief in natural sex must be a category mistake – the mistake of supposing that something which inherently refers to social norms is the kind of thing that can exist naturally (non-socially).

To clarify Butler's/Warnke's argument, we can note its similarity to Kant's key argument for the 'transcendentally ideal' status of space and time. Kant claims that space and time are forms which we impose upon objects of our experience, and hence they are not properties of things 'in themselves', things as they are independent of us. But why cannot space and time be both forms which we impose upon experience *and* properties of things in themselves? To exclude this possibility, Kant argues that things in themselves cannot have the spatio-temporal form of experienced objects, precisely because that form, as something imposed by us,

---

[50] Ibid, p. 135.

[51] Analogously, Foucault claims that 'the notion of "sex" made it possible to group together, in an artificial unity, anatomical elements, biological functions, conducts, sensations, and pleasures' (*The History of Sexuality: Volume One*, p. 154).

necessarily differs in kind from any form which things could have independently of us and our impositions.[52] Analogously, Butler and Warnke believe that any natural clusters of biological features just cannot be like the clusters which we perceive with reference to social norms concerning gender. Since sex is such a culturally perceived cluster of bodily features, it cannot also exist naturally, and must be entirely a cultural artefact (which could be changed, even eradicated, were gender norms to change).

According to the most compelling and fully elaborated argument from intersex, then, the treatment of the intersexed reveals the imposed, artificial, character of all sex ascriptions, and, correlatively, exposes that human bodies naturally have diverse properties among which none inherently group together to define those bodies as sexed (this inherent diversity being manifested unusually clearly in the case of the intersexed). On this argument, intersex does support the view that all human bodies, naturally, are internally diverse. Now, Irigaray might retaliate that arguments from intersex unacceptably presuppose a biological conception of the body, a conception which is detached from lived, embodied experience. After all, these arguments purport to show that bodies are composed of miscellaneous physical features which are understood, in broadly biological terms, to include and to be effects of genes, chromosomes, and hormones. But we can readily redescribe bodily diversity in terms of the more phenomenologically concrete notion of multiple forces introduced in Chapter 2. According to that notion, bodies have diverse forces, and they are naturally non-sexuate because none of these forces ever inherently group together to constitute a sexed character. This diversity of forces within a body can be expected to manifest itself, outwardly, in the diverse bodily features which Butler and Warnke identify. Yet, conceived as drives towards definite patterns of activity (towards, for example, sex or eating), these forces carry an intrinsic phenomenological reference: the notion of forces articulates our pre-theoretical experience of our bodies as assailed by various urges and impelled into diverse, sometimes incompatible, patterns of activity, patterns of activity which we generally find ourselves pursuing prior to any exertion of conscious control. Moreover, the idea that these forces are non-sexuate articulates the experience that our impulses and capacities are inexhaustible by any sexed identities we

---

[52] See Kant, *Critique of Pure Reason*, trans. Norman Kemp Smith (Basingstoke: Macmillan, 1929), p. 82; for (critical) exposition, see Sebastian Gardner, *Kant and the Critique of Pure Reason* (London: Routledge, 1999), pp. 107–11.

may assume. The notion of multiple forces thus redescribes, phenomeno-logically, the diversity within bodies which theorists of intersex have so far described in predominantly biological terms.

It transpires that Irigaray's conception of natural sexual duality and this quite antithetical conception of bodily multiplicity both have phe-nomenological support. This is because they articulate different dimen-sions of our pre-theoretical experience as embodied beings. As I sug-gested earlier, Irigaray articulates our sense of being constrained by somatic processes which unfold with an uncontrollable regularity of their own, which she conveys by describing these processes as manifestations of a nature which also grows at its own pace, following its own cycles. 'Our body itself carries those measures ... the laws of the body and of the cosmic world' (TBT, 90). Irigaray reminds us, too, that those aspects of our lives in which we sense our sexual specificity most strongly – for exam-ple, in women's case, in menstruation – are often the very aspects which we feel to emerge, uncontrollably and with rhythmic regularity, from within our physical being. In contrast, I have claimed, the idea that bod-ies consist of plural forces articulates our sense of having pre-volitional, diverse and often conflicting, motivations and impulses. This idea also articulates our sense that this diversity makes us non-sexuate, internally complex and fragmented in a way which feels incompatible with having a stable, smoothly unfolding, sexed character of the sort which Irigaray posits. According to the idea of multiple forces, the physical features of our bodies embody not (as for Irigaray) constraining, sexually specific, regularities but, instead, indefinitely varied possibilities, always exceed-ing what we can actualise at any time. Thus, the notion of multiple forces reflects a dimension of our embodied experience which is quite differ-ent from that which Irigaray foregrounds but which, I believe, is equally recognisable on reflection.

Insofar as we can recognise in our embodied experience both of the dimensions which these conceptions elicit, both conceptions can claim phenomenological support. To this extent, moreover, both conceptions can claim to give a true account of the real character of human bodies and of the nature in which they are situated. This restores the problem which Irigaray faced earlier: how to decide which conception of bodies is preferable. We can now see, though, that neither Irigaray's conception of natural bodily duality nor the opposed conception of natural bodily mul-tiplicity have conclusive phenomenological support, since each excludes recognisable dimensions of embodied experience – those which the other articulates. Taking it, then, (with Irigaray) that an account of nature and of bodies is satisfactory inasmuch as it articulates embodied experience, a satisfactory account must synthesise her belief in natural duality with the contrary belief in natural multiplicity. Such an account of nature and bodies will articulate embodied experience more fully than either of the extant accounts, and therefore has better claim to describe nature and bodies as they really are.

Now, one might object that no special work of synthesising these conceptions is necessary, since, although opposed in emphasis, they are not actually incompatible. One might think that a body could both contain multiple forces and follow a sexually specific rhythm. According to Irigaray's idea of sexuate rhythms, though, these rhythms are fundamental to a body's constitution and so must (from her perspective) generate that body's forces, which therefore must – manifesting a sexually specific rhythm as they do – themselves be sexually specific, occurring only in the female or male sex. But, we have seen, the conception of multiplicity includes the idea that forces are inherently capable of entering into varied combinations, and so can never be unique to male or female bodies. Perhaps one could say that the same forces take different forms depending on the rhythm of the body to which they belong. Yet if forces took different forms in this way, they would cease to remain the same. What different rhythms would alter in forces is the temporality of the process by which these forces discharge their energy and accomplish their ends. But since a force just *is* a propensity to pursue a given activity with a certain level of energy, a change in how a force discharges itself or unfolds would amount to an alteration in what that force is. Irigaray's idea of rhythms thus remains incompatible with belief in inherently diverse forces.

We can view the same incompatibility from the other side: if bodies are composed of forces, then this leaves no obvious room for rhythms to govern how these bodies develop. The temporality, or rhythm, of the process by which any force accomplishes its end is internally prescribed by that force's distinctive aim and level of energy. An internally multiple body thus consists of many independent centres of energy and temporal unfolding, and it has no ontological room for one overarching rhythm which would regulate all these centres. Yet another way to bring out the incompatibility here is to remember that diverse forces are (according to the conception of bodily multiplicity which I have been exploring) non-sexed because they never inherently group together with other forces to define a body as sexed. To the extent that a body is naturally composed of these forces, then, that body is naturally non-sexed. Irigaray's contrasting insistence is, of course, that bodies naturally *are* sexed, ultimately by their rhythms. One might now protest that, if these conceptions are so deeply antithetical, then they cannot be synthesised. I agree that bodily duality and multiplicity can only be jointly affirmed if they are *reconceived* as capable of co-existing. But we can reach this reconception only as part of a wider effort to synthesise Irigaray's later philosophy with the opposed belief in bodily multiplicity. The next section opens up a route for beginning to think about how these could be synthesised.

VI. Towards a Reconciliation of Duality and Multiplicity

In working towards a synthesis of Irigaray's later philosophy with the idea of bodily multiplicity, we can lean on writings by sexual difference feminists, some of whom have argued that the cultural accentuation and recognition of sexual difference would release and promote bodily multiplicity as well. These thinkers advance their arguments within a conception of sexual difference feminism as a project of symbolic transformation, but, by recasting their arguments in terms of Irigaray's later thought, we can form an initial idea of how natural duality and multiplicity might be jointly affirmed.

Sexual difference feminists derive their argument that a culture of difference would also recognise and celebrate multiplicity from Irigaray's early writings. In *Speculum* and *This Sex*, Irigaray claims that women have traditionally been understood as non-unified and internally multiple. She means, in part, that women's sexuality has been located at multiple parts of their bodies (TS, 28–9/27–8); that women's bodies have been seen as not clearly bounded but prone to merge with those of others, especially in pregnancy (S, 237/294–5); and that women have been thought to lack a clearly bounded sense of self, instead perpetually identifying with others (TS, 210/210). As Ellen Armour says of 'Irigaray's woman', 'her essential features are difference and deferral . . . Irigaray's woman is "essentially" different from herself and from other women'.[53] For the early Irigaray, therefore, any reaffirmation of female identity must reaffirm multiplicity as well, while also transforming the meaning of both concepts. Contributing to this, her earlier writings portray women's multiplicity not as unhealthy fragmentation, 'shards' and 'scattered remnants', but as

---

[53] Armour, *Deconstruction, Feminist Theology, and the Problem of Difference*, pp. 133–4. For a similar argument, see Mary K. Bloodsworth, 'Embodiment and Ambiguity: Luce Irigaray, Sexual Difference, and "Race"', in *International Studies in Philosophy* 31: 2 (1999), pp. 75–7.

positive openness to change, to others, to relationships, and to varied sexual impulses (TS, 30–31/29, 213/212, 217/215–16). Based on these writings by Irigaray, sexual difference feminists maintain that the affirmation of difference enables, and requires, us to rethink and revalue multiplicity as well. Rather than repressing diversity, a culture of sexual difference would enable new respect for and enjoyment of multiplicity as it arises both within each woman (internally) and between different women (externally).

Arguably, though, a culture of sexual difference would celebrate multiplicity to only a limited extent. Since this culture would revalue multiplicity insofar as it is symbolised as female, it would make a positive identification with multiplicity available only to women. Even if multiplicity, once revalued, could somehow be endorsed by both sexes, men and women could still only value, and try to embody, multiplicity insofar as this leaves their sexuate identities intact – otherwise, they would undermine the culture of sexual difference which gives multiplicity its new value in the first place. Although sexual difference feminists plausibly argue that a culture of difference would revalue multiplicity, then, their position entails that multiplicity could be valued only inasmuch as it is compatible with stable sexuate identities. We may therefore suspect that this culture would, after all, curtail people's capacity to explore their internal and external diversity.

Furthermore, this entire argument that a culture of difference would promote multiplicity rests on an understanding of sexual difference feminism as a project of reimagining and revaluing the concepts of femaleness and multiplicity which govern our culture. Irigaray, though, rightly supersedes this project to construe sexual difference as natural. The argument for compatibility between cultures of sexual difference and multiplicity must therefore be recast to show that duality and multiplicity co-exist naturally and require interlinked expression. Very roughly, this must involve arguing that our bodies not only have sexually specific rhythms which require expression but also are composed of multiple, non-sexuate forces which can achieve expression and development only in a culture which expresses and develops individuals' sexuate rhythms as well.[54] How might we begin to make such an argument?

In 'Becoming Woman: Or Sexual Difference Revisited' (2003), Braidotti starts to argue along these lines. Her stated aim is to combine

---

[54] Irigaray moves towards this position in *Between East and West* but still privileges sexual duality over multiplicity; see Chapter 6, Section III.

(the early) Irigaray's project of revaluing the female with a project which affirms a 'multiplicity of sexed positions'.[55] Braidotti maintains that, in asserting a female identity defined outside traditional parameters, one asserts a kind of self which embodies multiplicity and internal diversity, and which, in its lack of definite identity, is not only female but also (paradoxically) *post*-female. She relates this idea to Deleuze's notorious proposal for overcoming masculinity (*le masculin*) through the process of 'becoming-woman' (*devenir-femme*). He denies that we should become 'woman' in what he calls the 'molar' sense: this would mean assuming femininity (or femaleness – *féminité*) as a fixed, sedimented, identity defined in contrast to masculinity. Rather, Deleuze advocates becoming woman in the 'molecular' sense, which means that everyone – including women – should engage in experiments which induce their identity to dissolve in a flux of change, transformation, and internal diversification.[56] Braidotti objects that, if 'becoming-woman' means transcending any sexuate identity, then it will merely reinforce the dominant cultural tradition which denies any independent female identity.[57] She instead construes the cultural process of 'becoming-woman' as that of defining and affirming a *sui generis* female identity which would also exemplify multiplicity.

So far, Braidotti's argument appears squarely located within a conception of sexual difference as culturally, symbolically constituted (hence, she advocates repossessing and rewriting images of woman, images which, she believes, shape our bodies as 'cultural constructions').[58] However,

---

55 Braidotti, 'Becoming Woman: Or Sexual Difference Revisited', in *Theory, Culture and Society* 20: 3 (2003), pp. 47–8. See also her *Metamorphoses*, p. 106.

56 See Deleuze and Guattari, *A Thousand Plateaus*, trans. Brian Massumi (London: Athlone, 1988), pp. 275–7; *Mille Plateaux* (Paris: Minuit, 1980), pp. 338–42. Deleuze calls this process 'becoming-woman' because he thinks that identity is regulated by cultural systems which privilege the *masculin*. Embracing the 'molar' feminine/female position of non-identity is thus the first step towards the 'molecular' dissolution of identity. Deleuze thus grants feminism considerable importance, while insisting that, ultimately, it must go beyond concern for women (see Colebrook, introduction to *Deleuze and Feminist Theory*, pp. 2–3).

57 Irigaray, obliquely, makes the same criticism of Deleuze (S, 232/288; TS, 140–1/138–9; SG, 61/73); see Olkowski, 'Morpho-logic in Deleuze and Irigaray', in *Deleuze and Feminist Theory*, ed. Ian Buchanan and Claire Colebrook (Edinburgh: Edinburgh University Press, 2000), p. 102.

58 Braidotti, 'Becoming Woman', pp. 51, 44. Again, *Metamorphoses* refers to sexual difference as the 'distributor and organizer of social and symbolic differences ... the constitutive socio-symbolic cast in which human subjectivity is thrown' (p. 34). Although her well-known earlier paper 'The Politics of Ontological Difference' recommends that sexual difference be understood, and affirmed, as 'ontological' difference, Braidotti – unlike the later Irigaray – understands ontological difference as a difference in cultural identity.

strains in Braidotti's argument convey an alternative understanding of bodies as naturally multiple. In particular, drawing on Deleuze, she suggests that we have multiple corporeal characteristics and energies which have become blocked and inhibited by our cultural positioning as individuals with male or female identities which are defined hierarchically. But whereas Deleuze thinks that the dissolution of fixed sexual identities is necessary to unleash these energies, Braidotti claims that a non-hierarchical *redefinition* of these identities would loosen their meaning and so unleash our blocked energies. She suggests, then, that we have naturally multiple 'energies', 'forces', and 'desires': 'A body is . . . a slice of forces that have specific qualities, relations, speed, and rates of change . . . [bodies] are intelligent matter, endowed with the capacity to affect and be affected'.[59] These multiple forces have become inhibited through the institutionalisation of a culture which denies sexual difference, but a culture of sexual difference would release our nature from this inhibition, allowing it to proliferate. With this suggestion, Braidotti intimates the ontology and politics which we need in order to reconcile sexual difference and multiplicity – an ontology and politics which, together, hold that the historical denial of duality has also constricted our naturally existing multiplicity, and that the cultural expression of duality would simultaneously express multiplicity. We might wonder, again, whether a sexuate culture would prevent our multiplicity from expressing itself beyond the confines of stable sexuate identities, and so would only ever allow multiplicity to be partially realised. This problem can be addressed only in the context of a fuller elaboration of the ontology and politics which Braidotti has begun to sketch.

To provide this fuller elaboration, we need to reconceive human bodily duality and multiplicity as naturally co-existing, such that they can gain full cultural expression only in conjunction with one another. We therefore need a philosophy of nature which supports the appropriate conceptions of bodily duality and multiplicity. Just as Irigaray supports her belief in

---

She claims that women need a culture which allows them to affirm themselves, positively, as women – to fulfil their 'ontological' desire to be women. This requires a redefinition of symbolic female identity: 'The "feminine" is that which "I, woman" invent, enact and empower in "our" speech, our practice, our collective quest for a redefinition of the status of all women'; 'The Politics of Ontological Difference', in *Between Feminism and Psychoanalysis*, ed. Teresa Brennan (London: Routledge, 1989), p. 102. For Braidotti, then, women differ 'ontologically' not in their specific rhythm of growth but insofar as they achieve a *sui generis* cultural identity.

[59] Braidotti, *Metamorphoses*, pp. 102, 99.

humanity's natural duality with a philosophy on which all nature is rhythmic and bipolar, likewise, support for a conception of human bodies
which reconciles duality and multiplicity must come from a corresponding philosophy of nature. Resources for such a philosophy of nature can
be found in the work of German Idealist and Romantic thinkers who
elaborate speculative accounts of nature. Lest this move from Irigaray to
German Idealism and Romanticism seem idiosyncratic, we should note –
with Elaine Miller – that Irigaray is 'the heir to nineteenth-century *Naturphilosophie*' in her attention to natural growth, rhythms, and difference
(we have already observed her proximity to Goethe, with his philosophy of
self-intensifying, expanding, contracting nature).[60] Admittedly, Irigaray
is reluctant to acknowledge this inheritance, as Miller also remarks, suggesting that Irigaray's reluctance arises because she wishes to avoid any
association with the infamously hierarchical account of natural sexual
difference which Hegel offers in his *Philosophy of Nature*.[61] Yet, despite
this reluctance, Irigaray engages with and rethinks the speculative theories of nature espoused by German Idealist and Romantic thinkers at key
points in her later work. Specifically, she builds on both Hölderlin and
Hegel in thinking of nature as originally dual and in tracing the political
ramifications of this original duality.

Irigaray's engagements with German Idealism and Romanticism provide points of departure for redirecting ideas from these traditions
towards a revised feminist philosophy of nature which could, potentially, explain how human bodies can be both sexually dimorphic and

---

[60] Miller, *The Vegetative Soul: From Philosophy of Nature to Subjectivity in the Feminine* (Albany:
SUNY Press, 2002), p. 189. Rather than focusing on German Idealism, it might seem
more obvious, in theorising how nature can make bodies both multiple and dual, to
draw on Deleuze's writings. However, Irigaray leans more readily on German Idealism:
her references to Deleuze are sparse, oblique, and critical (see note 57), despite the
parallels between her thought and that of Deleuze – on which, see Tamsin Lorrain,
Irigaray and Deleuze: Experiments in Visceral Philosophy (Ithaca: Cornell University Press,
1999). Irigaray's influence by German Idealism makes it relatively easy to see how her
conception of nature can be rethought in light of other elements of this tradition.
Anyway, Deleuze's view of nature is influenced by that of the principal exponent of
German Idealist philosophy of nature, Schelling. Schelling's influence on Deleuze is
indirect – Deleuze refers rarely, albeit approvingly, to Schelling but draws very heavily
on Bergson, who was himself deeply influenced by Schelling via the nineteenth-century
French philosopher Jean Ravaisson; see Maurice Merleau-Ponty, *Nature: Course Notes from
the Collège de France*, trans. Robert Vallier (Evanston, Ill.: Northwestern University Press,
2003), p. 39.
[61] See Hegel, *Philosophy of Nature* (1830), 3 vols., ed. and trans. M. J. Petry (London: Allen
and Unwin, 1970), vol. 3, pp. 174–5). Irigaray criticises Hegel's account of sexual difference at S, 220–2/274–6.

indefinitely diverse, and could explain how these characteristics can find expression and recognition only in conjunction with one another. The shape of this feminist philosophy of nature, and of the attendant conceptions of the body and its cultural expression, can emerge only gradually as we trace and build upon Irigaray's responses to German Idealist and Romantic conceptions of nature. The next two chapters therefore examine Irigaray's readings of Hölderlin and Hegel, in preparation for the development in Chapter 6 of a philosophy of nature which reconceives human sexual difference and bodily multiplicity as co-existing and requiring interwoven cultural and political expression.

4

Irigaray and Hölderlin on the Relation Between Nature and Culture

I have suggested that Irigaray's philosophy of natural sexual duality is attractive insofar as she sees nature as dynamic and bodies as active and striving for expression, consequently proposing cultural change to give expression to nature generally and to female bodies, with their inherent rhythms, which have never achieved adequate expression in western culture. However, a revised version of Butler's approach to sex and gender, which rests on a notion of active, multiple, bodily forces, offers equivalent attractions: it regards bodily activity as responsible for a constant instability in gender norms which generates deep differences between women. This revised version of Butler's approach also prescribes that dualistic gender norms should be subverted to give greater expression to bodily forces. This latter approach to sex and gender is incompatible with that of Irigaray. These two approaches to sex and gender are premised on antithetical conceptions of human bodies as, respectively, internally diverse (and naturally non-sexed) or sexually dual. I have argued that each conception has some phenomenological support: the former articulates our embodied experience of having diverse pre-conscious impulses and energies; the latter articulates our sense of being constrained by bodily rhythms which have their own momentum, especially in respect of those processes (such as menstruation and pregnancy) which seem most plainly to be sexually specific. Following Irigaray's argument that an adequate account of human bodies, and of the nature within which they are located, must articulate pre-theoretical experience, we need an account of bodies and nature which coherently synthesises these opposed conceptions. Such a synthetic account would also combine the attendant attractions of both approaches to sex and gender.

Admittedly, the incompatibility of these conceptions of bodies, and of their social and political implications, means that they can be synthesised only if they are simultaneously rethought. Specifically, we must rethink bodily duality and multiplicity as being such that they can co-exist and require interlinked expression. For this purpose, I have proposed drawing on ideas from the German Romantic and Idealist tradition of *Naturphilosophie*. Irigaray draws on some ideas from the same tradition in theorising humanity's natural duality. We can therefore start to engage with philosophy of nature by exploring the elements within it which Irigaray appropriates and adapts. We can then identify alternative elements in this tradition which she ignores but which can help to advance the idea that bodies are naturally multiple as well as dual.

This chapter focuses on Irigaray's engagement with the German Romantic idea that nature is originally self-dividing, an idea pioneered by the poet and thinker Hölderlin and developed further by Heidegger. Section I introduces this strange idea of a self-bifurcating nature by returning to the problem of Irigaray's apparent determinism, briefly situating this problem within broader feminist debates about nature and cultural change. Irigaray's problem, to recall, is that she claims that western, non-sexuate culture is rooted in male nature, which seems to imply that this culture is immutably fixed. To remedy this problem, Irigaray needs to understand culture as capable of being changed and transformed, but without falling back on the conceptual hierarchy which privileges active, mobile culture over passive, static nature. She achieves this by arguing that culture acquires the agency to transform itself only because it arises from an internal division within nature itself. She supports this suggestion with a unique, complex, view of the nature/culture relationship which arises from her readings of Heidegger and Hölderlin.

Section II begins to trace how Irigaray elaborates her view of nature and culture by examining her critique of patriarchal culture's hostility to nature in *Thinking the Difference* (1989). Irigaray argues that this culture stems from destructive tendencies which are natural to men, and, to explain how patriarchal culture can be both anti-natural and rooted in nature, she suggests that this culture emerges because nature spontaneously turns against itself. In Section III, I explain how she derives this idea that nature turns against itself from Hölderlin's view that nature, as *physis*, originally divides itself. Irigaray explicitly refers to Hölderlin on a number of occasions, and she implicitly engages with his conception of nature and culture in several of her discussions on that theme – especially when she refers to Heidegger, whose later thought, as she acknowledges, was very heavily influenced by Hölderlin. Accordingly, Section IV shows how Heidegger rewrites Hölderlin's belief in self-dividing nature to say that nature inflicts violence (*Gewalt*) upon itself. This section also shows how Irigaray modifies both Heidegger and Hölderlin to say that nature is originally dual and that only specifically *male* nature tends to turn against itself; hence, as she sums up, 'sexuate difference ... is ... the one which first articulates nature and culture' (KW, xiv). As I explore in Section V, for Irigaray, this self-opposing tendency on the part of male nature can be overcome through the very cultural resources which (male) nature has generated as it divides itself. She therefore advocates cultural change to transform nature's originally self-destructive tendencies, but, since she conceives culture *as* natural, she avoids reinstating the traditional culture/nature hierarchy. Finally, Section VI moves beyond the parameters of Irigaray's philosophy to ask whether there are other elements in Hölderlin's initial idea of self-dividing nature which might help with rethinking bodies as multiple as well as dual.

I. Nature and the Immutability of Culture

As we saw in Chapter 1, Irigaray contends that western culture, which denies sexual difference and construes it hierarchically, has its roots in a visceral, bodily urge of men to assert themselves against women. Across a whole swathe of her later texts, Irigaray specifies that males have particular trouble negotiating separation from their mothers: the 'task ... of differing from another human ... is ... especially difficult for a man because of his maternal origin' (KW, xi). Men respond to this difficulty by construing mothers and, by extension, all women, as 'nature from which man has to differ' hierarchically, and which men must transcend and control (38). But, if non-sexuate culture thus arises naturally, out of males' spontaneous difficulties with birth and difference, then how can this culture ever be changed for the better? Irigaray's explanation for (what she sees as) western culture's protracted denial of sexual difference seems to undercut her proposals for social change. Yet this explanation is itself necessitated by her view that cultures give expression to bodies in their inherent characters. Compounding the problem, Irigaray's view that cultures express bodies is in itself attractive, insofar as it revalues bodies, and the nature which shapes them, by reconceiving them as actively self-expressive. This view already contributes to one of her overarching projects, that of changing culture to recognise the value and fundamental importance of nature, and to recognise how profoundly culture is invariably shaped by, and dependent upon, nature. She insists, for example, that 'it is from the natural that we should start over in order to refound reason' (ILTY, 37/68) and that thinking must 'understand its natural roots and resources' (SG, 86/101). Yet, if every culture has natural roots, then our current non-sexuate culture must be naturally grounded and so, presumably, resistant to improvement.

Irigaray's difficulty in reconciling the imperative to revalue nature with the imperative to change cultural ideas of sexual difference mirrors a broader dilemma within feminist philosophy. Partly informed by Irigaray, contemporary feminist thinkers generally agree that western culture and society have a pervasive tendency to devalue and denigrate nature relative to culture and to align nature symbolically with the female, which becomes equally devalued. Most feminist thinkers therefore concur that women's situation can be improved only through symbolic and social change to recognise culture's dependence upon, and continuity with, nature. However, if culture truly is continuous with nature, this implies that there must be some natural basis for current, patriarchal culture, and hence that this culture cannot readily be changed. This undesirable implication pushes feminists back to affirming culture's independence of, or underdetermination by, nature, yet that affirmation threatens to perpetuate the symbolic devaluation of the female, insofar as the female is aligned with nature.

Seeking to escape this dilemma, many feminist theorists contest the culture/nature antithesis, suggesting that, although culture has a natural basis, nature itself is always cultural. For example, Elizabeth Grosz argues that culture intertwines with a nature which consists of multiple tendencies and potentialities which, however, are not given prior to culture but only acquire determinate form through the impact of cultural processes.[1] Ultimately, then, Grosz believes that culture interacts only with a nature which is already a cultural artefact. In this way, she continues to privilege culture over nature, identifying culture as the basic and independently active reality, from which nature derives.[2] A more ambiguous assessment of nature's intertwining with culture is provided by Moira Gatens, who holds that there are determinate natural tendencies and forces upon which culture builds.[3] Although, for Gatens, these tendencies are

---

[1] Grosz, *Volatile Bodies*, pp. 21, 191, 227. On Grosz, see also Chapter 1, Section III.

[2] For this criticism of Grosz, see also Terri Field, 'Is the Body Essential for Ecofeminism?', *Organization and Environment* 13: 1 (2000), p. 44.

[3] Gatens, *Imaginary Bodies*, pp. 9, 69–73.

culturally pliable, she suggests that the culture which modifies natural tendencies is always given determinate direction *by* natural forces in their initial form. Gatens's approach promises to allow a more genuine inter-weaving of nature with culture, yet it prompts a string of questions. How far must culture be independent of natural tendencies in order to modify them? If culture is independent of those tendencies, then how far do they ever really direct it? Conversely, if natural tendencies do impart direction to culture, then can culture ever really modify those initial tendencies?

More recently, several thinkers have argued that this worry that nat-ural determination immutably fixes culture is misguided, premised on a mistaken image of nature as static and unchanging – an image which also motivates Grosz's and Gatens's endeavours to reconceive nature as malleable by virtue of being intertwined with culture. As this illustrates, feminist debates on nature and cultural change have often been con-taminated by unconscious acceptance of the traditional view that nature is fixed and inert vis-à-vis changing, self-renovating culture. Countering that view, Helen Fielding writes that

rather than an acknowledgement of sexual difference negating the possibility for change in the guise of an essentialist account of nature as unchanging matter, . . . it is exactly such acknowledgement that will provide for change since it includes a recognition of the corporeal self and its potentiality.[4]

If we rethink nature as active and self-changing, then we can recognise (and promote societal recognition of) culture's natural roots without implying that women's and men's respective symbolic standings are fixed and cannot be changed for the better. Indeed, as Fielding and others have hinted, Irigaray's own novel conception of nature as open-ended growth could provide the basis for such a rethinking of nature.[5] Although Irigaray believes that nature encompasses bodily rhythms and forms which determine our experience and cultural activities, she also believes that nature grows in an open-ended way, and so thinks that nature determines culture in a way which leaves culture similarly open to change and, in particular, improvement. She works out this thought by maintaining that nature not only grows but also, more specifically,

---

[4] Fielding, 'Questioning Nature', p. 21.
[5] Among those also writing on Irigaray's conception of nature are Stacy Keltner, 'The Ethics of Air: Technology and the Question of Sexual Difference', pp. 53–65 and Ann V. Murphy, 'The Enigma of the Natural in Irigaray', in *Philosophy Today* 2001 (Supp.), pp. 75–82. For an account of nature as mutable that is informed by Irigaray (without discussing Irigaray's view of nature as such), see Bigwood, *Earth Muse*, pp. 47–48, 139–45.

grows through self-division. We can access her elaboration of this idea by seeing how it underlies her critique of patriarchal culture and its ecological destructiveness in *Thinking the Difference*.

II. Nature and Culture in Irigaray's *Thinking the Difference*

Irigaray does not systematically set out her idea of self-dividing nature, but it is implicit in several of her later texts, most notably the essay 'A Chance to Live' (*Une chance de vivre*) in *Thinking the Difference* and the chapter in *To Be Two* (1994) entitled 'Between Us, a Fabricated World'. Whereas her discussion of nature and culture in the latter text is mediated through readings of Heidegger, Hölderlin, and Sophocles, the earlier text is couched in a more popular style: it was first presented as a talk to the Italian Communist Party. Besides popularising Irigaray's earlier ideas, *Thinking the Difference* also provides an accessible way in to her unique approach to the relation between nature and culture. Irigaray's burgeoning interest in this theme stems from her concern about the Chernobyl accident of 1986, which galvanised her to reflect on the ecological dangers posed by a culture which is (in some sense) severed from nature.

Irigaray begins by pointing to a widespread cultural unease which, she thinks, has crystallised around Chernobyl. Before Chernobyl, one could imagine that nature would regulate and alleviate the ill-effects of human activities. But, Irigaray claims, 'at Chernobyl, nature turned out to be a vehicle of greater destruction than any war' (TD, 3/21). She adds that this destruction stemmed from a 'combination of . . . artificial pollution and natural phenomena: hails, storms, even sun' (4/21). She has in mind the way that weather patterns dispersed radioactive fallout over a vast area. Irigaray takes this to show that the destructiveness of the Chernobyl disaster was so great – that 'the cultural disorder into which we are being drawn . . . has become [so] intolerable' (4/22) – as to draw nature itself into the same destructive cycle which characterises human culture. Ultimately, then, Irigaray regards Chernobyl as reflecting the deeper-lying problem that western culture is fundamentally destructive, towards nature particularly. She maintains that this destructiveness reflects the fact that western culture has been created by and for men.[6] She writes:

---

[6] As Whitford observes, Irigaray insistently links the conceptual pair creation/destruction to the sexual pair female/male; see Whitford, 'Irigaray, Utopia and the Death Drive', in *Engaging with Irigaray*, ed. Burke et al., p. 382.

'This warlike method of organizing society is not self-evident. Its origin is patriarchal. It is sexuate' (5/22) – or, as she later states, 'society . . . has certain characteristics which pass for universal but are in fact attributable to the sex of the people that compose it' (17/35).

Irigaray goes on to claim that this male or 'patriarchal' culture displays a preoccupation with death and destruction while neglecting, and failing to reflect upon, the primary importance for all human beings of their birth and dependency upon their mothers in early infancy.[7] She then enumerates some further features of patriarchal culture – its suppression of mother-daughter relationships and its tendency to deny women legal rights – but the fundamental task generated by her opening analysis is to explain in what way the destructiveness of western culture reflects its specifically male character.[8] Her explanation unfolds in two stages.

Firstly, and quite typically of her later work, Irigaray suggests that patriarchal culture has its roots in the particular difficulties of male infants in negotiating separation from their mothers. *Thinking the Difference* offers a relatively lengthy account of these difficulties, which she develops further in prior and subsequent writings on this theme. As these writings clarify, Irigaray understands separation from the mother to consist in both physical birth and the gradual process of becoming independent and forming a separate sense of self. According to Irigaray, this process of separation is inescapably painful for all infants – she speaks of 'the losses and scars involved in the separations from that first dwelling [*demeure*] . . . The wound we cannot heal, and cannot cure, is the cutting of the umbilical cord' (SG, 16/27–8). For boys, though, this separation is especially painful because boys are overwhelmingly aware of their sexual difference from their mothers. In contrast, girls directly experience themselves as being of the same sex as their mothers – as Irigaray puts it: 'Woman . . . becomes a subject immediately in relation to another subject who is the same as she: her mother' (TD, 19/36). Girls can therefore adapt to losing their mothers because they experience themselves as having the same ability to give birth as their mothers: 'the little girl . . . is able to engender like her mother' (JLI, 108). This shared ability ensures some continuity between mother and daughter, which makes their separation

---

[7] For another prominent feminist philosophical exploration of western culture's (male) preoccupation with death, see Adriana Cavarero, *In Spite of Plato*, trans. Serena Anderlini-D'Onofrio and Áine O'Healy (Cambridge, U.K.: Polity Press, 1995).

[8] On Irigaray's account of how patriarchy erases mother-daughter relationships and female genealogies, see Whitford, *Luce Irigaray*, ch. 4.

bearable. The principal difficulty for girls is not how to make separation tolerable but how to combine their sense of sharing a sexuate nature with their mothers with a robust sense of individual difference from their mothers.

Woman is not at all in the same type of subjective identity as man. In fact, she does not have to distance herself from her mother as he does: through a *yes* and above all a *no*, a *near* or *far*. . . . She finds herself faced with a wholly other problem. . . . She must be or become a woman like her mother and, at the same time, be capable of differentiating herself from her. But her mother is the same as she. . . . She cannot reduce her mother to an object without thereby reducing herself, since they are of the same *genre*. (TD, 18/36)[9]

Boys, for their part, are born into an immediate experience of sexual difference, which is painful because it makes the loss of their mothers much more profound. Irigaray clarifies: 'the son does not know how to situate himself in regard to she who engendered him with no possible reciprocity. He cannot conceive in himself. . . The situation is different for the daughter, who is potentially mother' (TD, 110–11/121–2). Lacking this experience of commonality with their mothers, boys must adopt a variety of coping 'strategies' (JLI, 107). Chief among these is to deny or disavow ever being dependent upon, or closely entwined with, their mothers. This denial forces boys to disavow, in turn, their own embodied nature, which bears testimony to dependency and finitude: 'man always seems to neglect thinking of himself as flesh, as having received his body' (E, 127–8/123). Boys cast corporeality and nature as something inferior to them, an 'object' to which they are opposed (TD, 18/36). These strategies instil in males an attitude of thinking themselves superior to nature, which they inescapably associate with the mother and, by extension, with all women. Irigaray calls these strategies, for short, the 'murder' of the mother – not (usually) a literal murder but an attitude of denying the

---

9 Irigaray differs from Nancy Chodorow, who claims that girls have difficulty separating from their mothers because mothers treat their daughters like themselves, instilling in the daughters the sense of a common gender identity; meanwhile, mothers instil in their sons a sense of difference by pushing them away. Chodorow's claims reflect the broadly sociological view that one's gender identity is shaped by one's relationships in early infancy, which, in turn, are shaped by the social division of labour and, in particular, women's primary responsibility for childcare. By contrast, Irigaray's approach is phenomenological, beginning from the infant's immediately lived experience of sexed identity and of corporeal difference from the other sex. See Chodorow, *The Reproduction of Mothering*, esp. ch. 6.

mother's importance and value at a symbolic level.[10] Underneath this attitude of repudiating the mother, however, there lingers in boys/men a fantasy of fusion with and proximity to the mother, a fantasy which boys/men never relinquish (precisely because they never acknowledge it) and which covertly invades and blights all their relations with women.

Irigaray's analysis of male difficulties in separating from the mother appears to rely on the implausible view that boys cannot tolerate separation from their mothers because they know that they will never be able to give birth, whereas girls know that they will be able to do so. As Mary Beth Mader notes,

> though the epistemological position of the child is not elaborated upon . . . the girl is taken to understand her physical resemblance to her mother, and to grasp the notion that she shares with her mother, allegedly, the same reproductive potential for engendering children herself. . . . Irigaray assumes that both the girl and boy are in an epistemological position to know that . . . women can gestate and bear children, or that those who gestate and bear children are women.[11]

This is implausible, as Mader observes, both because some girls will turn out never to be able to give birth and because young children are reasonably thought to lack knowledge of their future reproductive abilities. These epistemological difficulties recede, however, once we appreciate that Irigaray's whole account of young children's attitudes is grounded in her conception of sexual difference as a difference in rhythms. She understands the ability and inability to give birth as functions of the bodily forms which, themselves, constitute stages in the unfolding of men's and women's distinctive rhythms. So, if girls and boys sense that their physical capacities are the same as, or different from, those of their mothers, then this is just an aspect of their deeper sense that their bodily forms are growing according to a rhythm which is the same as, or different from, their mother's rhythm.[12] Over a period of time in their infancy, girls and

---

[10] See Irigaray, 'Women-Mothers, the Silent Substratum of the Social Order' (1981), in *The Irigaray Reader,* ed. Margaret Whitford (Oxford: Blackwell, 1991), p. 47. Defending Irigaray's notion of 'symbolic' murder, see Boulous Walker, *Philosophy and the Maternal Body,* p. 14.

[11] Mader, 'All Too Familiar', pp. 373–4.

[12] Irigaray's account may still seem to presuppose that the sexes fundamentally differ in the capacity to give birth (and not in their rhythms), since boys only have difficulties because being *born* of a woman puts them in a primary proximity to their mothers which neither girls nor boys (on her view) have to their fathers. For Irigaray, though, women's ability to give birth is just one manifestation of their rhythm. Hence, that boys are in primary proximity only to their mothers is already an effect of the rhythmic difference which also produces boys' psychical troubles.

boys can form a sense of their own rhythms, insofar as these structure and pervade the growth and changes in their bodies of which girls and boys are aware. In forming this inchoate awareness of their rhythms, girls and boys need not have any conceptual knowledge of what these rhythms are. Because infant boys and girls are in an intimate, sensuous, and embodied relationship with the mother, they can also – again, over a period of time – form a sense of the rhythm which regulates the changes in the mother's body. Consequently, boys and girls can also form a non-conceptual awareness of whether their own rhythm is synchronised or dissonant with that of their mother, and hence can sense whether or not their own rhythm is the same as hers.

Taking it that there genuinely are differences between sexuate rhythms, as Irigaray believes, and that boys will therefore experience their own rhythm as different from that of their mothers, this experience must aggravate general difficulties with separation. Moreover, to return to Irigaray's overarching narrative in *Thinking the Difference*, boys' and men's resultant strategy of symbolically murdering the mother can be expected to produce an ecologically destructive culture because, much of the time, boys/men will seek to detach themselves from whatever is corporeal and natural, towards which they will act in a way which denigrates and devalues it. Boys/men will let this destructiveness persist unchecked because they remain trapped in a fantasy according to which the natural, corporeal, and (by association) maternal remains ever-present and indestructible – the very collective fantasy which Irigaray sees as threatened by the severity of the Chernobyl disaster.

Thinking the Difference adds a second explanation of how western cultural destructiveness is male: this culture is rooted in male sexuality, which, Irigaray claims, obeys a different pattern to female sexuality, that of 'tension, discharge and return to homoeostasis' (TD, 21/38). It may seem problematic that Irigaray assumes that male sexuality has a determinate character independently of any cultural mediation. We should bear in mind, though, that she again regards male sexuality as a function of men's distinctive rhythm. To the extent that we are persuaded by her account of sexual difference as a difference in rhythms, then we should also accept that these natural rhythms will manifest themselves as naturally different patterns of sexual behaviour. Irigaray maintains that men's sexuality impels them to engage in destructive modes of behaviour that seek to raise tensions to a breaking point. She finds this reflected, especially, in modern technology, which – for example, in the rapidity of its development or its tendency to generate incessant mechanical noise – intrudes disrespectfully upon the natural rhythms of human bodies. Notably, Irigaray's analysis of male sexuality implies that it generates practises and technologies which operate detrimentally to *other* elements of male embodiment. It appears that, for Irigaray, male corporeality turns against itself, some aspects of this corporeality perpetrating violence against others. From this idea that male corporeality turns against itself, we can finally draw out the conception of self-dividing nature which underlies *Thinking the Difference.*

Irigaray believes that male nature has generated a kind of culture which opposes itself to nature, including to female bodies and to male bodies *qua* natural. There is, then, a part of nature – the male sex – which turns against itself. Western culture arises in this turning of (the male part of) nature against itself, thereby acquiring the (allegedly) enduring form of an anti-natural, ecologically damaging, culture.[13] By deriving these features of western culture from male nature, Irigaray carefully attempts to avoid reifying this culture as something independent of nature and to understand this culture, instead, as an internal torsion *within* the natural. This reconception of western culture – and, concomitantly, of nature as self-opposing – becomes more explicit in *To Be Two.*

In this latter text, Irigaray's consideration of nature and culture is found in the chapter 'Between Us, a Fabricated World'. She opens this chapter by quoting the choral song from Sophocles' tragedy *Antigone,* which begins (in the translation which she uses): 'There is much that is uncanny, but nothing that surpasses man in uncanniness'. Heidegger is Irigaray's primary interlocutor here: he discusses this chorus in his 1935 lecture course *Introduction to Metaphysics,* to which Irigaray is critically responding. However, in the background to her response is a further level of engagement with Friedrich Hölderlin, whose thinking about humanity centrally informs Heidegger's discussion of Sophocles. Hölderlin might not seem an obvious interlocutor of Irigaray's, but actually references to him recur at regular intervals throughout her oeuvre. For instance, she refers to his interpretation of *Antigone* in the introduction to *Between East and West* (BEW, 19/31), an introduction which

---

[13] Steven Vogel has objected that the notion of a culture's being cut off from nature is incoherent ('Nature as Origin and Difference: On Environmental Philosophy and Continental Thought', in *Philosophy Today* 1998 (Supp.), pp. 169–81). Since humans are natural beings whose activities express their natural powers, any culture that they create must itself rank as an expression of nature – even in its ostensibly most artificial manifestations such as motorways or nuclear power stations (p. 171). Irigaray overcomes this objection, suggesting that humans are natural but that their nature turns against itself (through men, but affecting women by extension). This generates a culture which is artificial and estranged from nature, yet which remains natural in its very artificiality.

largely reprises the argument of 'Between Us, a Fabricated World'.[14] This makes explicit that Irigaray is knowingly engaging with Hölderlin, as well as Heidegger, in that latter text. Moreover, Irigaray is aware of Heidegger's own debt to Hölderlin – as she says, Heidegger's later 'thought was "indissolubly linked"' to that of Hölderlin (E, 128/123). In particular, she notes that Heidegger thinks about man's 'hatred of nature' – which he addresses in the *Introduction to Metaphysics* under the rubric of human uncanniness – via 'reading and re-reading' the works of Aristotle and Hölderlin (FA, 75/71).[15] Since Irigaray is aware that Heidegger's thought on nature is deeply influenced by Hölderlin, her response to Heidegger in *To Be Two* inevitably, and deliberately, encompasses Hölderlin as well. We therefore cannot understand her reconception of self-opposing nature in this text without first gaining an overview of Hölderlin's speculations on this topic.[16] We can then explore how these speculations influence Heidegger, and how Irigaray eventually responds to both thinkers.

III. Hölderlin, Nature, and Humanity

Hölderlin's thinking about nature arose in the context of early German Romanticism. The German Romantics aspired to overcome what they saw as modernity's disenchanted view of nature by producing art which would depict nature as infused with 'beauty, magic and mystery'.[17] Hölderlin became increasingly critical of this project of artistically depicting nature as re-enchanted, which, as we will see, he came to find anthropocentric, presupposing the same separation between humanity and nature

---

[14] Irigaray also refers to Hölderlin's translation and interpretation of *Antigone* in *This SexWhich Is Not One*, when she proposes to teach a history of readings of the play, including that by Hölderlin (TS, 167/161).

[15] The other element of Hölderlin's thought that Irigaray regularly discusses is his idea (which greatly influenced Heidegger) that cultures can gain self-knowledge only by first becoming unknown or 'foreign' to themselves (FA, ch. 7). For Hölderlin, this interplay between self-ignorance and self-knowledge reflects the deeper interplay between distance from and proximity to nature in human life. For explanation, see Philippe Lacoue-Labarthe, *Typography: Mimesis, Philosophy, Politics*, ed. Christopher Fynsk (Stanford: Stanford University Press, 1998), pp. 241–7.

[16] This overview must be simplified, notably omitting any account of Hölderlin on poetry or the divine; I aim to present the details of Hölderlin's texts just sufficiently to reconstruct in them a coherent line of thinking regarding the status of humanity within nature.

[17] Frederick Beiser, 'German Romanticism', in *The Routledge Encyclopaedia of Philosophy*, ed. Edward Craig (London and New York: Routledge, 1998). For a classic statement of this early German Romantic programme of 're-enchantment', see Friedrich Schlegel, 'Dialogue on Poetry', trans. Ernst Behler and Roman Struc, in *German Romantic Criticism*, ed. A. Leslie Willson (New York: Continuum, 1982), pp. 100, 106–7.

which it purported to overcome. Hölderlin's increasingly critical attitude to the early Romantic project reflects his deepening conviction that humanity's very separation from nature arises through a *natural* process – humanity being merely the site where nature turns against itself. This conviction of Hölderlin's becomes crucial for Heidegger and, in turn, Irigaray.

Hölderlin's thinking about humanity's status within nature represents the progressive working out of his early theoretical reflections on nature, especially those contained in his crucial early fragment 'Judgement and Being' (1795). Here Hölderlin argues that all consciousness involves the subject relating to objects via judgement, through which it distinguishes these objects from itself. For subjects and objects to be related, however, there must be something unitary in virtue of which they can come into relation across their difference. For Hölderlin, then, consciousness as a subject-object relation necessarily presupposes a prior unity of subject and object, a unity which is no mere synthesis but an absolute unification which precedes any distinction. This unity is, he states, '[b]*eing* [which] expresses the combination of subject and object. Where subject and object are directly, not just partially, united, . . . there and nowhere else can there be talk of *being as such*'.[18] Hölderlin also refers to this as 'being in the true sense of the word'.[19] However, this 'blessed unity, being' cannot be known.[20] We cannot be conscious of being because all consciousness requires experience of objects from which we differentiate ourselves as subjects – a differentiation which is absent within being. Insofar as we are conscious, judging subjects, being is lost to us.

Now, unitary being, Hölderlin also maintains, is nature. He equates original being with nature for two reasons. Firstly, this is because he relies on the ancient Greek understanding of nature as *physis*, that which 'loves to hide'. Being is always disappearing from view, since it precedes all division of subjects and objects and cannot be known by consciousness. Because being is always receding behind the separation between

---

[18] Hölderlin, 'Being Judgement Possibility' (usually translated as 'Judgement and Being'), in *Classic and Romantic German Aesthetics*, ed. J. M. Bernstein (Cambridge: Cambridge University Press, 2003), p. 191. In defining being as original unity prior to subject and object, Hölderlin is opposing Fichte's idea that self-consciousness is what correlates subject and object. Hölderlin reasonably objects that self-consciousness is a form of consciousness and hence must post-date, and cannot precondition, the subject-object relation.

[19] Preface to penultimate draft of *Hyperion*, in *Friedrich Hölderlin: Sämtliche Werke und Briefe*, ed. Günter Mieth (2 vols.; Munich: Carl Hanser, 1970), vol. 1, p. 558.

[20] Ibid., p. 558.

objects and subjects, it can be said to 'love to hide', and so can be identified with nature as *physis*. Admittedly, as Heidegger notes in a lecture
on Hölderlin's poetry from 1939, Hölderlin still calls nature 'nature'
and not *physis*, and yet: 'The essence of Hölderlin's word "nature"
resounds . . . following the concealed truth of the primordial fundamental word *physis*'.[21] That is, Heidegger plausibly claims, Hölderlin thinks
nature as *physis*, self-concealing, without using the word. This leads
Hölderlin to believe that, as J. M. Bernstein puts it, 'nature as the ground
of the human cannot appear because it would have to be judged, but if
judged, then it is already in a state of dispersion'.[22] We can experience
nature only as the realm of objects standing over against us, but we cannot experience that *prior* nature which is united with us; as conscious, we
have always already lost that original nature. Hölderlin's second reason
for equating being with nature is interrelated with the first: he thinks
that being presents itself to us in the multiple objects into which it splits,
while remaining different from these knowable entities as the prior condition of their emergence. This prior being, as Heidegger explicates,
'can never be found somewhere within the actual as an individualised
actual thing . . . [it] withdraws from all producing, and nevertheless it
passes through everything with its presence'.[23] For Hölderlin, then, original being is not an entity, or even the totality of entities, but, rather,
is the process of spontaneous coming-into-appearance by which entities
become present to us. As such, being can again be equated with nature
as *physis*.

Through his analysis of how nature splits into subjects and objects,
Hölderlin identifies the objectification of nature as an inescapable consequence of reflection, where reflectiveness itself is an ineluctable concomitant of human consciousness. As his character Hyperion laments,

---

[21] Heidegger, ' "As When on a Holiday" ', in *Elucidations of Hölderlin's Poetry*, trans. Keith
Hoeller (New York: Humanity Books, 2000), p. 79. Françoise Dastur agrees: 'Nowhere
does Hölderlin quote Heraclitus' fragment saying that "nature likes to dissimulate itself",
but his understanding of nature is as near as it can be in modern times to the pre-
Socratics' approach to *physis*' ('Tragedy and Speculation', in *Philosophy and Tragedy*, ed.
Miguel de Beistegui and Simon Sparks (London: Routledge, 2000), p. 87).

[22] Bernstein, introduction to *Classic and Romantic German Aesthetics*, p. xxvi.

[23] Heidegger, ' "As When on a Holiday" ', p. 75. Translation modified following *Erläuterungen
zu Hölderlins Dichtung* (fourth, expanded edition; Frankfurt: Klostermann, 1971), pp. 52–
3. Heidegger extracts Hölderlin's two reasons for equating being with nature from his
locution that nature is 'wonderfully all-present' (*wunderbar allgegenwärtig*): nature grows
into presence in all things, but does so 'wonderfully' insofar as it recedes unknowably
behind them (' "As When on a Holiday" ', pp. 74, 79; for Hölderlin's original phrase, see
Poems and Fragments, trans. Michael Hamburger (London: Anvil Press, 1994), p. 372–7).

'an instant of reflection hurls me down. I reflect, and...the world in its eternal oneness is gone; nature closes her arms, and I stand like an alien before her and do not understand her'.[24] For Hölderlin, our conscious reflectiveness as humans marks us as distinctively cultural, historical beings, who are inherently estranged from original nature.[25] Despite the fact that original nature is unknowable for us, Hölderlin believes that we retain some sense of it as our basis and origin, for which we are always nostalgic. Consciousness, separation, and reflection presuppose an original unity of which we necessarily retain some vestigial awareness. This awareness impels us to strive to *re*unite with original nature – 'To reunite ourselves with nature, with a unique infinite totality, is the goal of all our strivings'.[26]

Hölderlin sees it as the task of poetic literature to trace human beings' effort to reconcile their conflicting impulses to reunite with nature and (*qua* conscious beings) to maintain separation from it. Within his studies of how poetic literature is to fulfil this task, Hölderlin focused, from the later 1790s, on understanding Greek tragedy. His fragment 'The Significance of Tragedies' (1802) conceives the tragic hero as compelled to reunite with nature. For example, in Hölderlin's own tragedy *The Death of Empedocles*, Empedocles, the hero, endeavours to live in relative harmony with nature by comparison to his surrounding culture. However, he inevitably becomes compelled to try to reform that culture, whereupon he finds that he has come to behave artistically – reflectively – vis-à-vis that culture. He finds himself embodying the antagonism between culture and what is natural and given, rather than embodying the unity of culture and nature. To escape this, Empedocles is forced to withdraw from social life, whereupon his desire for unity assumes the changed form of the suicidal urge to fling himself into Mount Etna.

Hölderlin's work on the *Empedocles* tragedy is important because it shows him working out the ontological and ethical implications of his idea that humanity's consciousness divides it from original nature. In drafting and redrafting this drama, Hölderlin came to identify two possible

---

[24] Hölderlin, *Hyperion and Selected Poems*, ed. Eric L. Santner (New York: Continuum, 1990), p. 4.
[25] According to Lacoue-Labarthe, Hölderlin's concept of culture – which exists, like his concept of *physis*, even when he does not use the word – derives from that of Schiller, who distinguishes between the ancient Greeks as 'beings of nature' and the moderns as 'beings of culture' (Lacoue-Labarthe, *Typography*, p. 238). Schiller thus introduces the idea that culture is a realm of artificial separation from nature.
[26] Preface to penultimate draft of *Hyperion* in *Sämtliche Werke und Briefe*, vol. 1, p. 558.

responses to separation from nature. The first, Greek response – that of Empedocles – is to dissolve the self and die. The second response is the 'Hesperian' response, which defines Western Europe after the decline of classical Greece and which accepts the living death of separation from nature.[27] The same contrast between the Greek and the Hesperian surfaces in Hölderlin's 'Remarks on Antigone' (1803). Here the moderns or 'Hesperians' are said to inhabit a culture which 'forces the eternally anti-human course of nature . . . more decidedly down onto earth'.[28] Rather than striving beyond existing life for unity with nature, post-classical Europeans are rooted in a culture which is premised upon the stoical endurance of separation from nature. Hölderlin seems to have come to see this Hesperian outlook as more appropriate, finding the Greek attitude hubristic, premised on an inflated assessment of humanity's status within the cosmos. He never systematically defends the Hesperian outlook, but we can reconstruct why he would have come to find it appropriate given the logic of his earlier thinking concerning nature.

If humanity is originally wholly one with nature, then their separation cannot arise from any activity on the part of humanity just as such. This separation must arise *from* nature, with which humanity is initially united. Nature must *divide itself* – into humanity on one side and an objectified derivative of itself on the other. To construe ourselves, human beings, as responsible for this division is to presume our capacity to act independently of nature as a whole – when in fact, Hölderlin avers, 'all the . . . streams of human activity . . . have their source in nature'.[29] From Hölderlin's perspective, it must be inappropriate for humanity to attempt to overcome separation (whether through suicide or artistic efforts to depict nature as enchanted). To suppose that humanity can overcome separation is to *assume* that humanity can act independently of nature (so as to oppose the self-division which nature has initiated). Even though all striving for unity is a striving to dissolve one's humanity, this striving remains, ultimately, premised upon anthropocentric assumptions. In fact, according to Hölderlin's thinking, we have become separated from

---

[27] Hölderlin writes that 'in his [Empedocles'] opponent' (an opponent who is the bearer of the 'Hesperian' attitude) ' . . . the subjective takes on more the passive shape of suffering, endurance, firmness'; see *Essays and Letters on Theory*, trans. Thomas Pfau (Albany: SUNY Press, 1988), p. 61.

[28] Hölderlin, *Essays and Letters on Theory*, p. 113.

[29] Hölderlin, letter to his brother, 4 June 1799, in *Sämtliche Werke und Briefe*, vol. 2, p. 820.

nature by *its* power alone, so it is not within *our* power to undo separation.[30] The appropriately modest response is to recognise our dependence and hence to endure separation – to wait, patiently, until nature may change its mode of being. Humanity, Hölderlin increasingly comes to believe, must undergo the suffering of division from nature.

Having previously positioned humanity as distinctly non- or anti-natural, Hölderlin increasingly draws out how nature persists within the non-naturalness of humanity. For Hölderlin, humanity is non-natural just because it is the place where nature divides itself, splits within itself. The human condition of opposition to nature is inflicted upon humanity by nature. Hölderlin's understanding of humanity may be characterised as thoroughly non-anthropocentric, in that it traces even humanity's anti-natural, cultural proclivities back to (self-dividing) nature. Even humanity's separation from nature is a product and manifestation of nature itself. This thoroughly non-anthropocentric view of humanity becomes decisive for Heidegger and Irigaray.

In understanding humanity as naturally non-natural, Hölderlin reciprocally views nature as self-opposing, self-dividing. He weaves this view together with a concept of nature as *physis* which deeply influences Heidegger, who writes on the notion of *physis* in Hölderlin's poetry in the same period as he writes on Aristotle's *Physics*. In both writings, Heidegger maintains that nature grows by rendering itself manifest, opening itself up to human knowledge, but thereby also concealing itself as the presencing process behind these manifestations. Similarly, for Hölderlin, nature splits into objects and subjects who can know these objects, but nature thereby makes itself unknowable in its original, unitary guise. By conceiving of nature as self-dividing, Hölderlin specifies *how* nature as *physis* grows – by splitting – and he clarifies that this splitting accounts for what Heidegger defines as nature's simultaneous self-manifestation and self-concealment. This idea that nature grows by splitting into culture *versus* nature will allow Irigaray to see nature as determining patriarchal culture in a way which still permits this culture to be transformed and improved. To see this, though, we must first look more closely at how Heidegger takes up and amends Hölderlin's ideas of nature and humanity, and how Irigaray responds to both thinkers.

---

[30] Perhaps Hölderlin's greatest statement of this thought is in 'As on a holiday . . .', where the poet attempts to precipitate reconciliation with nature on his own initiative and is cast down, humiliated, by the gods for this hubris; see *Poems and Fragments*, p. 399.

IV. Heidegger and Irigaray on Nature and Humanity

In his *Introduction to Metaphysics,* Heidegger comments on the choral ode to Sophocles' *Antigone* while discussing the essence of the human. He aims to return to the original, ancient Greek, definition of human being, a poetic definition which he finds expressed in the writings of Heraclitus, Parmenides, and in *Antigone.* Heidegger takes as *Antigone's* central definition that humanity is *to deinotaton,* which he translates as the 'most uncanny' (*Unheimlichste*). Humanity is singularly uncanny because it is the point at which nature (as *physis*) divides against itself. Although Heidegger does not mention Hölderlin at this point in the lecture course, Hölderlin's understanding of the human is evidently in the background – especially since Heidegger refers earlier to Hölderlin's unsurpassed understanding of 'the great age of Greek beginnings'.[31] Nonetheless, Heidegger departs from Hölderlin in giving central place in his analysis to the concept of humanity's violence (*Gewalt*), as we will see.

Heidegger begins by exploring the Greek concept of *deinon,* translated as 'uncanny' or 'terrible'. Firstly, being or *physis* is uncanny because it is irreducible to beings: it is the event of their emergence which, preceding all beings, cannot itself properly be said to 'be'. Heidegger also describes being in its emergent, eruptive, character as violent, as the 'overwhelming sway' (*überwältigende Walten*). Humanity derives from *physis* and, as such, is violent, too. However, humanity is distinguished in being violent towards the rest of the beings which emerge physically: humanity (as Sophocles' chorus tells us) intrudes violently into sea and earth, forcibly tames and exploits animals, and, above all, masters beings as a whole by imposing intelligibility upon them. Humanity, then, is the place at which the violence of *physis* turns upon itself, which makes humanity the most uncanny. As Susan Schoenbohm explains Heidegger's thought: 'As human, the violent is a power of *physis,* . . . indeed, *the* power of *physis,* which uses violence *against* itself; that the overwhelming sway turns against itself characterises the power of *physis*'.[32] Whereas Hölderlin focused on humanity's

---

[31] Heidegger, *Introduction to Metaphysics,* trans. Ralph Manheim (New Haven: Yale University Press, 1959), p. 126. It is worth recalling that in 1934/5, Heidegger lectured on Hölderlin's hymns 'Germania' and 'The Rhine': his thinking in *Introduction to Metaphysics* (1935) is already intimately connected with his appropriation of Hölderlin's poetic thought.

[32] Susan Schoenbohm, 'Heidegger's Interpretation of *Phusis* in *Introduction to Metaphysics*', in *A Companion to Heidegger's Introduction to Metaphysics,* ed. Richard Polt and Gregory Fried (New Haven: Yale University Press, 2001), p. 157.

separation from nature without defining this separation as *per se* violent, Heidegger foregrounds the violence both of *physis* and of humanity towards other beings. He envisions humanity as destined to actively struggle with other beings, primarily through the intellectual and poetic struggle to wrest intelligibility from them.

Heidegger also stresses that humanity is destined to misunderstand its violent powers as manifesting its independent agency (when in fact, these powers are really powers of *physis*). In 'his' very resourcefulness and violence, the human being cannot but mistake 'the power which pervades him, which alone enables him to *be* a man' for a power that 'he' has somehow brought about through his own resources.[33] But because, in fact, humanity's power derives from *physis*, humanity is destined to be defeated by *physis* in its struggle against it. Each human being, then, must die; through death, there occurs a closing of the 'breach' within being which humanity represents.[34] However, Heidegger suggests the possibility of embracing one's death, by actively wrestling against nature while knowing that the struggle is doomed. Whereas Hölderlin counselled acceptance of our limits, Heidegger urges violence towards the beings of nature; he cannot, at this point in his philosophical development, concede the worth of any non-violent ways of relating to other physical beings.[35]

Heidegger's emphasis on violence enables Irigaray to connect Hölderlin's conception of humanity's place in nature to her analysis of western destructiveness and its specifically male character. 'Between Us, a Fabricated World' largely adopts the 'mimetic' style well-known from her earlier work: she begins by quoting the Sophoclean ode and then paraphrases portions of Heidegger's commentary upon it. She writes

Man upsets the rhythm of natural growth. He plows the earth and obliges it to produce by force what it does not yield on its own ... Man imposes a yoke upon the life that unfolds in itself but whose foundations he does not inhabit. (TBT, 69)

Man is the *inquiétante* being who breaks out of the nature to which he was originally enslaved and dominates it, instituting a second, cultural and historical, world (See TBT, 70). Following Heidegger, Irigaray adds

[33] Heidegger, *Introduction to Metaphysics*, p. 156.
[34] Ibid., p. 124.
[35] Influenced by the earlier Irigaray, Patricia Huntingdon critically analyses the patriarchal flavour of Heidegger's imagery, in which manly creators must appropriate and harness the powers of female *physis*; see her *Ecstatic Subjects, Utopia, and Recognition*, ch. 2.

that man becomes 'exiled' and 'estranged' from his being in this cultural world, inevitably coming to identify himself as the creator of this entire sphere, when, 'in fact, he has only imitated the strength of the universe which surrounds him...man's mastery resembles the natural strength with which he wishes to measure himself'. His strength and violence are really that of nature, operating through him.

Besides paraphrasing Heidegger, Irigaray distances herself subtly from him – and, indirectly, from Hölderlin – by highlighting the sexually dual nature of the humanity through whom nature enacts violence upon itself. At first, she uses Heidegger's language of 'man' mimetically, but, as her essay unfolds, she marks increasingly firmly that *male* humanity is in question, not humans *per se*. Thus, she states that the violence of culture 'can be explained beginning from a male subjectivity' (TBT, 76).[36] She also writes that:

> The female is not called to carry out the task of constructing a world which is similar to man's: a violent, uncanny world, which exists through the domination of nature...To...cultivate herself without violence or power over what surrounds her – all of these correspond more to female being. (72)

Irigaray suggests that men are violent due to their special difficulty in accepting sexual difference: 'man chooses to ignore this irreducible difference...Is this not because he feels foreign to this life which lives without him, this life which reproduces itself...?' (70) Or, as she states later on, man's violence is

> probably related to man's relationship with the one who generates him: he will never generate in himself and must fabricate things outside of himself, in order to separate himself from the mother; he must manufacture externally, while she generates internally. (76)

For Irigaray, drawing on her analyses in *Thinking the Difference* and elsewhere, it is men's difficulty in accepting sexual difference which leads them to turn against women and, simultaneously, against the nature of which they themselves are part – as when men engineer technologies which damage their own nature.

---

[36] As with Irigaray's *féminin* and *masculin*, I translate her *femminile* and *maschile* as 'female' and 'male' (*To Be Two*, like *Democracy Begins Between Two*, originally appeared in Italian). As Kirsteen Anderson, one of Irigaray's translators from Italian, notes, 'Italian does not distinguish between "male" and "masculine" and "female" and "feminine"; both meanings are covered by "maschile" or "femminile"' (DBT, vii).

While Irigaray agrees with Hölderlin and Heidegger that nature turns against itself, she holds that only males mediate this turn. Man's, but not woman's, nature is to be uncanny and violent. Through men's activities, women become embroiled in a non-natural mode of life which is fundamentally alien to them. Evidently, Irigaray can only identify men as the sole mediators of nature's violence because she believes in an original sexual duality within nature, against which men, as one pole of this difference, react. This contrasts with Hölderlin's view of nature as original, absolute unity. Believing in an original duality, Irigaray understands male violence to proceed, typically, through the denial of duality and the forcible imposition of homogeneity upon women and other natural beings. Hölderlin, on the other hand, conceives humans as separated from nature insofar as their power of judgement leads them to divide, analyse, and reflectively partition natural beings. From Irigaray's perspective, Hölderlin's idea that nature is primordially unitary falsely denies the original status of sexual difference.

As well as rejecting Hölderlin's view of nature as unitary, Irigaray's discussion in *To Be Two* reprises her earlier criticisms of Heidegger's notion of *physis* within the more complicated thematic of a *physis* which grows through self-division. To recall, she objects generally that Heidegger overlooks the fact that *physis* is dual, containing two rhythms. With respect to humankind more specifically, it is divided into two sexes whose growth obeys different rhythms. *To Be Two* reiterates that there are two human rhythms of which only one, the male, spontaneously becomes motivated to unfold through self-division. Nonetheless, the male sex imposes its divided mode of growth upon the female sex by disseminating an oppositional culture within which all humans can only live and grow in a split, artificial manner.[37] For Irigaray, the splitting that Heidegger depicts as universal to humanity actually becomes generalised starting only from male humans. In this respect, her account of male violence in *To Be Two* also embodies a modification of Heidegger's idea that *physis* conceals

---

[37] Irigaray's other central objection to Heidegger, as we saw in Chapter 3, is that he defines *physis* only in terms of form (*morphē*), as emergence into appearance, ignoring its material composition; this, she argues, is because he insists that *physis* inherently becomes intelligible to humanity. After *Introduction to Metaphysics*, Heidegger drops the view that humanity must violently wrest intelligibility from nature, but, for Irigaray, his ongoing emphasis that *physis* inherently renders itself intelligible to humanity remains continuous with his earlier view and so retains a violent undertone: '*hylē* [is what] man would always have to open, expose, and unveil to make possible any manifestation or meeting' (FA, 103/95).

itself. For Irigaray, what above all conceals itself is the *duality* of *physis*, insofar as one half of this duality inevitably comes to deny duality, and to deny nature precisely insofar as it recalls duality.

One advantage of Irigaray's belief in humanity's original duality is that it makes nature's turning against itself considerably less mysterious than it is on Hölderlin's initial conception. The opening up of a division within primordial unity must necessarily be a mysterious event, since this unity itself contains no grounds for bifurcation. In contrast, Irigaray's analyses in *To Be Two* and *Thinking the Difference* make it quite intelligible why the male half of a pre-existing difference should turn, reactively, against (the rest of) nature. One might object that there remains a mystery as to how humanity originally becomes sexually dual: that is, that Irigaray has simply pushed the mysterious event of division back to reside in some sort of movement whereby sexual difference naturally emerges. However, although Irigaray does regard sexual difference as mysterious, she sees it as mysterious precisely in being *irreducible* to any prior unity (TBT, 111). For Irigaray, sexual difference does not emerge from any prior movement: it is, precisely, original.

Two interrelated disadvantages of Irigaray's analysis of male violence should also be observed. Firstly, this analysis implies that western culture has uniformly denied sexual difference, following men's (allegedly) inbuilt propensity to deny natural duality. Typically, then, Irigaray's analysis fails to accommodate the diversity and instabilities of western culture. Secondly, she regards this culture as a product of men and an alien imposition upon women, remarking, for example, that: 'The removing of woman from herself originates in ... man's domination over nature ... as we can read ... in the tragedy of *Antigone* ... [a domination which produces] a loss of identity for the woman' (KW, 167–8). For Irigaray, women can participate in patriarchal culture only by estranging themselves from their own, inherently non-divisive, nature. This implies that the contributions of female thinkers, philosophers, and writers must either be faultily complicit with patriarchy or marred by reflecting a high level of alienation (an implication which justifies Irigaray in discussing women thinkers as seldom as she does).[38] If she could acknowledge that there are many non- or anti-patriarchal elements in western culture, then she could recognise that this culture bears the marks of not only men's but also *women's* nature

---

[38] Rare exceptions are the medieval female mystics (S, 191–202/238–52), Simone de Beauvoir (JTN, 9–14/10–15), and the biologist Hélène Rouch (JTN, 37–44/45–54).

as it struggles to express itself. Since she does not acknowledge these elements, her analysis comes close to portraying women as passive recipients of a culture which men, as agents, create. (A third problem with Irigaray's analysis is that it suggests that all men, without exception, are and have been destructive. I will return to this issue shortly.)

Despite these defects, Irigaray's discussion of nature and culture in *To Be Two* deepens her earlier analysis of male destructiveness, specifying that the male sex is the place where nature enacts violence upon itself. Male violence – and patriarchal culture, with its separation from and hostility to nature – derive from a nature understood, philosophically, both as sexually dual and as effecting a violent turn against itself. Irigaray does not, then, regard patriarchal culture as natural in the sense of being grounded in biology, but, since she still grounds this culture in nature (as reconceived philosophically), she avoids hypostasising culture as a separate, independent sphere. We can now, at last, identify how this philosophical reconception of nature enables Irigaray to construe patriarchal culture as both naturally arising and changeable – for, despite her emphasis upon this culture's natural roots, she insists throughout *To Be Two* that this culture can be changed for the better.

V. The Place of Nature in the Culture of Sexual Difference

In *To Be Two*, Irigaray stresses that western violence represents only one possible cultural direction, and that men could learn to cultivate respect for the sexually different other, and for other natural beings. Men could learn to practise 'self-mastery' (TBT, 172) – self-restraint in the face of their desire to act violently and deny difference. Indeed, Irigaray suggests, rather overoptimistically, that this alternative cultural direction has been taken in 'the Far East'. But how has this (supposed) difference between western and eastern cultures been possible if men, as a sex, are inherently prone to destructiveness? And how is the attitudinal change which she envisages possible in the west if, as Irigaray has maintained, men spontaneously become the site through which nature turns upon itself? She explains that: 'The fact that [man's] impulses, inclinations and desires are violent does not necessarily mean that this is an inherent part of male being, but that violence can come from an historical construction' (71). Likewise, at one point in *Thinking the Difference*, she avers that men's destructiveness stems from the absence of a 'sexual culture [*culture sexuelle*], a (partially dialectical) pattern of cultural relations between the *genres*' (TD, 17/35). But if, after all, patriarchal culture explains male psychical difficulties, then what explains the formation and tenacity of patriarchal culture?

Irigaray's apparently contradictory statements regarding the contributions of nature and culture to male violence can be reconciled if she believes that men have only a natural *tendency* to violence. To be sure, Irigaray herself does not explicitly speak of men having this tendency. She does, however, speak of male 'instincts' (see, for example, ILTY 27/54), and plausibly a spontaneous 'instinct' to destructiveness means the same as a spontaneous 'tendency' to destructiveness. If Irigaray does, at least tacitly, believe that men have only a tendency in this direction, then male violence is not inevitable because, although men's destructive tendency will actualise itself if left or permitted to unfold spontaneously, this tendency need not manifest itself in its spontaneous form if appropriate conditions are put in place to redirect it. Such conditions can affect how the tendency exercises itself, giving a social and cultural mediation to the way in which it becomes manifest. (Consequently, it is at least possible that 'Far Eastern' cultures could have set up conditions which enable men to restrain their spontaneous tendencies.) Irigaray need not, then, envisage a linear causal relationship between male violence and a destructive culture. Rather, men's violent tendencies will unfold in their spontaneous guise only in the absence of a sexuate culture, an absence which leaves men devoid of encouragement to recognise and value sexual difference. The little boy finds himself in a 'space of unfathomable mystery' only because his culture, which is non-sexuate, deprives him of reasons to value his mother's difference from himself. If female identity were recognised as *sui generis*, with values and virtues of its own, and if male identity were recognised as another, correspondingly specific, identity, then the difficulty of sexual difference would become negotiable for boys/men.

Given, though, a patriarchal culture which has only come into being in the first place as the effect of nature's tendency to turn against itself, how can this culture ever be changed into a sexuate culture so as to affect, and restrain, the natural tendency from which it results? Irigaray's answer is that western culture has arisen as something genuinely non-natural through nature's turn against itself, a non-naturalness which enables this culture to undergo internal transformation and to act back upon the (male) nature which has hitherto sustained it. Here Irigaray denies that she is falling back upon the traditional idea that culture is independent of nature – for her, the anti-naturalness of western culture has itself arisen naturally. Moreover, she insists that a sexuate culture would not act back on male nature by eradicating its self-dividing tendency. This would only intensify the traditional antagonism of culture to nature. Rather, a sexuate culture would *cultivate* men's natural tendencies – allowing them to remain in existence, but transforming them and orienting them in a new, relatively benign, direction.

Irigaray's later writings constantly emphasise our need to cultivate our human nature, playing, in part, on the etymological link between 'culture' and 'cultivation'. She stresses that a sexuate culture, by cultivating human nature, would allow it to flourish instead of repressing it.[39] However, this culture also has to restrain men's natural tendency to deny sexual difference; seemingly, therefore, this culture *must* encourage men to abstract themselves from and suppress, rather than express, their nature. Indeed, Irigaray writes that 'man has not [yet] pulled himself out of his immediate existence [*être-là*] to consider himself as half of humanity . . . he has not pulled himself out of his intuitive natural immediacy' (ILTY, 39–40/73). In fact, though, she believes that sexuate culture would not force men to break with their nature but would redirect their natural tendencies – in particular, by redirecting, against *itself*, men's inherent tendency to oppose their own nature. Somehow, men's tendency to deny and negate difference and nature must be rerouted so that it denies and negates itself, permanently checking itself and impeding itself from coming into operation, except insofar as it is exercised in suspending itself. This sounds paradoxical. If men's destructive tendency is turned into an agency which checks itself, then what remains for this agency to check? Conversely, if some destructiveness remains which needs checking, then it seems not to have been thoroughly rerouted anyway. I defer until Chapter 5 (Section IV) a fuller explanation of Irigaray's apparently puzzling proposal, but, to anticipate, she argues (building on Freud's account of how our 'death drives' can be rerouted into conscience) that part of men's destructive energies must be turned inwards to constitute a restraining psychical system. By exercising restraint, this system actually still expresses men's destructiveness (and self-destructiveness), but its object is those destructive propensities of men's which have not been captured into this system. Generally, then, the institution of this psychical division allows men's self-dividing tendency to gain some continued expression, in the form of an exercising of self-restraint.

Irigaray's own emphasis is mostly on the role of sexuate culture in motivating men to adopt this system of self-restraint. As she says in *The Way of Love*, culture must encourage men to impose 'negativity' upon

---

[39] 'Being Two, How Many Eyes Have We?', p. 148.

themselves and not, as formerly, upon the world around them (WL, 78). Men's natural tendencies must 'be subjected to the negative in order [that] . . . welcoming the other and having dialogue . . . become possible'. A culture of sexual difference would achieve this result by presenting female identity as *sui generis*, with its own value, and so as deserving of respect. This would give men the initial motivation to oppose their own urges, which would institute a psychical pattern of self-restraint which opens up space to acquire further respect for difference. This, in turn, would reinforce men's motivation to assume the 'task' of 'sublimating [their] instincts and drives' – of turning those instincts back against themselves (ILTY, 27/54).

Where would women stand with respect to this sexuate culture? Irigaray's later works always affirm that a sexuate culture would allow women to express and realise their own nature for the first time. This is not only because this culture would, in terms of content, positively represent the symbolically female, but also because it would recognise and seek to articulate nature and bodies in their natural characters. In this respect, this culture would embody women's own mode of being, which is naturally undivided, consisting in 'a movement of growth that never definitively removes itself from corporeal existence in a natural milieu' (ILTY, 38/71). The singularity of the sexuate culture which Irigaray envisions, then, is that it would express the natures of both sexes, but by appropriately different routes. For women, this culture would directly express their natural mode of being. For men, whose nature inherently tends to oppose itself, sexuate culture would express their self-opposing nature by stimulating it to check itself. This would simultaneously clear space for men to realise and express the embodied and sexuate aspect of their nature, which they themselves were formerly prone to suppress.

At this point, we can return to the problem that Irigaray seems to see all men, without exception, as naturally destructive. We can now see that her position is slightly more complex: although all men will spontaneously tend to become destructive, this tendency can be redirected, so that all men need not in fact be destructive. Nonetheless, since Irigaray believes that this redirection has not yet happened (in the west, at least), all (western) men must, historically, have been destructive, for her. Plainly, this belief in exceptionless male destructiveness greatly underestimates the wide variety of modes of male self-identification and behaviour (now and in the past). Again, it is Irigaray's failure to acknowledge the diversity of western culture which has damaged her analysis. If she were to acknowledge that there have been many non-patriarchal elements in this culture, then she would have to say that these elements have already redirected the potential destructiveness of significant numbers of men, to at least some extent.[40] This would be quite compatible with claiming that the most enduring and dominant symbolic patterns in western culture have been patriarchal and anti-natural.

Irigaray, though, takes the stronger view that western culture has been overwhelmingly violent and anti-natural, and that this is due to our own – cultural – failure to redirect nature's tendency to turn against itself, as it manifests itself through men. A sexuate culture could counteract this tendency and push men towards a new respect for difference. *Both* men and women should work to bring about this cultural transformation, for both sexes have become thoroughly cultural beings, even though in women's case this mode of being has, hitherto, been externally imposed on them. Accordingly, Irigaray emphasises that women's primary task is to work towards a culture which reflects and extends their mode of being, and to avoid being deflected from this task by patriarchy. 'To remain faithful to herself, . . . animated by . . . her own words, . . . this corresponds to the most decisive conquest for women' (KW, 166). Inversely, men's chief task is to learn to transform and reorientate their spontaneous mode of being. 'Whereas a woman too often abandons her own gender, man is too enclosed in his. The "sin" of each is not the same' (KW, 155).

In urging that we – as human, cultural beings – should intervene to reorientate (male) nature's self-destructive tendency, Irigaray explicitly rejects Hölderlin's counsel that we should wait patiently for possible change in nature's own mode of being. Referring to Hölderlin, she writes that we should 'not wait passively for the god to come, but [instead] . . . conjure him up among us . . . as resurrection and transfiguration of blood, of flesh' – that is, as a culture that is continuous with nature (E, 129/124). In their divergent recommendations, Hölderlin and Irigaray might at first glance appear to occupy the two horns of the dilemma which, as I noted earlier, bedevils recent feminist philosophy: whether or not to affirm that culture has natural foundations. Hölderlin denies that culture has any independence of nature, but he consequently espouses quietism. Irigaray advocates cultural change but would therefore seem obliged to grant culture some independent agency with respect

---

[40] Moreover, one source of these ambiguous and non-patriarchal elements could be women's own nature as it strives for self-expression. This would counteract the idea – which Irigaray comes perilously close to endorsing – that women are passive recipients of patriarchal culture.

to nature. Yet she avoids making that move: although she allows culture the agency to transform and cultivate nature, she does so without conceiving culture as independent of nature, instead reconceiving it as dependent on nature for its agency. This agency arises naturally, through internal division within nature. Irigaray treats nature as the basic element within the culture/nature dyad, distancing herself from the patriarchal tradition which typically devalues nature, depicting it as secondary to the cultural, spiritual realm. She thereby succeeds in refusing the nature/culture hierarchy while advocating cultural change.

VI. Retrieving Hölderlin's Concept of Self-Differentiating Nature

Irigaray has adapted Hölderlin's and Heidegger's idea of self-dividing nature in the context of her idea that humanity is naturally dual, exhibiting two sexuate rhythms, where only one of these two sexes spontaneously acquires a tendency to grow through self-division. Her adaptation has the advantage of making it explicable why nature should turn against itself (through the mediation of men). Less positively, since her entire discussion of the nature/culture relation is premised on the assertion of original duality, this discussion presupposes that human bodies do not have any character of non-sexuate multiplicity. Moreover, while Irigaray's idea that male nature tends to turn against itself explains the enduringly patriarchal (and ecologically damaging) character of western culture, this idea also leads her to overestimate the seamlessness of this culture's denial of sexual difference. Her account of the nature/culture relation is therefore not fully acceptable. Nonetheless, core aspects of this account are worthwhile and should be included – suitably rethought – in any conception of nature and culture which seeks to recognise bodily multiplicity alongside duality. Specifically, the ideas of Irigaray's that are worth preserving are these: that one sex spontaneously develops a tendency to grow through self-division; that this sex disseminates a broader culture of artificiality; that, through this culture, an originally dual nature becomes caught in a denial and repression of its own duality; and that cultural resources can redirect how the male sex grows and so restore duality to expression. How might these ideas be recontextualised within a philosophy which also recognises both bodily multiplicity and instabilities within western culture?

We can productively return to other ideas of Hölderlin's on which Irigaray does not draw but which play a role in his thinking of self-opposing nature. By returning to these ideas and pulling out their implications regarding the nature of bodies, I will begin to sketch out a new framework for thinking of bodies as both dual and multiple. In doing this, I will be going beyond Irigaray's own philosophy, but I shall attempt to preserve her valuable ideas and resituate them within the framework which emerges from the implications of Hölderlin's ideas.

Importantly, there are two aspects of Hölderlin's conception of nature as *physis* or being. Partly, he envisions nature as an original unity, void of any distinctions, and which is necessarily still and peaceful (*friedlich*) in its lack of differentiation. He speaks of original nature as the 'peace of all peace' and 'infinite peace', the loss of which is painful to us, and reunification with which would end 'the eternal conflict between our self and the world'.[41] Because Hölderlin conceives original nature to have this unitary aspect, Irigaray opposes his conception and instead asserts nature's primordial duality. However, Hölderlin also envisions nature more dynamically, as the movement by which difference emerges, the process of splitting. Although he claims that nature, which 'was... *one*, now conflicts with itself' (via the conflict between humanity and natural objects), his idea that nature necessarily and spontaneously splits into these conflicting poles entails that nature can never remain unified but must endlessly embark on a process of differentiating itself. Through this process, nature continuously splits, passing from unity to duality. As his thought develops, Hölderlin becomes more strongly aware of this aspect of nature, as is reflected when he comes to find that our separation from nature (as humans) is not only painful but also a necessary consequence of nature's own self-differentiating character, a consequence which we must endure. As a whole, then, his view is that nature is not only unitary but also *self-differentiating*.

Because Hölderlin only gradually came to acknowledge this self-differentiating aspect of nature, he never fully examined its implications. But if nature is self-differentiating, then, whenever it splits into any determinate duality, it must lose not only its former unity but also its engagement in the process of splitting, since this process must cease once the definite form of any duality is attained. This suggests that nature must be impelled (in some way) to develop beyond any duality which it achieves, in order to restore itself not only to unity but also to that engagement in splitting which is necessary to it. By extracting from Hölderlin's attention to nature's unity these ideas that nature is self-differentiating, and that

---

[41] Hölderlin, preface to penultimate draft of *Hyperion* in *Sämtliche Werke und Briefe*, vol. 1, p. 558.

nature seeks to develop beyond all definite dualities, and by combining these ideas with Irigaray's criticism of patriarchal culture, we can start to sketch a new account of the nature/culture relation. This account preserves the positive features of Irigaray's account while dropping its defects: her denial that bodies are (in part) naturally multiple and her overgeneralised view of cultural history.

Let us suppose, then, that nature is self-differentiating and that the dualities in which it manifests itself include the sexual duality found in humans (and some other organisms). This supposition acknowledges the natural sexual duality which Irigaray affirms, but it treats this duality as not original but just one manifestation of nature *qua* self-differentiating. Following Irigaray, once sexual difference has arisen, one sex (the male) can be expected to become motivated to deny this difference and to generate a kind of culture which is severed from nature.[42] Again as Irigaray argues, this culture, once it is generated, can be transformed so that it redirects the male sex's difference-denying tendency and restores sexual duality to expression. By gaining cultural expression, sexual duality would be realising itself fully for the first time. Now, this duality which would be being allowed full self-realisation is, remember, only one manifestation of self-differentiating nature. As I have suggested, though, nature *qua* self-differentiating must always strive to develop beyond any particular duality in which it has come to manifest itself. Moreover, it is reasonable to think that nature will strive to pass beyond dualities more strongly the more fully it has manifested itself in those forms in the first place (because a fuller manifestation in any one form amounts to a firmer truncation of nature's broader onward movement). Therefore, by giving sexual duality full realisation and so allowing nature to fully manifest itself in sexually dual form, a sexuate culture would stimulate nature to develop beyond this duality.

In what specific manner would nature strive to pass beyond its manifestation in duality? Since nature would be striving to restore itself to engaging in the process of self-differentiation, it would, presumably, strive to go beyond sexual duality by splitting again – that is, by splitting up the elements of the duality into which it has entered, hence by splitting up each male or female body. Let us take it that, within this picture of nature, each

---

[42] Presumably the males of nonhuman animal species will also have difficulties with sexual difference, and greater difficulties the more fully their species realises this difference. But, according to Irigaray, humans are uniquely cultural and therefore the males of nonhuman animal species will not respond to their difficulties by generating a mono-sexuate and anti-natural culture. For more on this, see Chapter 6, Section II.

body is made female or male by having a specific character which differs from the character shared by all bodies of the other sex. The idea, then, is that the character of each sexed body would split into two elements or characteristics, which, in turn, would each split into two more characteristics, which would split in turn (and so on indefinitely). Each individual body would therefore come to consist of a diversity of internal characteristics which, since they arise from the breakup of that individual's sexed character, would constitute that individual body as *non*-sexed. Hölderlin's concept of self-differentiating nature thus appears to imply that a sexuate culture would release and stimulate a natural development towards ever-increasing internal diversity within human bodies. However, I am not envisaging that humans would embark on a gradual process of evolving from being sexuate to being non-sexuate over the course of successive generations. Rather, a sexuate culture, once created, would encourage movement beyond sexuation on the part of each individual body which participates in that culture, a movement which would occur within that individual body's lifetime – perhaps quite quickly, with sexuate culture stimulating bodies to rapid change.

Hölderlin's concept of self-differentiating nature may still seem to acknowledge the natural multiplicity of bodies less fully than we might wish, since this concept appears to suggest that multiplicity does not exist in bodies originally but can only arise *after* the inception of a sexuate culture. Because (*ex hypothesi*) sexual difference has not hitherto been allowed to express and so fully realise itself, it seems that nature cannot hitherto have had the chance to develop beyond duality, so that the bodily multiplicity which results from that development can never yet have emerged. This conflicts with the fact that the idea of bodily multiplicity already has phenomenological resonance for us, and with the fact that intersexed bodies – which, arguably, attest to multiplicity – have long been around.

However, we are overlooking the full import of Hölderlin's concept. Just by having arisen within humanity, albeit in culturally unexpressed form, sexual duality has already achieved partial realisation. After all, according to Irigaray, sexual duality realises itself more fully in humanity than in other animal species just because humanity has the potential to express its duality culturally – even though it has not yet actualised this potential. To the extent that nature has been able to realise itself in this (human) duality at all, it must also have striven beyond that duality. Consequently, inasmuch as sexed human bodies have existed at all, they must always have striven to develop a diversity of internal characteristics, a diversity in virtue of which these bodies cease to be sexuate. Yet, because sexual duality has not hitherto been culturally expressed and has therefore not been *fully* realised, nature, too, has been unable to *fully* acquire the striving to pass beyond (that is, to break down) sexual difference, and so has been unable to develop completely into the form of internally diverse characteristics within bodies. Because sexual difference has been left to turn against itself and prevent its own self-expression and full self-realisation, nature has also been deprived of (more exactly, has deprived itself of) the opportunity to fully develop into the form of bodily multiplicity. So, although bodily multiplicity has arisen within us such that no individual can ever have been merely sexed, this multiplicity has arisen in only an incomplete or truncated form (evidently, it remains to be seen what my claim here will concretely amount to). Sexuate culture, then, would not *bring about* internal diversity in bodies – this diversity must have existed for as long as has sexual duality itself – but sexuate culture would *increase* the already partially existing diversity of bodies by strengthening nature's striving to develop into this form.

Several questions immediately arise. (1) I have just claimed that human bodies have always been, in part, internally diverse and so non-sexuate. But then how is it possible that these bodies have always been sexed, as I have also claimed? My thought is that bodies have always striven to become internally diverse and so to break down their sexuate character, but they have only achieved this partially. Consequently, their sexuate character has always remained partially intact as well. Sexuation and non-sexuation have always co-existed in human bodies. (2) But how *can* sexuation co-exist with internal diversity when that diversity only exists at all to the extent that it breaks down sexuate character? We need to suppose that bodies have always tended to break down their sexuation (or, more exactly, that nature has always propelled bodies to do so), but that this tendency has only been partly or weakly realised, and so bodies' sexed character has always remained in place as well. Hence, bodies have always oscillated between phases when they move to break down their sex, and phases when this movement expires and their sex re-establishes itself. However, (3) if bodies' tendency to develop multiple characteristics would be strengthened were sexual duality to be fully realised, then doesn't my position have the fantastic implication that a sexuate culture would stimulate all bodies to develop – physically – beyond being sexed? To avoid this implication, we need to suppose that there is an active counter-tendency of bodies to reinstitute their sexed character against their own tendency to dissolve it. If there were such a tendency of bodies to reinstitute their sexed character, then the full realisation of bodies' sexual specificity would not only strengthen their tendency to develop beyond sex, but (it can be expected) it would also strengthen their tendency to hold onto and reclaim the sexed character which they have now fully acquired. This assertion of two tendencies within human bodies need not be *ad hoc*; I will try, in Chapter 6, to show that it is actually a concomitant of the idea of self-differentiating nature.

Finally, let me say more about what I mean, concretely, when I refer to this tendency of bodies to dissolve their sexual specificity. I have asserted that, to the extent that this tendency is realised, it will result in bodies developing a plurality of non-sexed characteristics. If we follow Irigaray and suppose that the characters which differentiate the sexes are their rhythms, then we can also suppose that whenever bodies move to break down these rhythms into subordinate elements, what these bodies develop is a plurality of centres of rhythm. That is, bodies come to contain a plurality of principles each of which regulates a distinctive kind of unfolding and activity. These plural centres of unfolding have begun to sound suspiciously like multiple forces or centres of energy. If so, then, concretely, the diverse non-sexed characteristics of a body consist in its diverse drives to pursue specific kinds of activity. Beyond this rather tentative suggestion, though, we must await subsequent chapters for a fuller account of what these diverse bodily characteristics concretely consist in.

Because Hölderlin's concept of self-differentiating nature implies that bodies have always tended to become internally multiple as well as to remain sexed, this concept suggests a way to correct Irigaray's overgeneralised picture of culture without exaggerating culture's diversity as Butler does. Insofar as sexual difference persists, unrealised, within the culture which fails to express it, such diverse, non-sexed characteristics as our bodies have developed must persist, too. These diverse bodily characteristics can be expected to strive to express themselves – in their character of non-sexuate diversity – by provoking shifts and alterations within culture, moments of diversification which, precisely, give expression to the *diversity* of these characteristics. Without a prior culture of sexual difference, though, these diverse characteristics cannot develop fully, and must therefore have been insufficient in force and number to rupture the basic direction of culture. These elements have had strength only to introduce intermittent shifts and deviations into a culture which has retained an overall pattern of denying sexual difference.

These suggestions about the shape of a philosophy which reconciles natural duality and multiplicity may look hopelessly speculative and sketchy, posing a host of questions. As yet, we lack conceptual resources to elaborate this philosophy more fully because Hölderlin himself failed to develop his concept of self-differentiating nature completely. Nonetheless, this concept – when fed into Irigaray's view that male nature spontaneously tends to turn against itself but that this tendency can be redirected – contributes an important opening into an account of bodies as naturally both dual and multiple. The next chapter explores the further contributions which can be gleaned from Irigaray's readings of another German Idealist philosopher: Hegel.

5

Irigaray and Hegel on the Relation Between
Family and State

Irigaray has drawn on Hölderlin to develop the idea of self-dividing nature and so explain how patriarchal culture can be rooted in nature and yet open to change and improvement. The other German Idealist philosopher on whom she principally draws is Hegel, although she does so chiefly in the context of the political analyses and proposals which are increasingly important to her writing from the later 1980s on. She remarks that: 'For a very long time, but more continuously since 1981, I have been looking at Hegel's work' (ILTY, 12/31), and she particularly praises what she calls Hegel's 'gigantic speculative project', that is, his 'global consideration of issues that relate to natural law, civil law, and divine law' (SG, 128/142). Her own analyses of law and politics are, indeed, so deeply grounded in Hegel's thought that they cannot be understood unless they are first situated in relation to her readings of Hegel. This chapter aims to introduce these readings and show how they give rise to Irigaray's proposal that laws and political arrangements should express sexual difference – in particular, by allocating rights and obligations only to individuals *qua* members of a sex, and by organising all institutions along sexually differentiated lines. While the Hegelian background to these ideas does not in itself make them attractive, it does, I will suggest, provide conceptual resources with which to address some of the questions which Irigaray's political proposals provoke.

Since Irigaray draws on Hegel's political philosophy, and explicitly criticises his philosophy of nature for its hierarchical account of sexual difference (see S, 220–2/274–6), it may not seem that her Hegelian influence shows her building on the philosophy of nature as she has done with respect to Hölderlin, and, indirectly, Heidegger. Irigaray does, however, turn to Hegel above all to deepen her understanding of how natural human tendencies and drives can be *transformed* and redirected in a way which does not involve their suppression or elimination. She claims that 'Hegel always bet on the continuity between living nature and the spirit . . . [he explores] life's passage to spirit . . . the living development of individuals' (SG, 140/154). 'The ensemble of the Hegelian system, apart from a few errors and uprootings, in fact resembles', she adds, 'living plant growth. . . . Could the general model of his philosophy secretly be *vegetal?*' (112/127). She finds in Hegel, then, an account of how natural drives or tendencies can be developed and cultivated, rather than suppressed and disavowed. Although Irigaray is not engaging directly with Hegel's philosophy of nature here, she is appealing to an aspect of his thought – his account of education – which depends on his theory of nature. To see this, we can consider how his account of education fits into his philosophical system as a whole. A central branch of this system is his philosophy of nature, in which he argues that nature passes through a series of stages, from the most material types of phenomenon to those which are most infused with mind or spirit (*Geist*). At the culmination of this progressive chain, he makes the transition to his philosophy of mind – his systematic account of human mental life and mind-dependent phenomena such as culture and political institutions.

Hegel stresses that mind only distinguishes itself from nature across a gradual series of stages – 'the transition of nature to mind is not a transition to something wholly other, but only a coming-to-itself of the mind which is outside itself in nature'.[1] Mind only gradually redefines itself independently of the natural givens which initially pervade it. This redefinition happens, in part, through social institutions educating and redirecting our desires so that their content ceases to be simply given by nature. For example, for Hegel, marital relationships do not wipe out spouses' sexual feelings but draw out and reinforce the proto-rational element of mutual respect and commitment which is immanent within those feelings.

> Marriage . . . contains *first* the moment of *natural* vitality [*Lebendigkeit*] . . . But *secondly*, in self-consciousness, the *union* of the natural sexes, which was merely *inward* (or had being only *in itself*) and whose existence was for this very reason merely external, is transformed [*umgewandelt*] into a *spiritual* union, into self-conscious love. (PR §161/200–1)

---

[1] Hegel, *Philosophy of Mind* (third ed., 1830), trans. A. V. Miller and William Wallace (Oxford: Clarendon, 1971), p. 14.

Likewise, 'civil society' (the sphere of economic activity and public institutions which regulate economic life) does not discipline its members to suppress and eradicate their self-interested desires but encourages them to recognise and embrace the adherence to the common good which is already implicit in these desires. Thus, just as Irigaray looked to Hölderlin for an account of how nature divides itself, so she looks to Hegel for a detailed account of how individuals' natural tendencies – and, specifically, men's naturally self-opposing and violent propensities – can be transformed by appropriately designed social institutions.

Although Irigaray claims that her philosophy 'does not consist in a destruction of Hegel's thought since he indicates the method' of educating desires (SG, 138/152), she also criticises him for failing to advocate the education of desires consistently. She believes that he repeatedly lapses into encouraging humans to break with their nature (for instance, in the theory of sexual difference which he outlines in the *Philosophy of Nature*). Most commentators on Irigaray's relationship to Hegel have noted her criticisms of him, and they have concluded that, in urging that social and political life should allow people to express and realise their corporeality, Irigaray breaks with (what these commentators take to be) the Hegelian view that the organisation of social life should reflect non-natural, exclusively spiritual, principles.[2] This picture oversimplifies Irigaray's relationship to Hegel, portraying it as purely antagonistic. Actually, her view is that Hegel urges humans to deny and suppress their natural desires only intermittently, and contrary to his own principles of 'fidelity to nature' and 'always starting from sensible, concrete, immediacy' (142/156). Moreover, she objects that at other times he slips into the reverse view that social institutions should leave natural drives to follow their initially given course. In general, then, she wishes to apply his model of education more consistently than he does himself, and when she criticises him it is for insufficiently consistent adherence to his own model.[3]

In this chapter, I pursue Irigaray's engagements with Hegel in the following stages. Since her first discussion of him in *Speculum* focuses

---

[2] See Chanter, *Ethics of Eros*, ch. 3; Cheah and Grosz, 'Of Being-Two: Introduction', pp. 7–9; Morny Joy, 'Love and the Labor of the Negative: Irigaray and Hegel', in *Resistance, Flight, Creation: Feminist Enactments of French Philosophy*, ed. Dorothea Olkowski (Ithaca: Cornell University Press, 2000), esp. p. 123; Naomi Schor, 'French Feminism Is a Universalism', in *Differences* 7: 1 (1995), p. 31; Lisa Walsh, 'Her Mother Her Self: The Ethics of the Antigone Family Romance', in *Hypatia* 14: 3 (1999), pp. 113–15.

[3] I am simplifying here, since, to apply Hegel's model consistently, Irigaray also has to revise this model, as we will see later.

primarily on his account of the conflict between the ancient Greek institutions of family and city-state in his *Phenomenology of Spirit* (1807), Section I reconstructs his account of this conflict. As I will argue, his ultimate aim in this account is to criticise the ancient model of citizenship on the grounds that it unrealistically denies humans' natural, individual desires. Section II examines Irigaray's readings of Hegel's account of ancient Greece in *Speculum* and in later writings (*Ethics* and *Sexes and Genealogies*) which amplify *Speculum*'s claims. Deepening Hegel's criticisms of the ancient form of citizenship, she argues that its predication on a denial of nature reflects men's inherent tendency to repudiate the 'natural blood relationships' on which family life is based. However, her argument as presented in *Speculum* implies that natural blood relationships provide the model for a more just form of social organisation, which sits badly with her own (implicit) view that these natural relationships are self-undermining. This tension prompts Irigaray to examine Hegel's account of how social institutions can educate and redirect natural tendencies. In Section III I look at Hegel's account in his *Philosophy of Right* (1821) of the central, interlocking set of modern social institutions – the state, civil society, and the family. On Irigaray's reading, Hegel endorses the modern state because it recognises and accepts natural desires as individuals live them out within the family, but he fails to advocate that these desires be politically cultivated and transformed. He therefore ends up acquiescing in the injustice to women which natural family relationships breed. As Section IV explores, Irigaray therefore proposes that the state should instead educate men's natural propensities, an education which requires the reorganisation of social life by laws which recognise the right of all men and women to express themselves, culturally, as sexually specific individuals. These laws would enable the development of a broader culture of sexual difference within which men's desires would undergo transformation, and within which men and women could begin to conduct family relationships justly.

Irigaray's readings of Hegel thus generate her vision of the good society, a society which, she believes, would fully express the nature of both sexes for the first time, permitting all individuals, unprecedentedly, to achieve 'happiness' (*le bonheur*). In Section V, though, I argue that Irigaray's political proposals have serious defects: (1) she inherits, without questioning, Hegel's belief that the family is grounded in naturally heterosexual desires; (2) she continues to deny that human bodies (besides being sexed) contain a non-sexuate multiplicity of forces; (3) she unrealistically exaggerates the power of law over society; and (4) the cultural changes she proposes threaten to make sexuate identities unhappily constricting (a problem which I shall consider more in Chapter 6). Positively, Irigaray's political views remain worthwhile for offering a concrete account of how society could allow women to express their nature, instead of forcing them to comply with pre-existing, implicitly male, institutions.

I. Hegel's Account of Ancient Greek Society

Irigaray's first engagement with Hegel in *Speculum* sets the parameters for all her subsequent interpretations of him and so, too, for the development of her political thought generally. She focuses on the account of the conflict between the polis and the family which he gives in chapter VIA of his *Phenomenology*, 'The True Spirit. The Ethical Order'. As with all her readings of canonical philosophers in *Speculum*, Irigaray closely follows Hegel's discussion, paraphrasing and imitating his own words to foreground particular aspects of his argument. Understanding her early reading of Hegel therefore requires some familiarity with his initial account of this conflict.

Hegel sees the polis and the family as the two central social institutions of ancient Greece, whose conflict precipitates the collapse of Greek life and its supersession by Roman society. In narrating this conflict, Hegel centrally aims to show how the ancient Greek form of political community made itself unstable, and ultimately unviable, by refusing validity to family life. His account is thus intended both as a historical description of ancient Greece and as a normative critique of its political institutions. It should be noted that the details of his account of ancient Greece are opaque and contested; in what follows, I reconstruct his account to make it as clear and internally coherent as possible (although this inevitably forces me to use a language different from Hegel's own, which is technical and often barely penetrable).

Hegel claims that the citizens of the ancient polis were 'immediately' united with their community: they identified wholeheartedly with the good of their community, as articulated in its laws (PhG, 265/326, 289/354). This was possible because ancient citizens lacked any sense of 'singular individuality' (*einzelne Individualität*). Certainly, according to Hegel, they regarded themselves as distinct from one another – as 'particular' (*besondere*) community members with special traits and distinct social tasks – but they lacked any sense of having purely individual interests, separate from their interests as members of the community, just in virtue of being particular individuals.[4] Since members of the polis lack a sense of having separate individual interests, the purely individual interests which they do, nonetheless, have (as Hegel appears to assume) must find fulfilment *outside* the polis – within the separate institution of the family. 'The individual who seeks the pleasure of *enjoying his individuality*, finds it in the family' (PhG, 276/339). The family, he claims, is the 'law of individuality' (267/329), where the person's 'individuality, his blood, still lives on' (277/340). This view of the family seems peculiar: surely, one thinks, the family *is* a community. Indeed, Hegel claims that the family forms a community which resembles the polis in that family members, too, lack any sense of separate interests beyond those they have *qua* family members (269/331). But the familial community differs from the political community in being 'unconscious' (*unbewut*): that is, family members cannot explicitly articulate the content of the communal norms they follow, because these norms are not expressed in publicly accessible laws, but only tacitly enshrined in unspoken traditions and practices. These tacit familial norms (prescribing veneration for ancestors and household gods) comprise the 'divine law' (*göttliche Gesetz*), which Hegel contrasts to the 'human' (*menschlich*) – public and explicit – law of the polis.

Why do the family's communal norms remain tacit and inarticulate? Hegel replies that these norms are grounded in family members' *natural* relationships to one another, what he repeatedly calls their 'blood-relationships' (*Blutsverwandschaften*). The family is, then, a '*natural ethical* community' (268/330). It is based, first and foremost, on the natural sexual relationship between husband and wife, a relationship which generates in them an awareness of, and adherence to, a shared good. Hegel assumes, then, that the family is a heterosexual unit, grounded in desires presumed to be naturally heterosexual. Because the content of the common good which family members share is given by their natural relationships, they can access it only by participating in these relationships – their ethical attitude, Hegel therefore states, is inevitably 'mixed with a natural relation and with sensation' (273/336). So, familial norms necessarily remain tacit due to their basis in natural relationships (between men and women, and, derivatively, parents and children, and among siblings).[5]

---

4 So Michael Hardimon explains in *Hegel's Social Philosophy* (Cambridge: Cambridge University Press, 1994), pp. 146–53. As Hardimon clarifies, Hegel also thinks the Greeks had no sense of purely individual rights or capacities for moral judgement or social criticism.

5 Terry Pinkard explains: 'Whereas the government must deliberate about its policies . . . the members of the family simply know what to do. This is understood by the Greeks as

Having understood that, for Hegel, family relationships derive from nature, we can see why he regards the family as both a community and a place where purely individual interests and desires can be met.[6] Family relationships are natural in that they arise from desires for sex, reproduction, and sustenance which people inherently have just *qua* individuals, not as community members. More precisely, people have these desires as *physical*, corporeal, individuals. So family relationships stem from individuals' inherent corporeal desires, yet these very relationships which people generate in gratifying their desires become the source of a communal identity, an identity as a member of a family. Their adherence to this identity prevents people from consciously acknowledging the individuality of the desires which have led them to belong to a family in the first place.

Continuing his account of ancient Greece, Hegel analyses how polis and family clash. He emphasises that the two institutions are sexually divided: only men progress out of the family into political life. He attributes this division, rather vaguely, to the sexes' 'diverse dispositions and capacities' (276/338). Clearly, the point is not that men, on reaching maturity, permanently relinquish family life, but that they abandon their earlier identification with their familial community and henceforward participate in family life without conceiving this participation as essential to their identity. The sexual division between the two spheres of Greek life, according to Hegel, brings them into conflict: women cannot identify with the political community and consequently can see no validity in actions which promote its good, while conversely men can see no validity in actions promoting the good of families. Hegel finds in Sophocles' *Antigone*, to which he alludes, the perfect illustration of the problem. In this tragedy, Creon denies Antigone's right to bury her dead brother Polyneices, which she wishes to do just because he is her brother; conversely, Antigone denies Creon's (and the polis's) right to value people solely for their contribution to public life and hence to condemn Polyneices for having traitorously declared war on Thebes.

---

being due to the family's having its basis in nature, in the natural facts of sex and reproduction. The Greeks took these natural facts (as facts about "the way things are") to specify determinate duties and social roles, "the way things are done")' (*Hegel's Phenomenology: The Sociality of Reason* (Cambridge: Cambridge University Press, 1996), p. 139).

[6] Hegel speaks indifferently of interests or individual purposes (*Zwecke*), desires (*Begierden*), and needs (*Bedürfnisse*).

Hegel goes on to argue, however, that because the agents of polis and family are drawn into conflict incessantly, they come to realise that the institutions they oppose exist necessarily – 'the two laws [are] linked in essence' (283/347) – and so must have some validity. This realisation fills men and women with guilt for having violated valid institutions, and their guilt prompts the further realisation that it is the institutions which they themselves supported which have brought about these violations. '[T]his much is immediately evident, that it is not *this individual* who acts and is guilty... [but rather] the laws and customs... of his station' (282–3/346). In realising that the institutions from which they acted are at fault, agents have acquired an individual capacity for social criticism, and they can no longer embrace their social institutions wholeheartedly in the way essential to the ancient Greek way of life. This marks the end of classical Greek society and the transition to a more individualistic way of life.

A note of nostalgia suffuses Hegel's portrayal of the polis, hanging over from his tendency, in earlier writings, to idealise the ancient republics as paradigms of social integration and civic virtue. But the overall narrative of *Phenomenology* VIA *criticises* ancient Greek political life for being predicated upon an unrealistic disavowal of the separate physical interests of individuals. In more Hegelian terms, we could say that he criticises the polis for involving a merely immediate unity of individuality and universality (289/354). In criticising the polis for its disavowal of individual corporeal interests, Hegel is also criticising it for denying validity to family life, originating as the latter does from individuals' inherent corporeal interests and desires.[7] His analysis implicitly contrasts to ancient Greece a preferable scenario in which citizens conceive it as integral to their political identity that they also have separate interests and hence recognise the necessity and legitimacy of interspersing politics with pursuit of those interests, and with participation in the familial relationships which arise as a result. In his *Philosophy of Right*, Hegel argues that this scenario materialises in modern society, in which citizens no longer oppose, but recognise, family life and its ethical norms.

---

[7] My claim that Hegel is criticising the polis separates me from some recent feminist readers, who believe that he supports the polis against the family, as reflected in his view that Antigone is guiltier than Creon. Butler, for example, points out that Hegel calls Antigone's crime of breaking the public law 'inexcusable', in contrast to what he sees as Oedipus's comparatively 'excusable' crime of overstepping familial law through his incestuous marriage to Jocasta (*Antigone's Claim*, pp. 33–4). Arguably, though, Hegel emphasises Antigone's guilt not to blame her vis-à-vis Creon but to identify her as someone who suffers her guilt with an exemplary nobility and depth.

II. Irigaray's Reinterpretation of the Conflict Between Polis and Family

Irigaray discusses *Phenomenology* VIA in the section of *Speculum* named '... the eternal irony of the community...' (hereafter 'Eternal Irony'), after Hegel's famous dictum that 'womankind' is 'the eternal irony [in the life] of the community' (PhG, 288/352). As I noted earlier, Irigaray's reading of Hegel in *Speculum* is cast in mimetic and highly allusive language. Again, therefore, my exposition is reconstructive and draws on the later, relatively lucid, summaries of her reading of Hegel's *Phenomenology* in 'An Ethics of Sexual Difference', in *Ethics*, and in 'The Female *Genre*' and 'The Universal as Mediation', in *Sexes and Genealogies*.

Broadly, Irigaray endorses Hegel's account of the polis both as historical description and as normative critique. She accepts his criticisms that the polis unrealistically denies its citizens a sense of their separate interests and illegitimately opposes familial norms, approvingly stating that: 'The course of Hegel's *Phenomenology* describes well how spirit develops in our culture'; he 'diagnosed the fact that the ethical order was heading precipitously down, notably in the unresolved opposition between human law and divine law' (SG, 114/128, 110/124).[8] While approving Hegel's general characterisation and criticism of the polis, she deepens his criticism with a further charge that the polis is constituted through men's violent repudiation of family life, which they then re-organise into a form which is unjust and injurious to women. Yet we will see that, as she develops this charge, she combines it with an affirmation of the original, pre-patriarchal, 'blood relationships' of the family which is politically unproductive, and which fits uneasily with her incipient idea that these 'blood relationships' inherently turn against themselves to generate the polis.

---

[8] Actually, Irigaray is more critical of Hegel than this might suggest. In *Speculum*, she maintains that he supports the polis against the family, which she takes to be shown, again, by his claim that 'the purest fault is that committed... by the female [*féminité*]' (S, 223/277). Her early reading of Hegel exemplifies her broader position in *Speculum* that philosophers' ambiguities – including their criticisms of patriarchal values – feed into their ultimate denial of sexual difference. Her later summaries of her view of Hegel's *Phenomenology* are more sympathetic: for example, she praises him for 'discussing the failing that has marred our whole culture... the lack of ethical relations between the sexes' (ILTY, 20/40). Since Hegel's texts do not warrant the claim that he supports the polis against the family, I ignore this critical strand of Irigaray's early reading (a strand which ties in with her criticisms of his account of sexual difference as a hierarchical difference between active, inwardly differentiated, males and passive, inwardly undifferentiated, females: see his *Philosophy of Nature*, vol. 3, p. 175).

Underpinning Irigaray's sharpened assessment of the faults of the polis is her subtly transformed conception of the ancient family. She portrays this revised conception of the family as already present within the *Phenomenology*, submerged under Hegel's dominant conception of it. This hidden conception of the family, she believes, is implicit in Hegel's repeated references to family relations as 'blood relationships' (*liens au sang*), which suggest that he sees blood as incarnating the inherent physical desires of an individual.[9] Confirming Irigaray's suggestion, his *Philosophy of Nature* outlines a theory on which blood is the expressive vehicle of individual desires – in much the same way that, say, black bile contains and expresses melancholy according to the theory of humours.[10] Irigaray infers that, because Hegel sees blood as this expressive vehicle of individual desires, his 'blood relationships' must involve individuals allowing and encouraging one another to express, fulfil, and cultivate the individual desires expressed in their 'blood', or more broadly the fluid rhythms and materials which make up their bodies. Family members, Irigaray says, 'recognise one another in their singular self' (S, 216/269); 'that individuality, that *still living subject* of blood simply took place' (220/274).

To occupy a 'blood relationship' to another person means, for Irigaray, to respect and attend to the good that person has as a separate, embodied individual – to 'the singularity of her desire' (E, 117/114). Although blood relationships are ethical, they can only arise from natural – sexual or parent-child – relationships, relationships which arise from 'the passion "of the blood", . . . the carnal act'. Only these relationships bring individuals into the close physical proximity which allows them to appreciate and interpret the corporeal manifestations of one another's desires. It is this conception of family members as acting from naturally arising principles of respectful attentiveness to one another's individual, physical desires which Irigaray discerns underneath Hegel's dominant conception of family members as espousing a (naturally arising) common good. She considers this hidden conception more historically accurate than Hegel's

---

9　Irigaray's discussion of Hegel is suffused with plays on the notions of 'red blood' (*sang rouge*) and 'white blood' (*sang blanc*), as other readers have noted (see, especially, Whitford, *Luce Irigaray*, pp. 118–20). As Whitford says, '*sang rouge* is opposed to the *semblant*, or the "other of the same", which is a homophone for *sang blanc*' (p. 118). For Irigaray, red blood expresses the physical desires of individuals, forming the substrate of family relations in which individuals respect one another's desires. Women are reduced to having 'white blood' when the polis transforms families into communities which treat all women as mothers, depriving them of any sense of their individual differences.

10　Hegel, *Philosophy of Nature*, vol. 3, p. 360.

dominant conception – and, above all, better attested by Greek tragedies, from which Hegel drew his own faltering insights into the true character of the ancient family.[11] Significantly, though, Irigaray remains faithful to Hegel in that she imagines 'blood relationships' to take place within heterosexual families.

Irigaray's revised conception of the family leads to her new understanding of polis/family conflict, in which the polis denies validity to family relationships in the sense of 'blood relationships' oriented to family members' good as corporeal individuals. This revised account of polis/family conflict, sketched in 'Eternal Irony', embodies a deeper criticism of the polis than Hegel originally presented. Irigaray suggests that ancient Greek citizenship, premised on the idea that citizens have no separate individual interests or desires, is a quintessentially male identity – an identity which men are uniquely motivated to assume. Men assume this identity as part of a broader repudiation of nature, 'a split . . . that leaves nature without gods, without grace' (E, 119/115). Men want, then, to deny that their natural, corporeal existence – and the individual desires and interests which, for Irigaray, follow from natural existence – are essential to their identity. But since the family is premised upon recognition of and attentiveness to its individual members' separate interests, men become motivated to break with the family and institute, or enter, a type of community – the polis – which is predicated upon its members lacking a sense of separate, particular interests. The polis, then, emerges from men's deliberate break with the family: 'the stratification above/below of the two ethical laws, of these two existences of sexual difference, . . . comes from the Self' (S, 223/277). In *Speculum*, Irigaray does not explain why men wish to deny the importance of their corporeality, but in *Sexes and Genealogies* she clarifies that this wish stems from their infantile difficulties in separating from their mothers, given the reality of sexual difference (SG, 136/150). These difficulties, as we have already seen, lead boys to disavow their early intertwinement with their mothers and, at the same time, their corporeality.

To support this interpretation of the origins of the polis, Irigaray builds on Hegel's allusion to Oedipus. He hints that Oedipus is the

---

[11] According to Irigaray, ancient tragedies narrate 'the historical passage from matriarchy to patriarchy' (S, 217/270) and define the family in terms of 'blood bonds' (most conspicuously in Aeschylus's *Oresteia*). Her idea that Greek tragedy reflects this historical transition is influenced by the anthropologist Johann Jakob Bachofen; see his *Myth, Religion and Mother-Right* (1861), trans. Ralph Manheim (London: Routledge, 1967).

paradigmatic political agent, whose exclusively civic identification causes him to violate the entire structure of norms constituting his family, by committing parricide and incest.[12] Irigaray extends this hint that the typical citizen's sexual life is 'Oedipal': 'the family of Oedipus would be quite exemplary' (S, 216/268). Because citizenship rests on a repudiation of relations with the mother, it simultaneously allows men to keep up the unconscious fantasy of being fused with their mothers (since, for Irigaray, the disavowal of relations is precisely what allows this fantasy to persist unchallenged). Inevitably, therefore, ancient Greek citizens re-enact their fantasy of fusion in all their sexual relationships, equating the women they desire with their mothers; Oedipus only dramatises this. As Irigaray summarises in *Sexes and Genealogies*: 'Citizens as a kind [*genre*] are cut off from their corporeal roots even as they remain tied, as a body, to their mother-nature. This being unresolved, they let it weigh on their relations to women, whom they reduce to maternity' (SG, 136/151).

Irigaray thus explains the historical emergence of the polis from the family, and, simultaneously, the exclusive maleness of the polis, as conjoined consequences of men's peculiar difficulty in separating from their mothers. Interestingly, then, she does not reject Hegel's claim that ancient Greek institutions were sexually divided due to the sexes' naturally 'diverse dispositions and capacities' (PhG, 276/338). Instead she identifies the sexually specific disposition which generates this division as men's tendency to consciously exaggerate, but also unconsciously resist, their separation from their mothers. This disposition arises *naturally* (from the natural sexual difference which propels boys/men to develop this disposition).

Irigaray's attribution of an 'Oedipal' form of sexuality to ancient citizens underpins her further argument that their sexual conduct progressively transforms the family into an oppressively communal institution, which forbids its members any sense of individual identity. Men inhabit their families according to a fantasy of fusion with their various female members, who come to lose their own sense of individuation because men's attitude destroys their 'genealogies'. For Irigaray, mothers and daughters can only individuate themselves by referring to a sense of generational difference – of being differently located in a genealogical chain. Because women in ancient Greece imbibe from

---

[12] Hegel remarks that 'the son does not recognize his father in the man who has wronged him and whom he slays – nor his mother in the queen whom he takes as his wife' (PhG, 283/347).

male citizens an identical understanding of themselves as mothers, they lose the psychical ability to separate themselves from one another – 'the female is aware of no difference between itself and the maternal' (S, 224/278). Antigone exemplifies this, repeating her mother Jocasta's suicide:

Whatever her current arguments with the laws of the city may be, another law already draws her along her path: identification with her/the mother. *But how are mother and wife to be distinguished?* Fatal paradigm of a mother who is wife and mother to her husband. (219/272)

The Oedipal attitude of citizens converts the family into what Irigaray later calls a 'primitive undifferentiated unity' (SG, 140/154), which prevents anyone from individuating him- or herself relative to the other members. Reduced to this condition, family members can no longer act from the ethical principle of attention to one another's interests as embodied individuals. Instead, family members start to promote their common good – the only good their fused identities allow them to recognise. So, Irigaray's narrative suggests that when Hegel defines the family as a community like the polis, he confuses the *secondary*, 'Oedipal' form of the family – acquired only once the polis has broken from family life – with the family in its original form, as a natural ethical structure whose members are oriented to one another's individual good.

Hegel criticised ancient Greek citizens for an unrealistic lack of awareness of their separate individual interests and for illegitimately opposing the norms of the family, which are valid just as the family is necessary. Irigaray endorses this criticism of ancient Greek citizenship, but adds that this form of citizenship arises precisely in reaction *against* the attention to individual, physical interests which the family practises. Citizen identity is constituted through a dramatic repudiation of natural corporeal relationships. Moreover, male citizens go on not only to oppose valid familial norms, but also to transform the family into an oppressive institution which inflicts psychical fusion upon all its members, most harmfully its female members, who derive no emotional benefit from this transformation.

Irigaray's deepened criticism of the polis is accompanied by an overvalorisation of the ancient family in its (allegedly) original form. Whereas Hegel criticises both citizens *and* family members – the latter for their inability to appreciate the good of the community as a whole – Irigaray does not chastise family members for refusing to recognise political norms. She praises Antigone for defying state authority and insists on the ethical asymmetry of Creon's and Antigone's actions (E, 118–20/115–16; TD, 67–70/81–5). Behind Irigaray's approval for the family lies the presupposition that its respect for embodied, individual interests makes it a legitimate social institution. Politically, this implies that society should be rebuilt around the family in its original, just form – a programme indicated in a few of Irigaray's later writings, such as her enthusiasm for the 'era of female law' (*droit féminin*) (JTN, 89–91/111–13). Yet this programme is unfeasible from her own standpoint, which already implies that the family cannot endure as a stable basis of social life. This is because the same natural relationships between individuals which (according to Irigaray) originate familial ethical relationships of mutual attentiveness include the natural relationship between mothers and sons which motivates sons to deny their corporeal separateness and reject family life. Because familial ethical life exists on a purely *natural* basis, it leaves boys/men to acquire and act on their tendency to turn against family life. The family is internally unstable, inherently tending to generate the political agents who resist and transform it. In this sense, Irigaray's analysis of ancient Greece seems tacitly to incorporate a pessimistic philosophy of history in which natural, just, ethical relationships necessarily engender the political community which repudiates and destroys them. She therefore needs to identify an alternative model of co-existence between family and state – as she states in *Sexes and Genealogies*, her overarching political concern becomes that of thinking how family and state, or 'divine' and 'human' law, can co-exist (SG, 127–8/141–2). On this model, the state must neither oppose family relationships nor leave them to run their natural – and naturally unjust – course, but instead it must 'cultivate' these relationships out of their natural form.

III. Irigaray's Criticisms of Hegel on the Modern State

To ascertain how the state might cultivate the family, Irigaray turns, firstly, to Hegel's model of developmental growth, and, secondly, to his account, in the *Philosophy of Right*, of how state and family should be re-organised to overcome their ancient opposition (an account which she discusses in *Sexes and Genealogies* and in earlier chapters of *I Love to You*). As I explained earlier, Irigaray endorses Hegel's general model of how mind emerges from nature, gradually, by participating in a society whose institutions educate desires out of their initially given form. She also hopes to learn from this model how the state could re-educate the natural tendencies of male family members. However, she believes that Hegel abandons his model of educational development when he considers the relationship between family and state.[13] He

> breaks the chain of life's becoming, of life's passage to spirit within the couple, the family.... Hegel is doomed to do what he wished not to do, because of a paralysis of will between the *genres* in the family.... This failure of thought [*impensé*] ... maintains a break in the spiritualization of the living and of nature. (SG, 140/154)

Instead of showing how family life could be 'spiritualised', or how the desires which men spontaneously develop within the family could be re-educated, he argues that the state should leave these desires to follow their spontaneous course, which leaves the intra-familial relations between men and women in a state of 'paralysis'. To understand Irigaray's interpretation of Hegel here, we first must return to his *Philosophy of Right.*

As in the *Phenomenology*, Hegel's discussion of family and state in the *Philosophy of Right* blends description with justification, since he believes that the affectionate nuclear family and the liberal constitutional state, as realised in post-Enlightenment Europe, are ideally rational and legitimate, overcoming the conflict which ruined their ancient Greek precursors. Although, for Hegel, the modern state and family differ markedly from their ancient precursors, they share with them certain essential features which continue to define them *as* state and family. The state remains the sphere in which the common good of the community as a whole is determined and executed, while families remain small-scale communities arising from relationships of natural (and still presumptively heterosexual) desire between particular individuals. Families, then, remain ethical communities whose members share a sense of their common good and lack any sense of purely individual interests – in Hegel's terminology, the family embodies the principle of 'immediate universality'. As in ancient Greece, this 'universality' arises from the natural relationships

---

[13] Irigaray also hints that Hegel abandons his developmental model in his *Philosophy of Nature* when he portrays sight – and, by extension, representation, consciousness, and mind – as emerging through a break with the 'red blood' which embodies physical, individual desires. For Hegel (as she quotes): 'In the case of the eye ... the arteries are continued into finer branches, which no longer contain *red* blood' (S, 214/226). She concludes that 'the *eye* ... would have no need of blood to see, any more perhaps than the Mind does to think (itself)' (S, 226/281). She implies that Hegel provides this account of sight to help justify men in breaking from family life to constitute the polis.

which men and women initiate to fulfil their sexual and reproductive drives: marriage arises from the 'moment of *natural* vitality', specifically the process of reproduction (*Begattung*) (PR, §161/200). These natural relationships sustain in men and women 'the consciousness of... unity with [one] another', in the inchoate, rationally inarticulable, shape of the feeling of 'love' (§158A/199).

It is characteristic of modernity, though, that the family and state are structured so that they embody recognition of one another: modern citizenship incorporates recognition of the validity of what Hegel calls the 'principle of self-subsistent particularity', and, reciprocally, modern family members recognise the state by educating their children for public life.[14]

The state is the actuality of concrete freedom. But *concrete freedom* requires that personal individuality and its particular interests should reach their full *development* and gain *recognition* of their right... and also that they should, on the one hand, *pass over* of their own accord into the interest of the universal, and on the other, knowingly and willingly acknowledge this universal interest even as their own *substantial spirit*, and *actively pursue it* as their *ultimate end*. (§260/282)

This reconciliation between 'particularity' and 'universality' is possible, for Hegel, because individual interests no longer find satisfaction only in the family but also in the newly arisen realm of 'civil society'. Material production, formerly conducted within the family, has branched off to comprise this distinct area of social life, which can 'mediate' between the extremes of family and state. Because civil society interconnects, oversees, and protects *all* the economic agents of the community, it can educate them to adhere to the good of this community as a whole:

The selfish end in its actualization... establishes a system of all-round interdependence, so that the subsistence and welfare of the individual and his rightful existence are interwoven with, and grounded on, the subsistence, welfare, and rights of all, and have actuality and security only in this context. (§183/221)

In contrast, family members can only ever endorse the good of the small-scale community which is their own family. Civil society guides its

---

[14] Hegel's 1802–1803 *Natural Law* essay already suggests that the state must become reconciled with the private sphere by (1) recognising the private sphere's necessity and validity, and (2) sacrificing part of itself to the private sphere; see his *Natural Law*, trans. T. M. Knox (Philadelphia: University of Pennsylvania Press, 1975), pp. 103–5. Hegel models this schematic solution on Aeschylus's *Eumenides*, in which the Athenian polis learns to appease and revere the chthonic female deities whom its agent, Orestes, has wronged.

members to become aware that their pursuit of individual ends simultaneously serves the common good as well. So although family life *per se* remains antithetical to politics, it becomes reconciled with the state by ceding its productive functions to civil society. In turn, civil society allows family members to contribute indirectly to political life by educating their children for the economic activity which makes political life possible.

Because people's pursuit of their separate interests now typically elevates them to adhere to the common good, members of the state can, reciprocally, recognise the validity of pursuing private interests, which no longer signals the dissolution of political community. Members of the state recognise the 'principle of particular individuality' in several more determinate ways, most centrally by conceiving it as integral to political membership that one also has purely individual interests which merit satisfaction. Also crucially, the state legally protects, supports, and regulates the family and civil society. In short, 'the end of the state is both the universal interest as such and the conservation of particular interests within the universal' (§270/290).

As in *Speculum*, Irigaray in her later writings broadly accepts Hegel's description of the interlocking functions of family and state – as she notes, he 'define[s] love between men and women … as it exists within a culture of the patriarchal type' (ILTY, 20/41). But she denies that the state/family relationship which Hegel describes is legitimate, maintaining, on the contrary, that it is inherently unjust, necessitating women's confinement within the family. Hegel's description captures this aspect of modernity, stressing women's exclusion from political and economic life. Hegel, though, tries to justify this exclusion by – notoriously – deriving it from women's essential domesticity:

Man … has his actual substantial life in the state, in learning, etc., and otherwise in work and struggle … so that it is only through his division that he fights his way to self-sufficient unity with himself. … Woman, however, has her substantial vocation in the family, and her ethical disposition consists in this [family] *piety*. (PR, §166/206)

This idea that women are essentially domestic vacuously redescribes, rather than genuinely explains, the sexual division of labour which Hegel observes. This might suggest that he has no good reasons for endorsing women's confinement in the home, merely accepting it out of nineteenth-century prejudice. Irigaray claims, however, that there *are* strong philosophical reasons why Hegel attempts to justify women's restricted role.

He dimly perceives that the family/civil society/state configuration he endorses results *necessarily* in the exclusion of women from economic and political life, and though he is unable to grasp the mechanism of this, he sees that he must justify this exclusion for his defence of the modern social order to succeed. Irigaray, in contrast, proposes to identify the mechanism which makes women's confinement in domesticity necessary to modern society, in a way which will clearly expose its injustice.

According to Irigaray, the central problem with the social configuration Hegel describes is that it leaves the family in a 'natural' state. The modern family 'is where spirit fails to penetrate into nature to spiritualize it' (SG, 139/154), so that 'the natural immediacy of the couple is not spiritualized' (135/150). This looks odd: for Hegel, the family is not exclusively natural, as its constitutive natural relationships directly inspire its members with an ethical attachment to their common good. But this fact that familial ethical relationships originate in nature is exactly what Irigaray objects to, on grounds prepared by her reading of Hegel in *Speculum.* She argues that, due to its natural basis, the family both elicits in men the tendency to deny their early, embodied proximity to their mothers, and leaves them free to maintain the fantasy of fusion with their mothers, which they re-enact in all sexual relationships. The predictable results are that men engage in the various destructive behaviours which manifest their hostility to nature and embodiment, and that men convert the family into 'a *substantial* unity in which the individual units fuse' (130/144). 'The family...forms a unity. It must do in the absence of a dialectic between the sexes' (139/154). Men impose the identity of mother on all women, and so women lose a sense of having individual interests or identity. Since a sense of individual interests is necessary for economic participation, the naturally based family effectively deprives women of the capacity for extra-domestic life. Male family members, by contrast, remain capable of entering civil society, since they position themselves above the sea of familial homogeneity which they create. 'In the bosom of the family, man drowns in a primitive undifferentiated unity. He can regain his individuality only when he leaves the family. This means that the living development of individuals in the family is interrupted, split' (140/154). Irigaray's criticism of the naturally based family restates her point from *Speculum* that the natural family inherently subverts its originally just organisation, but this point is now explicitly formulated *as* a criticism.

Irigaray's basic objection to the social order Hegel commends, then, is that it provides legal and political sanction for the family as a naturally grounded and hence unjust institution.[15] She concludes that

> the family falls back in several ways into non-spiritualised nature: the woman insofar as she is . . . reduced to the flesh of man and to reproduction, man insofar as he is . . . split between belonging to the familial unity and working for the culture of the people, while yet remaining, secretly, the son of his wife. (136/150)

By protecting natural family life, the state colludes in excluding women from economic and political existence. Notably, Irigaray continues to accept Hegel's picture of the family as a unit which is both natural and heterosexual. She also accepts that injustice to women arises primarily from male nature as it spontaneously develops within the family so understood. Presupposing that family relationships are 'natural' in these interrelated ways, Irigaray sets out to establish how political institutions could avoid the modern state's acquiescence in the injustices which flow from these relationships. Her solution is to apply Hegel's model of the social education of desires more consistently than he does himself. When consistently applied, this model suggests that the state should 'cultivate' family relationships by re-educating male desires so that they oppose, not women and nature, but their own spontaneous manifestation. This re-education requires change to laws so that they recognise 'sexuate rights', as Irigaray calls them. Let us see how she develops these arguments in her political writings.

IV. Law and the Education of Natural Desires

Irigaray's latest writings increasingly emphasise the need to overcome the natural basis of family relationships, which renders them unjust.

> If [sexual relationships] are left solely to natural identity, to reproduction, to the parental function, the alliance between man and woman does not achieve human maturity, and the singular identity of each one disappears in the familial unity. . . . [Then t]he family does not correspond to the place where human maturity can be accomplished. It remains a more or less animal tribe. The path to

---

[15] This means that, although the modern state recognises the family, as the ancient polis did not, the modern state remains exclusively open to male citizens who understand themselves as partially split from family life. Within the ostensibly harmonious structure of modern life, a weakened version of the ancient family/state opposition persists, in Irigaray's view (BEW, 16/27).

the realisation of human identity should, rather, be found . . . [in a] carnal sharing which is capable of passing beyond [*dépasser*] instinct, . . . capable of going beyond the regression or disappearance of [individual] consciousness in a return to a so-called nature that ignores all difference (BEW, 114–15/151–2).

It might sound as if Irigaray is proposing that male family members must learn to respect women according to principles of justice which they hold on non-natural grounds, and independently of their natural desires (their *désirs*, *instincts*, or *pulsions*). She stresses, though, that the 'sharing' which family members must undertake should be a 'carnal' sharing, not a renunciation of carnal relationships. She is not urging men to transcend their natural desires, but to *desire* what is just. In the scenario she envisages, then: 'Nature no longer subdues itself but adapts itself, in its rhythms and necessities, to the path of its becoming, its growth' (116–17/154). In particular, men's natural desire to reject sexual difference, their mothers, and nature must 'adapt itself', or, as Irigaray also says, be 'cultivated' (*cultivé*), 'sublimated' (*sublimé*), and 'educated' (*éduqué*) (ILTY, 27/55–6). How is this to happen?

In *Sexes and Genealogies*, Irigaray claims that, for the 'home' to be spiritualised, 'there must be representation in law of the rights of each sex insofar as they are different' (SG, 140/154). Thus, she believes that the re-education of desires requires the institution in law of 'sexuate rights'. In many recent political texts, she urges change to national and international legal codes and charters so that they allocate individuals only sexually specific rights, urging a process of 'redefining rights appropriate to the two sexes to replace the abstract rights of non-existent neutral individuals, and reinscribing these rights in the civil code . . . we must modify civil law to give the two sexes their own identities as citizens' (TD, xv–xvi/15–17). For Irigaray, the introduction of 'sexuate rights' is a necessary condition for the cultural development of a *sui generis* female identity. The cultural existence of such an identity is, in turn, necessary for the re-education of male desires, because – as we saw in the last chapter – if an independently valuable female identity is culturally recognised, then this gives boys/men respect for women and so motivates them to quell their spontaneous urges to deny sexual difference.

The first question is why Irigaray deems law especially important in creating the conditions for a culture of sexual difference. Regarding this culture, she states that it is 'necessary to give woman, women, a language, images and representations . . . appropriate to them: on a cultural, and also on a religious level . . . [they need] a world in the female, a world different from that of man as regards . . . relationships with work, nature, culture' (DBT, 131). Not only would the images and representations presented by this culture articulate a *sui generis* female identity, but also the existence of this identity would be conveyed by the very fact of women's autonomous activity in developing a body of cultural representations. Here, it should be noted, Irigaray is not urging the construction of a separate female culture in addition to the existing male culture. Since the latter, for her, is predicated on the denial of female identity and culture, the construction of a female culture cannot occur without provoking a transformation in how men express and articulate themselves. Thus, Irigaray is arguing for a transformation in our overall social culture, so that it accommodates a duality of traditions and practises in every field.

Irigaray believes, though, that certain legal conditions must obtain before a 'world in the female' (and then, in turn, a new 'world in the male') can germinate. Specifically, there must be recognition in law of the basic right of men and women to articulate and realise themselves culturally. She refers to this as the 'right to life' (SG, 132/146, 142/156), which she equates (in these passages from *Sexes and Genealogies*) with the right to develop and cultivate one's nature as a sexually specific being. Were this right secured, men and women could engage in the differentiated cultural activities through which they need to express themselves as sexually specific beings. Evidently, Irigaray construes this 'right to life' not as a negative right but as a positive right to assistance from society in realising oneself culturally.[16] How, though, does her idea of a 'right to life' relate to the idea of sexuate rights? The right to life seems to be a universal right obtaining for both men and women, which jars with the apparent import of Irigaray's proposal for sexuate rights, according to which all rights should be sexually specific. Let me first clarify how the 'right to life' is universal before assessing its relation to the notion of sexuate rights.

The suggestion that the right to life is a universal right may well be surprising. After all, Irigaray generally opposes the pursuit of universal rights and the politics of sexual equality which she associates with it (an opposition which is most strongly expressed in JTN, 9–14/10–15). She construes egalitarian feminism – exemplified, for her, by Simone de Beauvoir's thought – as the pursuit of women's equal participation in

---

[16] For example, she claims that the media should have a legal obligation to direct half their broadcasts towards women (JTN, 89/111), presumably reflecting women's legal right to the conditions of their cultural self-realisation.

traditionally male activities. Irigaray denounces this political strategy on the grounds that it uncritically presupposes the positive value of these traditional activities, overlooking the extent to which they have been symbolically defined in opposition to the female, so that women can participate in them only by tacitly adopting a male self-identification – which condemns them to being second-best approximations to men (TD, 79/93). She also objects that women's participation in traditionally male activities will not only dislocate them symbolically but also bring them distress and 'alienation' at the level of their physical being (JTN, 84–5/106). Without a culture, embodied in a set of institutions and activities, which reflects their own pattern of physical growth and unfolding, women will be unable to achieve a level of self-realisation equivalent to that open to men.

Nevertheless, that Irigaray believes a culture of sexual difference to be necessary for women to achieve a level of self-realisation equivalent to that of men implies that she is less unequivocally opposed to equality than her denunciation of it suggests. Her criticism of equality feminism for denying women comparable self-realisation only makes sense if she retains some commitment to equality, albeit interpreted in a different sense than in conventional egalitarian feminism.[17] After all, in making this criticism, Irigaray is objecting that the attainment of the goals of equality feminism would *prevent* women from attaining equality in the ability to realise themselves, culturally, as sexually specific beings.[18] Rather than rejecting equality altogether, she is offering a new interpretation of the respect in which equality is desirable: 'it is ... *in terms of difference* that we should be seeking equivalence and equality of rights' (DBT, 90; italics added).[19] She calls this novel form of equality 'equivalence', to distinguish it from the traditional construal of equality as access to pre-existing activities. Genuine sexual equality will be attained only when women and men develop their sexual difference, articulating it within a culture which provides them with appropriately differentiated traditions and practises. Irigaray sums up: 'it is important to elaborate a still nonexistent culture

---

[17] In emphasising Irigaray's commitment to equality, I do not mean to diminish her challenge to conventional varieties of egalitarian feminism. Rather, my point is that she challenges conventional egalitarian feminism by *reinterpreting* the ideal of equality.

[18] Penelope Deutscher argues similarly for Irigaray's ongoing commitment to equality in 'French Feminist Philosophers on Law and Public Policy: Michèle le Doeuff and Luce Irigaray', in *Australian Journal of French Studies* 34: 1 (1997), pp. 38–9.

[19] Irigaray exemplifies a tendency noted by Amartya Sen: 'theories that are widely taken to be "against equality" (and are often described as such by the authors themselves) turn out to be egalitarian in terms of some other focus' (*Inequality Reexamined* (Oxford: Clarendon Press, 1992), p. 3).

of the sexual which respects the two *genres*' (JTN, 80/99), so 'the strategy of equality... should always aim for the recognition of differences'
(84/105).

Were the right to life to be recognised, then, it would be universal,
because it would serve to secure an equivalent level of self-realisation for
individuals of both sexes. How does this proposal for a right to life relate
to Irigaray's proposal for sexuate rights? We should first examine what
her proposal for sexuate rights amounts to. She concretises this proposal
by itemising some of the specific rights she desires for women, which she
sorts into four basic groups. Women should have: (1) the right to economic equality and equal representation on all civil and religious bodies;
(2) the right to defend their own cultures and traditions if threatened
by male practises; (3) the right to what Irigaray calls 'human dignity',
principally comprising the right to positive representations of women in
public places; (4) the right to 'inviolability', embracing both the right to
choose motherhood freely (including the right to abortion) and the right
to 'physical and moral integrity' (virginity for girls) (JTN, 86–89/106–
11). By implication, rape of women or girls should be punishable not
as a violent crime *simpliciter* but as a violation of rights to inviolability
or integrity which are specific to members of the *female* sex (see DBT,
71). If all rights are to be sexually specific, then crimes, as infringements
of rights, must also be defined in sexually specific terms. Perhaps disappointingly, Irigaray says little about this implication, or about the special
obligations which she also thinks that laws should allot to women and
men, beyond a brief mention of women's special responsibility to protect
their children, especially daughters, from abuse (JTN, 88/110).

There is a problem with Irigaray's proposals: it is not obvious that she
really intends the four basic rights which she enumerates to belong exclusively to women at all (though some of the subordinate rights should – for
example, abortion rights). That would deny men rights to social and economic participation, cultural self-defence, dignity, and physical integrity –
which surely cannot be Irigaray's intention. Despite her own statements,
it looks as if she must regard the core legal rights she adduces as rights
of which *every* member of society should be assured. Indeed, these four
rights are plausibly regarded as protecting conditions which are jointly
necessary for men and women to be able to realise themselves through
appropriately sexually specific cultures. This is especially clear in the case
of the right to defend the cultural traditions with which one is affiliated.
Irigaray may well be suggesting, then, that certain key rights to economic
participation, cultural self-defence, dignity, and physical integrity must

be granted as a consequence of granting the more basic right to 'life', since these further rights secure a set of conditions which is necessary if women and men are to exercise their right to life effectively. If so, then her claim that these four core rights should apply exclusively to women contradicts her argument for the centrality of the right to life. A coherent reading of Irigaray should therefore eschew the familiar interpretation of 'sexuate rights' as a proposal that there be no neutral or universal rights, and reinterpret this notion as suggesting that all rights should be 'sexuate' in that they should serve, directly or indirectly, to secure women and men the ability to express their sexed natures culturally.

I have considered Irigaray's notions of sexuate rights and of the right to life so as to clarify how the legal recognition of sexual difference is necessary for a culture of sexual difference and so, in turn, for the intra-familial re-education of male desires. This legal recognition is not necessary in the way which Irigaray's writings often imply, namely, to define a *sui generis* female identity by allocating to its bearers a distinctive set of rights. Rather, by recognising that all individuals have a right to cultural self-realisation as sexually specific beings, law could provide the background against which women could begin to develop the sexually specific sets of traditions, images, and activities which they need (as Irigaray herself says: 'Law is protection for life and the means to cultivate interiority' (ILTY, 53/95)). By developing these representations, women would be able to articulate a *sui generis* female identity (and would also contribute to its articulation by the very fact of their cultural activity). This *sui generis* identity would be one that all women could see themselves as embodying, and could strive to personify more fully. Irigaray refers to this identity as a female *genre* or kind, a type in its own right, not merely a defective version of the male *genre* or of a humanity implicitly understood on the model of the male. Here it is worth noting that – as Deutscher has shown – Irigaray thinks that the content of the female *genre* would necessarily be shifting, as different women produce different articulations of female identity, adapting pre-existing articulations with reference to their own individual experience. As such, when identifying oneself as embodying the female *genre*, one would be situating oneself in a field of differences among those of this *genre*, rather than having to see oneself as identical to all other women.[20]

---

[20] See Deutscher, *Politics of Impossible Difference*, pp. 85–9. She summarises: Irigaray's concept of *genre* offers a 'transformed model of identity as an open-ended, deferring spectrum of difference' (p. 87).

Irigaray suggests in *I Love to You* that it is in the couple, as the nucleus of the family, that women must primarily try to embody (in their particular, different ways) this female identity as made available to them culturally.

> This couple [which] forms the elementary social community . . . is where sensible desire must become potentially universal culture. It is where the *genre* of the man and of the woman may become the model of male human kind or of female human kind while remaining linked to the singular task of being *this* man or *this* woman. (ILTY, 28/55)

Women's embodiment of their *genre* within family life would galvanise men to respect them, as bearers of an independently valuable female identity. Thus, Irigaray continues, women's embodiment of their own *genre* enables 'the couple formed by the man and the woman' to 'realis[e] the passage from nature to culture, from the singular to the universal, from sexual attraction to the actualisation of gender, [which] ensures the salvation of the community and of nature, both together'. Because men would then develop respect for women, they would be motivated: (1) to quell their destructive desires (to move from nature to culture); (2) to relate to women *as women* and not, unconsciously, as mothers (so passing out of a state of unconscious, visceral, 'attraction'); (3) to accept sexual difference and therefore see themselves as bearers of a male identity which is 'universal' in the sense that it is shared and embodied – in countless particular ways – by all men. Hence, men would begin to develop a new kind of 'world in the male', centring around a specifically male *genre*. Women, meanwhile, would be progressing from nature to culture in at last being allowed and encouraged to express themselves culturally, and to do so as people who embody, in different ways, a universal female *genre*. This would 'save the community' – by ensuring justice – and would simultaneously 'save nature', since men would have ceased to act from their ecologically malign urges.

Irigaray thinks that women's embodiment of their *genre* in the family must constitute the first step towards these wider changes because the family, precisely, is where men's desires are currently left to develop spontaneously and, once formed, to wreak broader destructive effects. Since political change – in the guise of change to legal frameworks – is necessary to introduce this female *genre* into social (including familial) life, Irigaray can characterise the change to the family which she seeks as a process of political 'cultivation' of the family. This process is, equally, describable as one whereby the state – through the public, codified law – transforms the desires of male family members (a transformation which Irigaray envisages affecting adult males first and foremost, then, derivatively, any male children).

One might wonder whether men, in learning to quell their negative, destructive desires – to 'overcome [*surmontent*] their immediate instincts and desires [*pulsions*]' (ILTY, 51/89), are learning to separate themselves from or suppress their natures in the way Irigaray professes to oppose. But we should recall that she thinks that male nature inherently tends to turn against itself. As such, in turning against their own self-opposing nature – learning to constrain, 'limit', and 'measure' it (BEW, 115/152) – men are actually *expressing* their self-opposing nature at the same time. If this seems paradoxical, let us consider Freud's comparable conception of the cultural function of conscience and the superego. In *Civilization and its Discontents* (as in other later writings), he postulates a 'death instinct' in all individuals, which manifests itself in aggressiveness, and is therefore equally a 'natural aggressive instinct'.[21] This aggressiveness can be directed either outward onto others or inward onto the self. Insofar as aggressiveness spontaneously turns outwards, it leads us to resist the constraints of civilised co-existence with others. Consequently, civilisation (*Kultur*) requires that this aggression be turned back inwards. Individuals must learn to attach part of their death instinct to their conscience and superego, so that this instinct finds some satisfaction just when individuals punish themselves – and make themselves suffer – for their destructive, anti-social, urges. As Paul Ricoeur explains Freud's position: 'Culture . . . uses my own self-violence to bring to naught my violence against others . . . [it] employ[s] internalized violence against externalized violence'.[22] Individuals must learn to restrain themselves from being destructive, but in exercising this restraint they gratify their destructive instinct after all; more precisely, this instinct gains partial gratification, gratifying part of itself by repressing another part of itself. Likewise, for Irigaray, men's tendency to destructiveness – and to *self*-destructiveness and self-opposition – gains partial satisfaction just by checking itself from spontaneous expression. So, in encouraging men to restrain themselves,

---

[21] Freud, 'Civilization and its Discontents', in *Civilization, Society and Religion*, trans. James Strachey (Harmondsworth: Penguin, 1985), p. 313.

[22] Paul Ricoeur, *Freud and Philosophy: An Essay on Interpretation*, trans. Denis Savage (London: Yale University Press, 1970), pp. 306–9. As Ricoeur notes, in 'Civilization and its Discontents' (1930) Freud no longer considers self-inflicted violence to be pathological as he had in *The Ego and the Id* (1923); now, instead, he sees it as a necessary part of civilisation.

sexuate culture would be urging men not to suppress their violent nature but to give it limited expression as 'self-violence'. A sexuate culture would redirect men's nature so that it manifests itself only to the extent that it ceaselessly checks itself, but not in other, more harmful, ways.

As I mentioned earlier, Irigaray intends her conception of the re-education of male desires as a consistent application of Hegel's model of the cultivation of desires. Hegel believes that institutions educate our narrowly self-interested desires by drawing out the element of 'universality' latent within them and reorganising the self-interested aspects of these desires around their universal element. Irigaray indicates that this understanding of education reflects Hegel's conception of 'dialectic' as a process whereby two opposed concepts or items (in this case, the universal and individual aspects of desires) become reconciled. 'Hegel's method is based on contradiction, on contradictory propositions' (SG, 139/153). Irigaray redefines dialectic as a process whereby one of two different persons, groups, or elements learns to *limit* itself. 'Sexual difference is . . . the motor of a dialectic', she writes, in which 'the negative as limit is present from the very fact of respect for natural reality as constitutive of the subject' (ILTY, 51/89–90). Irigaray's reformulation alludes to Hegel's own stricter use of 'dialectic' to designate the process whereby a concept or item comes to be negated by something outside it (a process which, for him, precedes the subsequent, 'speculative', phase of reconciliation).[23] Irigaray suggests, then, that the education of desires should not be understood on the model of a reconciliation of opposites – of individuality and universality, and therefore of men's and women's initially self-interested desires and their common good – for this model suggests that the family is a 'natural ethical' community, needing no deliberate cultivation at all, and which can rightly be left in undifferentiated natural unity. Rather, she contends, education should be understood on the model of learning to limit one's desires, as men must learn to do within the family – 'man [must] educate his instincts and drives' (ILTY, 28/56). In order to consistently apply Hegel's model of education to the state/family relationship, Irigaray is actually obliged to modify this model as well.

---

[23] As a whole, Hegel postulates moments of 'understanding' (in which a first concept or element arises), 'dialectic', and the 'speculative'. The three moments together make up a process which is called 'dialectical' – in a broader sense – because it advances through the resolution of oppositions. Hegel finds dialectical processes throughout the universe. See Hegel, *Encyclopaedia Logic* (1830), trans. T. F. Geraets, W. A. Suchting, and H. S. Harris (Indianapolis: Hackett, 1991), §79–82/125–33.

V. Evaluating Irigaray's Political Proposals

Irigaray's political analyses and proposals are worthwhile in several respects, but they also have considerable problems. Positively, they inter-twine with and complete her important rethinking of nature as dividing itself via men, where this self-dividing tendency can be redirected by political means. Thus, these analyses confirm that she can coherently see patriarchy as derived from male nature while urging political change. Moreover, through her readings of Hegel, she clarifies that men's self-dividing tendency spontaneously manifests itself in the family because this tendency reflects attitudes which young boys develop to their mothers and which men display in the intimate relationships with women through which they re-enact their early relations to their mothers. The re-education of male desires must therefore happen primarily within family relationships, although, as Irigaray sees it, this requires legal change to alter the total socio-cultural context in which family relationships take shape. As she summarises her overall picture in *I Love to You*:

In the face of the universal that law represents, each person or individual... receives the right to be woman or man... The natural, then, no longer has to abolish itself in the spiritual, rather the concrete spiritual consists in the cultivation [*culture*] of the natural. An appropriate civil law is required as mediator for this cultivation. This law concerns the needs and desires of real persons considered as such: for life and its respective qualities, for instance. (ILTY, 51/ 90–1)

Irigaray's political proposals are also worthwhile in being premised on the idea that humans need to express and realise themselves, as sexually specific beings, through culture. She conceives cultural self-realisation to bring 'happiness' or 'felicity' to men and women (ILTY, 14–15/35; DBT, 165–73). This reflects her broader view that human beings, as natural beings, are engaged in processes of growth which follow different rhythms in each sex. She also believes that human beings are distinctive as a species in needing to grow and develop through specifically cultural self-expression. Therefore, for Irigaray, men and women need to express their distinctive rhythms within different sets of cultural activities and traditions. Although she recommends that men learn to practise self-restraint, she sees this self-restraint as giving partial expression to one aspect of male nature (its self-dividing tendency) while also making space for men to rediscover and express other aspects of their nature, namely, their rhythm of growth. Finally, she also hopes that her proposed political changes, by restraining men's ecologically damaging behaviour (and that of women insofar as they have become embroiled in male patterns), would 'save' the natural environment (ILTY, 28/55), restoring humans to a proper sense of their location within, and dependence upon, this environment.

Among the problems with Irigaray's political analyses is her assumption that families arise spontaneously from the naturally arising desires of men and women for one another.[24] As she says at one point, 'a family is born when two persons...decide to live together on a long-term basis, to "set up a home" ' (BEW, 105/139). Throughout her analyses of the family, her language presumes that these two 'persons' are always a – heterosexual – man and woman. Arguably, though, the fact that most families are heterosexual reflects not any pull of nature but the pressure of social and political expectations and institutions. But if the predominance of heterosexuality is not natural, then Irigaray's plan to cultivate the heterosexual family, as part of giving expression to nature, ceases to make sense. Instead, what comes to make sense is a politics, like that of Butler, which aims to dismantle the gender norms which channel individuals into inversely symmetrical and presumptively heterosexual gender identities, thereby making space for individuals to freely express various sexual urges. Irigaray might object that this would hasten the 'crisis' or 'explosion' of the family which she thinks contemporary life is inducing (106–7/141). This is question-begging, assuming that families must be based on heterosexual couples and can exist in no other forms.

One might try to defend Irigaray's account of the family against these criticisms. Perhaps, one might argue, she believes that the family has only become predominantly heterosexual because men have unresolved relations to their mothers, which they feel compelled to re-enact through relations with women. In a culture of sexual difference, where boys could resolve their relations to their mothers satisfactorily, they would also be freed from this compulsion towards heterosexuality. But this is simply not what Irigaray envisages: she believes that men should be re-educated to pursue their *heterosexual* relationships differently: 'The first and principal

---

[24] This assumption is present, too, in the Hegelian account of the family on which Irigaray leans. Butler has argued that Hegel's imagery of 'blood relations' – from which Irigaray derives her own conception of the naturally arising family – functions, defensively, to conceal the incestuous character of Antigone's family (because of her father Oedipus's incest, Antigone occupies the same relation to her father and to her brothers). Hegel's imagery creates the illusion that Antigone's family is untroubled and heterosexual; see Butler, *Antigone's Claim*, p. 13. By implication, Irigaray's conception of the family, too – through its imagery of blood bonds – is premised on uncritical acceptance of normative heterosexuality.

task in order to . . . refound a family lies in the labour of love between a man and a woman' (BEW, 119/157). Her assumption that heterosexuality is natural is grounded in her belief that sexual duality is natural, and that the difference between men and women produces between them a 'natural attraction' (ILTY, 146/227). In contrast, were she to accept that each of us naturally has a multiplicity of bodily forces as well as a sexuate nature, then ways might open for her to argue that the cultural recognition and expression of sexual difference could also enable men and women to pursue more freely desires which reflect their multiplicity. But making such arguments is just not part of Irigaray's political agenda as presently conceived.

Problems also beset Irigaray's conception of the mechanisms by which cultural change is to occur. Firstly, she regards it as a precondition of a culture of sexual difference that men restrain their tendencies to create patriarchal culture. Yet men cannot learn to do this unless they already inhabit a culture of sexual difference. Irigaray could render this circle non-vicious by suggesting that the transition to a culture of sexual difference can happen gradually: once legal change introduces the beginnings of such a culture, men will begin to change, which will hasten the development of this culture, further encouraging men to change, and so on. Yet how is legal change to happen in the first place? Irigaray's proposed legal changes rely on the existence of a legislator – Irigaray herself? – but her own draft codes, such as the 'Draft Code of Citizenship' which she and Renzo Imbeni submitted to the European Parliamentary Commission, have not been taken up.[25] This is no coincidence. To be effective, or to take effect, a law must be (tacitly) supported by at least a majority of individuals. But to support a law, individuals must already value that to which it confers a right. For Irigaray's sexuate law to come into force, then, individuals must (at least tacitly) already recognise their need to express themselves *qua* sexuate. But, if so, they will already be pursuing this self-expression and hence contributing to the formation of a sexuate culture. So, there must already be a sexuate culture before Irigaray's right to life could take effect; the institution of the right to life would reflect, but cannot create, this culture. Irigaray's political proposals would be improved,

---

[25] The European Commission for Women's Rights gave an 'opinion' on Renzo Imbeni's report on citizenship, a report which incorporated his and Irigaray's draft code, but, as Irigaray observes, the 'opinion' endorses only those of their proposals which could be reinterpreted in conventionally egalitarian terms (DBT, 81–4).

then, if she simply asserted that women need to begin developing a 'world in the female'; this would encourage men to respect sexual difference, facilitating increased efforts by women to create their own world, and so on.

A last problem is whether Irigaray's proposed culture of sexual difference would confine each of us to acting only in ways deemed compatible with our sexuate identity. Some readers have worried that her proposed laws defining the specific rights of female citizens embody a conception of female identity in line with which all women would be expected to act.[26] This worry need not arise, since sexuate rights should not be construed as sexually specific rights but as rights protecting 'life' in the sense of cultural self-realisation as a sexually specific being. The fact remains that Irigaray anticipates the development of a specific set of cultural traditions and images expressing a *sui generis* female identity, or *genre*. But, as she sees it, each woman would appropriate and contribute to these traditions and images in a different way, with the result that the content of the female identity would be open-ended and changing, not unitary. All these contributions, though, would have to differ in content from men's contributions to (male) identity, contributions which, Irigaray thinks, women should not take up as vehicles for their cultural self-expression. Irigaray does, then, seek to restrict women to participating in the tradition of representations of *female* nature. But, according to her, this is no restriction, since women have no forces or desires other than those that constitute them as female. We might well feel sceptical here, and inclined – against Irigaray – to think that a desirable culture would give us opportunities to act and express ourselves among others without regard to our sexuate identity. To this, Irigaray can reasonably object that any attempt to go beyond sexual difference without first constructing and valorising a *sui generis* female identity will inadvertently reproduce patriarchal conceptions of sexual difference, which, precisely, deny any such female identity. Whether Irigaray's projected sexuate culture would be unacceptably restrictive of women's (and men's) possibilities for action thus remains uncertain, and requires further examination.

---

[26] Cornell complains that Irigaray's sexuate law 'denies women the freedom to reimagine their sexual difference' (*At the Heart of Freedom*, p. 122). Nicola Lacey, too, objects that Irigaray's legal proposals invoke images very similar to conventional stereotypes of women, which 'would, if institutionalised . . . in law, have the effect of fixing women within identities' which Irigaray professes to challenge (*Unspeakable Subjects*, p. 215).

The problems with Irigaray's proposals for re-educating male desires and re-organising the family/state relationship mean that we should not straightforwardly endorse them. Rather, we need to resituate their valuable elements within a framework which presupposes neither natural heterosexuality nor the exclusive existence of natural duality, and which omits Irigaray's misguided emphasis on law. In the next chapter, I will attempt this resituation by drawing upon other elements from the tradition of *Naturphilosophie* on which Irigaray is silent – elements which I extract from Hegel's and Hölderlin's friend and interlocutor, F. W. J. Schelling. These elements can provide the basis for rethinking nature as a process of self-differentiation which passes through duality and multiplicity as stages.

6

From Sexual Difference to Self-Differentiating Nature

I have suggested that, given the problems with Irigaray's philosophy of sexual difference, we need to rethink it significantly, so as to argue that the historical suppression of sexual duality has simultaneously suppressed the natural multiplicity of our bodies, while a culture which expressed duality would equally express this multiplicity. To help with this rethinking of Irigaray's ideas, I proposed borrowing from *Naturphilosophie*, a tradition on which she herself draws. Having seen how she adapts Hölderlin's and Hegel's ideas of nature, we can review how, as a whole, she uses ideas from *Naturphilosophie* to support and flesh out her belief in natural duality. Through this review, we can start to bring together some alternative elements within this philosophical tradition which can support and flesh out the idea that human bodies are naturally internally multiple as well as sexed.

Irigaray takes up Hölderlin's idea that original nature (*physis*) divides itself into subjects and objective nature, but she argues that this self-division only spontaneously occurs in men. She explains that this self-division is caused by men's difficulties in separating from their mothers in infancy, given that the experienced sexual difference between (the rhythms of) boys and their mothers exacerbates the difficulties which this separation always involves. Irigaray maintains that men's self-division is manifested in their rejection of nature – both their own and that of women and the surrounding environment – and in their development of a technological, artificial culture. Her adaptation of Hölderlin thus presupposes that there is an original sexual duality in nature rather than the primordial unity of being which Hölderlin posits. However, an element of Hölderlin's view of nature which Irigaray overlooks (by focusing, critically, on his notion that nature is originally unitary) is the idea that nature ceaselessly differentiates itself. As I explained in Chapter 4, this idea can provide a basis for rethinking human bodies as naturally both sexed and internally multiple, since it suggests that nature always seeks to pass beyond the fixed dualities into which it enters and, therefore, that bodies must always tend to break down their sexed characters and to acquire a multiplicity of characteristics instead.

Irigaray's readings of Hegel, which are linked with her explorations of self-opposing nature, focus on his idea that mind distinguishes itself from nature gradually, through immersion in social institutions which re-educate individuals' desires out of their initially given form. Building on this idea, Irigaray proposes that the state should re-organise the family into a form in which it can re-educate the male propensity to self-opposition, a propensity which spontaneously emerges and manifests itself within family relationships. Specifically, Irigaray proposes the introduction of 'sexuate law' (law recognising our universal rights to self-expression and self-realisation as sexually specific individuals) to transform the overall cultural context in which family relationships take shape. Within a culture in which female identity is recognised as independently valuable, family relationships would inspire men to respect women and to redirect their self-opposing tendency so that it restrains itself. Irigaray's readings of Hegel, again, presuppose that humanity is naturally sexually dual, such that boys have particular difficulties separating from their mothers and such that men and women experience a 'natural attraction' which draws them into the families within which men's spontaneous tendencies can either be reinforced or redirected.

Irigaray's assumption that there is this natural duality limits the persuasiveness of her political analyses, especially by committing her to a vision of a transformed family life which remains premised on the heterosexual couple. If we re-examine Hegel's conception of education against the backdrop of Hölderlin's idea of self-differentiating nature, though, an alternative begins to show. For Irigaray, the re-education of male drives would lead to the full expression and realisation of *both* men's and women's natures. But if sexual duality is only one manifestation of self-differentiating nature, then, once nature is fully realised in dual form, it will press more strongly beyond duality. In particular, human bodies will acquire a stronger tendency to develop multiple, non-sexed characteristics. The re-education of male drives within the family, which Irigaray envisages, would therefore create the conditions in which individuals' tendency to multiplicity would be strengthened, as would, too, their tendency to develop sexual desires of a kind which reflect this multiplicity. I will clarify later what the general form of these desires might be, but let me indicate that, since these desires arise from the breakup of the sexed character which (according to Irigaray) makes us heterosexual, these desires would not be exclusively or presumptively heterosexual. Reconceived, then, as expressing a nature that is self-differentiating rather than simply dual, a sexuate culture need not reinforce the heterosexual family as Irigaray presumes but could strengthen men's and women's motivation to find different, 'non-traditional', forms of family life which can accommodate their desires as *non*-sexed, internally multiple, beings.[1]

Elements can be extracted from the thought of Hölderlin and Hegel which lead away from Irigaray's exclusive insistence on natural duality, and which provide a glimpse of how we could think of bodily duality and multiplicity as co-existing in nature. In general, as I argued in Chapter 3, it is necessary to affirm both duality and multiplicity because the structure of our embodied experience gives evidence of both. Yet, although this gives us grounds, in general, to support an ontology which reconceives duality and multiplicity such that they can co-exist, it does not follow that we must endorse the particular conciliatory ontology which arises from Hölderlin's idea of self-differentiating nature. This ontology remains unacceptably speculative: Hölderlin has given us no overwhelming reasons to think that nature really does consist in a process of self-differentiation which manifests itself in, then pushes beyond, sexual duality. We need, moreover, to deepen our understanding of what this view of nature actually amounts to. To provide this deepened understanding, and to identify reasons for endorsing this view of nature, we should turn to the work of Hölderlin's and Hegel's contemporary, Schelling.

Schelling initiated the project of a specifically philosophical form of inquiry into nature in the 1790s, and elaborated his successive accounts of nature in a theoretically sustained way (unlike Hölderlin), while attending to the status of sexual difference and the possibility of a non-hierarchical conception of sexual difference (unlike Hegel). Most relevant are Schelling's 1799 *First Outline of a System of Philosophy of Nature* (hereafter the *First Outline*) and the separate introduction to this work,

---

[1] I put 'non-traditional' in scare quotes because, as Linda Nicholson has argued, the supposedly 'traditional' family – comprising two heterosexual parents with children – is in fact a relatively recent phenomenon which has never obtained universally, and which has no greater claim to legitimacy than supposedly 'alternative' kinds of family ('The Myth of the Traditional Family', in *Feminism and Families*, ed. Hilde Lindemann Nelson (London: Routledge, 1997), pp. 27–42).

published a few months later. These texts are Schelling's richest and most important contributions to the philosophical study of nature. By reconstructing, in sufficient detail, the account of nature which these texts offer – according to which nature consists in self-inhibiting productivity – we can fill out the content and implications of a view of nature as self-differentiating, and also, following Schelling, argue that this view, although speculative, has philosophical justification and cannot be dismissed as arbitrary or fantastic.

In the first two sections of this chapter, I shall expound Schelling's account of productive, self-inhibiting, nature. Section I explains the motivations for this account in the philosophical debates of Schelling's time, indicating how these motivations remain relevant today, giving us grounds to endorse his account, at least in broad outline. I then explain his basic account of the tension between productivity and inhibition within nature, a tension, according to Schelling, which gives rise to the myriad 'products' – particular, finite, natural objects – which we encounter around us and which always exhibit a polar structure. I then examine the hierarchical conception of sexual difference which Schelling advances based on his account of natural polarity. Section II argues that this hierarchical conception is contradicted by Schelling's own understanding of the relationship between productivity and inhibition, which, ultimately, implies that these are not separate forces but that nature originally differentiates itself into both. In turn, this implies that nature must strive beyond all the particular objects in which it manifests itself, in order to reassert itself as the activity of self-differentiation – a view which converges with Hölderlin's idea of nature. Based on this view of nature, I will explain how we can rethink Irigaray's account of nature and bodies, examining, in Sections III and IV, how this rethinking allows us to rework her proposals for cultural and political change as well.

Before beginning my exposition of Schelling, let me clarify the status of my claims about the relation between Irigaray and *Naturphilosophie*. As we have seen, there are elements in Hölderlin's idea of nature on which Irigaray deliberately, although not always explicitly, draws; she also draws, more explicitly, on Hegel's idea of the education of desires. In drawing on Hegel's idea of education, Irigaray is still engaging – indirectly – with the philosophy of nature, both because she draws on Hegel's idea within the context of her thinking of self-dividing (male) nature, and because Hegel's idea presupposes his theory of nature and of the relation between mind and nature. But although Irigaray appeals to these elements of the tradition of *Naturphilosophie*, she ignores the idea of self-differentiating nature which is articulated by Hölderlin and – more fully – by Schelling. In exploring this idea, and reconsidering other aspects of *Naturphilosophie* with this idea in the background, I am intentionally going beyond Irigaray, but towards an account of nature and bodies which preserves – in suitably rethought form – the valuable portions of her later thought.

I. Schelling's Philosophy of Nature

In his *First Outline*, Schelling claims that nature is originally, infinitely, productive, and generates particular 'products', by which he means the entities and processes – trees, rocks, processes of chemical transformation, weather systems – with which we are familiar from our everyday experience of nature. Whenever Schelling refers to natural 'products', then, he simply means any definite natural entities or processes; I will follow his usage throughout. Schelling stresses that these 'products' exist only as resting points within nature's productive flow, points which he compares to eddies in a stream. But he puzzles over how nature's activity comes to fix itself, albeit temporarily, in these finite products. To explain this, he postulates an original force of inhibition (*Hemmung*) within nature. He tends to consider this inhibiting force to be separate from nature's original productivity, but, I will show, he cannot consistently sustain this separation.[2]

The best way to approach the details of Schelling's conception of nature is to reconstruct its intellectual motivations. This reconstruction must be somewhat convoluted, since Schelling's philosophy of natural productivity itself represents the third reworking of the project of philosophy of nature which he first sketched in his 1797 *Ideas for a Philosophy of Nature*. We must first trace why Schelling embarks on this project as originally conceived before we can appreciate why he successively rethinks the project to arrive, finally, at the 1799 theory of natural productivity.

One principal question generated by Kant's idealism gives rise to Schelling's project of philosophy of nature.[3] This question arises from

---

[2] David Krell notes that, as Schelling's *First Outline* unfolds, 'the distinction between free activity and necessitous inhibition becomes extremely tenuous' ('Three Ends of the Absolute: Schelling on Inhibition, Hölderlin on Separation, and Novalis on Density' in *Research in Phenomenology* 32 (2002), p. 63).

[3] The details of Schelling's project, and its relation to Kant, are complex and contested. My exposition minimises these complications, since I aim to explain Schelling's position only sufficiently to show how it supports a rethinking of Irigaray's philosophy. See, for some discussion of Schelling's initial position in *Ideas for a Philosophy of Nature*, George di

Kant's opposition between subjectivity and nature. Kant argues that ordered experience and knowledge are only possible if the subject of experience applies categories, such as causality, to the materials of sensation, an application which can occur only in virtue of the subject's spontaneity, or freedom. Yet these very categories constrain us to experience nature – including ourselves inasmuch as we are part of nature – as a realm of objects whose interactions are causally determined (in the way described in Newtonian physics). The problem, then, is that Kant's 'separation of the sphere of freedom from a wholly deterministic nature leaves no way of understanding how . . . we can gain an objective perspective on law-bound nature and at the same time can be self-legislating'.[4] How is free subjectivity possible within causally determined nature? Schelling's solution is to conceive nature as *itself* free and spontaneous – as he states: 'To philosophise about nature means to lift it out of dead mechanism . . . to animate it with freedom and to set it into its own free development' (FO, 14/79).

Admittedly, Kant himself tries to resolve his difficulty by claiming that ordered experience requires not that we actually *are* free but only that we be capable of thinking of ourselves as free. Moreover, his *Critique of Judgement* suggests that this requires us also to think of organisms, and of nature as an organised totality, as if they exhibited 'purposiveness' – a self-organising capacity which prefigures the mind's capacity to order its own experience. Nevertheless, Kant is emphatic that this is only a way of thinking about nature; we cannot know whether or not nature in itself, independently of us and of our ways of representing it, really is purposive.[5] Schelling, on the other hand, believes that we as subjects of experience must really *be* free and that this freedom is only possible if nature really is spontaneous as well, a natural spontaneity which we can therefore rightly claim to know as it is, really and independently of us. In this, Schelling goes beyond Kant's strictures on the limits of knowledge to outline a philosophy purporting to describe nature as it really,

Giovanni, 'Kant's Metaphysics of Nature and Schelling's *Ideas for a Philosophy of Nature*', in *Journal of the History of Philosophy* 17 (1979), pp. 197–215, and, on the development of Schelling's philosophy of nature over time, Richards, *The Romantic Conception of Life*, pp. 128–45.

4 Andrew Bowie, *Introduction to German Philosophy* (Cambridge, U.K.: Polity Press, 2003), p. 35.

5 See Kant, *Critique of Judgement* (1790), trans. Werner S. Pluhar (Indianapolis: Hackett, 1987), §65–§67, pp. 255–9. Kant expresses his idea that we can only think of nature as if it were purposive by calling judgements of purposiveness 'regulative', not 'constitutive' (§67, p. 259).

independently, is.[6] Schelling's move is not illegitimate: as Frederick Beiser argues,

> only on the assumption that *there is* an organism [a purposiveness in nature] is it possible to explain the *actual interaction* between the subject and object.... To leave the concept [of purposiveness] with a purely regulative ['as if'] status simply left the mystery of their actual interaction.[7]

Schelling's justification of his belief in spontaneous nature with reference to this question from Kant's philosophy gives us independent reasons to endorse that belief, since this question recurs, in more general form, outside the immediate context of Kant's thought. Taking it that we, as human beings, do relate actively to the world in knowing it (by actively making the world intelligible in varied ways, the variety of which reflects our spontaneity), this capacity for spontaneous relating becomes inexplicable if nature is devoid of spontaneity. Since we are natural beings, the nature which we embody must *itself* be spontaneous for our spontaneous agency to be possible. This broad line of argument for spontaneous agency in nature reappears in Irigaray. In *To Be Two*, she claims that perception always involves the active contribution of the perceiving individual, so that perception has 'a history, a becoming, an interiority' (TBT, 40). Perception reflects the individual's 'freedom' (41). That in the individual which freely shapes their perceptions is their rhythm, she says here; rhythms, for her, are free because they unfold spontaneously. But this spontaneous unfolding of human rhythms is only possible, she maintains, against the backdrop of 'the cosmic rhythms in which ... sensibility participates' (42). The 'pulsating movement' of human rhythms, she writes, is: 'Already determined by cosmic rhythms – night or day, light or dark, cold or hot' (WL, 166). Like Schelling, Irigaray roots human spontaneity in that of nature, which she locates in its rhythms. Generally, then, Schelling's argument that human spontaneity could not exist amidst inert nature shows that we should endorse his general idea of nature as spontaneous.

However, Schelling also needs to explain how we can obtain knowledge about the detailed character of nature's spontaneity and the entire

---

[6] '[T]he purposiveness of natural products dwells *in themselves*,... it is *objective* and *real*' (IPN, 32/96). On this realism of Schelling's philosophy of nature, see Andrew Bowie, *Schelling and Modern European Philosophy: An Introduction* (London: Routledge, 1993), p. 31, and di Giovanni, 'Kant's Metaphysics of Nature and Schelling's *Ideas*', p. 215.

[7] Frederick Beiser, *The Romantic Imperative* (Cambridge, Mass.: Harvard University Press, 2004), p. 167.

form of organisation which nature spontaneously tends to assume. Or, as he puts it, 'the existence of such a nature *outside me* is still far from explaining the existence of such a nature *in me*' (IPN, 41/107): given that our representations have an organised structure of their own, how can we know when they accurately describe the real structure of nature? Kant had denied that knowledge of nature in itself could be had, holding that we can know nature only as mediated by our forms of representation, our 'epistemic conditions', among which are the categories.[8] Schelling argues, though, that if we can show that nature necessarily unfolds into a series of structures which is (qualitatively) identical to the series of categories which we use to order our experience, then we can legitimately claim to know about nature in itself. Since we can legitimately claim knowledge of our own representations, we can equally legitimately claim knowledge of the real organisation of nature insofar as it is identical to that of our representations. Schelling concludes: 'As long as I am myself identical with nature, then I can understand what living nature is as easily as I can understand my own life itself' (36/100). This conclusion might sound strange – and anthropocentric – but, again, Schelling has good general reasons to believe that nature's structure really must resemble that of thought. Since the character of nature's spontaneity must be such that it prefigures (and so explains) active human thought, any patterns into which human thought necessarily enters can be expected to recur in nature.

This position gives rise to Schelling's initial version of *Naturphilosophie* as presented in the *Ideas for a Philosophy of Nature*. He begins by surveying the sciences of his time, extrapolating from this survey that all natural phenomena are best understood as polarised between two forces of attraction and repulsion. On this basis, he criticises Newtonian atomism, arguing that matter itself can only be understood as composed of attractive and repulsive forces. He contends:

Dynamic chemistry . . . admits no *original* matter whatever – no matter, that is, from which everything else would have arisen by composition [as in Newtonian atomism]. On the contrary, since it considers all matter originally as a product of opposed forces [*entgegengesetzter Kräfte*], the greatest possible diversity of matter is still nothing else but a diversity in the relationship of these forces. (IPN, 221/252)

These forces, according to Schelling, have the same structure as subjectivity, which alternately becomes attracted to knowing about items in the

---

[8] Henry Allison, *Kant's Transcendental Idealism* (New Haven: Yale University Press, 1983), pp. 10–13.

world outside it, and then repels these items by returning into self-knowledge (176/214–15). Hence, the general results of contemporary science show that nature is structured like the subject and is therefore knowable as it really is. As Schelling famously writes: 'Philosophy is . . . nothing other than a *natural history of our mind* . . . The system of nature is at the same time the system of our mind' (30/93). Importantly, he has not started by simply asserting the existence of polar forces and then attempting to deduce from these the particular phenomena which exist within nature. Rather, he takes empirical findings as his point of departure but argues that we can only properly understand the phenomena identified by science if we see them as organised by dual forces, where this duality prefigures the dynamic structure of subjectivity. Rather than indulging in unbridled speculation, Schelling is at this point trying to provide a basic framework for understanding nature which is not only philosophically plausible in the context of German Idealism but is also consistent with, and makes sense of, current empirical findings.

Schelling advances swiftly to his second version of *Naturphilosophie* in *On the World-Soul* (1798). Here, he argues that the basic forces composing nature can only exist if nature is organic and purposive as a whole (and, in that sense, has a 'soul'). Because, throughout nature, these basic forces stand in organised relations and levels of equilibrium, there must be some organising principle which regulates them.[9] Disagreeing with Kant, then, Schelling insists that nature, as a whole, really is purposive.[10] This organicist approach rapidly mutates into the position of the *First Outline*. At this point, Schelling abandons his idea that the forces of nature must be understood upon the model of subjectivity. He reconceives philosophy of nature as a discipline quite independent of the philosophy of subjectivity. He now considers his philosophical claims about nature to be sufficiently justified by their joint role in (1) describing how natural spontaneity must necessarily unfold and (2) making it possible to engage with, and reformulate, the findings of the empirical sciences.

The central claim of the 'speculative physics' which Schelling sketches in 1799 is that nature is originally productive. It originally consists in

---

[9] As Richards puts it, the attractive and repulsive forces can only 'structure a complete system of formative powers [if they are] . . . reciprocally interactive, now in balance, now productive of new chemical or physical developments' (*The Romantic Conception of Life*, p. 139).

[10] See Dieter Sturma, 'The Nature of Subjectivity: The Critical and Systematic Function of Schelling's Philosophy of Nature', in *The Reception of Kant's Critical Philosophy: Fichte, Schelling, and Hegel*, ed. Sally Sedgwick (Cambridge: Cambridge University Press, 2002), p. 222.

sheer, unlimited, productive activity (*unendliche productive Tätigkeit*). This productivity 'limits' (or 'fixates', *fixirt*) itself to constitute the various particular products and processes. These products, Schelling insists, must be recognised as not permanently fixed entities but only transitory resting points within nature's unending productivity (FO, 32/98). According to Schelling, the typical mistake of the empirical sciences is that they take for granted these transient products' superficial appearance of permanence and overlook the productivity underlying this appearance, which makes these products possible but also renders them merely transient (18/83). Empirical science, he writes, ignores 'the inner driving activity [*Triebwerk*],... that in nature which is *non-objective*' (I, 196/32). The aim of philosophy of nature is, then, twofold: firstly, to theorise nature's free productivity and trace how it must express itself; secondly, to re-examine nature's finite products, not merely empirically but also in their relation to the original productivity which Schelling calls 'being' (FO, 13–14/78).[11] So, although Schelling is concerned that his account of nature should not contradict empirical scientific claims, he nevertheless reformulates those claims so that they describe natural phenomena as manifestations of productivity. Schelling seems to assume that scientists accurately identify and explain many features of the natural world but give a misleading overall characterisation of these features because they start with inadequate metaphysical assumptions (specifically, they fail to recognise nature's productivity). Since Schelling has a philosophical starting point and can therefore recognise natural productivity, he assumes that he can correct scientists' metaphysical assumptions and reformulate their accounts of phenomena in a correspondingly improved way.

The key question which Schelling's *First Outline* confronts is *how* nature's productivity becomes confined in particular products. Puzzlingly, Schelling argues that nature's productivity would pass through an endless array of products infinitely quickly unless it encountered some 'retarding' force (FO, 187/266; see also 77/143). As Andrew Bowie explains Schelling's point: 'As simple productivity [nature] would never become determinate, it would dissipate itself at infinite speed. There

---

[11] Schelling prefigures Heidegger by identifying original productivity with a self-constructing being or 'principle of being' within all entities, a being which itself 'is' not (FO, 13–14/77–8). Because 'the individual entity, as a conditioned thing, can only be thought as a determinate limitation of the productive activity ... *being itself* must be *thought* as the same productive activity *in its unlimitedness*' (I, 202/40).

must, then, be a *conflict* of forces within nature, in which the "inhibiting" of the productivity by itself leads to products'.[12] The distinction between productivity and products must itself be explained by a prior *Dualität* or *Duplicität* of underlying forces within nature – a duality between productivity and a force opposed to it. To use Schelling's own analogy, a river only forms eddies when its flow encounters resistance (I, 206/45–6). He therefore argues that nature's productivity must be opposed by a counter-force of inhibition (*Hemmung*), so that particular products can arise through the resulting conflict between productive and inhibiting forces. Each product or process reflects a particular level of equilibrium between these opposed forces (FO, 29/93). 'Each formation is itself only the . . . appearance of a determinate proportion which nature achieves between opposed, mutually limiting actions' (35/101). Schelling thus thinks that every product or process is polar, in the sense that it has two poles, one reflecting a determinate level of productivity, the other reflecting an inversely proportional level of inhibition. Actually, to say even this is to simplify, since, for Schelling, no pole ever embodies just one force: '*the condition of* all *formation is duality*' (I, 213/54; emphasis added). Within any polarity, each pole expresses *both* forces, but the first pole expresses more productivity than inhibition, the second more inhibition than productivity. These balances of forces are inversely symmetrical, which is precisely what brings the two poles into a stable relation of polarity.

This account of nature may seem almost unintelligibly abstract, but Schelling proceeds to re-examine scientific accounts of physiology, magnetism, electricity, and chemistry, to see how phenomena in each of these domains manifest the polarity of forces. In his view, this array of manifestations of polarity arises because, in each case, natural productivity bursts beyond the polar product in which it has momentarily become confined (FO, 140/209). *Qua* infinitely productive, it must ultimately transcend this limitation; it can never be exhausted at any given stage, even when it temporarily appears to have assumed a stable form (46–7/111).[13] Having passed beyond its limitation, productivity must become re-inhibited, and so a whole series (*Reihe*) of products results.

---

[12] Bowie, *Schelling*, p. 36; emphasis added.

[13] As Jason Wirth says, Schelling argues 'that any fixed position is, as such, inhibited and thereby lifeless and false' (*The Conspiracy of Life: Meditations on Schelling and His Time* (Albany: SUNY Press, 2003), p. 199). Schelling celebrates the renewed 'collapse of form and the bursting forth of heretofore contracted energies' (p. 213).

According to Schelling, at the apex of this series stands sexual difference (*Geschlechtsverschiedenheit*).[14] He sees sexual difference as the supreme manifestation of natural polarity, and he stresses that it is not confined to humanity but pervades the entire organic realm: 'Throughout the whole of [organic] nature absolute sexlessness is nowhere demonstrable' (36/102). Even within the seemingly fixed, polar, structure of sexual difference, natural productivity drives the sexes to seek to overcome their polar opposition through reproductive activity (40–2/106–7). However, Schelling maintains, this activity is never fully successful – it necessarily becomes re-inhibited and so issues in a new product, the couple's offspring. This offspring is itself sexed, occupying one pole of the sexual opposition: it cannot embody the resolution of the opposition, for that would end all the striving and activity in nature (I, 230–1/64).

Schelling's philosophy of natural productivity grants sexual difference central importance within nature, as the culminating manifestation of the polarity which nature's forces assume throughout. Since Irigaray, similarly, sees (human) sexual difference as the fullest realisation of nature's bipolarity, it might seem that Schelling's philosophy of nature supports her conception of natural duality and not the idea of self-differentiating nature, as I have claimed. On closer inspection, though, Schelling's and Irigaray's conceptions of natural sexual difference are antithetical. Schelling explicitly conceives sexual difference as an opposition (*Gegensatz*), within which each pole reflects a particular balance of productivity and inhibition. Productivity predominates in one pole, inhibition in the other; in this respect, the two 'poles' or sexes are opposed in character. In the *First Outline*, Schelling does not explicitly define the contrast between productivity and inhibition in sexual terms. However, the resonance of this contrast with the history of philosophy ensures that these terms inescapably carry tacit male and female connotations. By implication, productivity – which Schelling also calls nature's 'subjectivity' (I, 202/41) – predominates in the male sex, while inhibition predominates in the female sex. This preponderance of activity on the male side suggests that it is the male who actively initiates sex and reproduction, and through whom natural productivity strains beyond the sexual polarity in which it has become fixed. Schelling's belief in an opposition between

---

[14] Schelling espouses a pre-Darwinian version of evolutionary theory, maintaining that nature undergoes *Evolution* through its series of products (FO, 15–16/80; I, 204/43). He intends to explain the fact that evolution occurs gradually, over long periods of time, by the fact that natural productivity must be retarded (*retardirt*) so that it produces at finite speed.

productivity and inhibition thus leads, eventually, to a hierarchical account of sexual difference which Irigaray would strongly, and rightly, contest. But if Schelling's philosophy of nature is wedded to this hierarchical account, then how can it be enlisted to help in rethinking Irigaray's philosophy?

Here it is helpful to recall the potentially positive aspects of Schelling's philosophy of nature so far. His general motivation for this project, as we have seen, is to overcome the conceptual opposition between free humanity and unfree nature, by developing an account of nature as spontaneous and as developing through a series of forms which express its spontaneity. Although he begins by supposing that this series must be understood as paralleling the organisation of the human understanding, his *First Outline* begins by simply affirming nature's spontaneity itself, which can then be characterised as productivity insofar as it necessarily expresses itself in finite entities or 'products'. From here, Schelling reasons to the necessity of inhibition and hence of (levels of) polarity, of which sexual difference can be identified as the fullest manifestation. Schelling's account is partly speculative (I, 195/32), created through reasoning about the necessary implications of nature's spontaneity. This reasoning, as he says, is *a priori*, independent of experience (197/34). But he also endeavours to demonstrate that his account enables a fruitful reformulation of the findings of the empirical sciences (197–8/36–7). Insofar as his account follows from the premise of natural spontaneity – a premise which is, arguably, necessary to explain human freedom – and enables a philosophical reformulation of empirical knowledge, we have grounds to endorse this account, even though it is partially speculative. Schelling thus provides grounds to pursue, rather than dismiss, the project of speculative theorising about nature, a project which promises to assist the feminist goal of reconceiving human duality and multiplicity as co-existing. However, the actual account of sexual difference which Schelling produces seems less than helpful. How can his promise of assistance be fulfilled?

II.   Productivity, Inhibition, and Sexual Differentiation

Schelling's philosophy of nature becomes helpful for rethinking Irigaray only when it is reread in light of some of its implications, which point beyond his tacit symbolisation of productivity and inhibition as male and female. In particular, as I will argue in this section, Schelling's belief that inhibition necessarily exists throughout nature implies that the inhibiting force cannot ultimately be held to be separate from the productive force. This implication, which Schelling wrestles with, resists, but sporadically pursues throughout the *First Outline*, entails a transformation of his entire conception of natural productivity and evolution – a transformation which renders his philosophy of nature much more congenial to feminism.

As we have seen, Schelling believes that natural productivity necessarily becomes inhibited such that it becomes merely one force within an endlessly ramifying polar opposition. He claims that the 'highest task' of philosophy of nature is to explain the existence of 'original heterogeneity', that is, of the inhibiting force (FO, 10/73). He asks:

> *What cause brought forth in nature the first dynamic externality* [that is, opposition of forces to one another]? *. . . Or what cause is it that has first cast the seed of motion into the universal rest of nature, duplicity into universal identity, the first spark of heterogeneity into the universal homogeneity of nature?* (158/230)

Yet although Schelling asks himself this question recurrently throughout the *First Outline*, he comes to no definite conclusion – its solution remains, as he admits, an 'irresolvable difficulty' (17/82).[15] The problem is that although natural productivity must necessarily become inhibited, Schelling defines natural productivity as 'pure identity', 'unity' which is directly active, and from which any inhibiting force must therefore be separate. But what, then, is the origin or cause of this inhibiting force? Although productivity lies at the basis of all of nature, inhibition cannot itself be a manifestation of productivity, since productivity can only assume determinate manifestations with the prior co-operation of inhibition. How, then, can inhibition get into a nature which is assumed to be, originally, wholly active?

Intermittently, Schelling explains inhibition by arguing that, after all, it is *internal* to natural productivity. He suggests, for instance, that: '*The homogeneous* itself becomes divided [*entzweit*] in itself, [so] no homogeneous state can be *absolute*' (FO, 10/74). And, towards the end of the text, he again notes that 'to *produce* heterogeneity means: to create duplicity in identity. But duplicity, too, is only cognisable in identity. Identity must therefore itself in turn proceed from duplicity' (179/256). That is, there must be an original 'diremption *within* the homogeneous itself' (185/263). The originally homogenous activity of nature must spontaneously divide itself into a force which carries its activity in pure form

---

[15] For Schelling's repeated statements of this question, see FO, 10/73, 77/143, 172/245, 179/256.

and another force which inhibits this first force. From this perspective, Schelling redefines it as the central task of philosophy of nature to explain how nature's successive polarities derive from this primal opposition, which inherently emerges from original productivity: '*How has the one original opposition developed itself into all the individual oppositions in nature?*' (184/262). Here, he no longer treats products as manifestations of a unitary productivity which is yoked to an outside inhibiting force, but, rather, treats products as direct manifestations of a nature which has split into two. Nevertheless, Schelling fails to sustain this conclusion consistently; this is because, were he to do so, he would have to make drastic revisions to his entire model of how nature evolves.[16]

In his introduction to the *First Outline*, Schelling goes further towards recognising that inhibition is not separate from productivity. He argues that productivity cannot be affected by inhibition as something separate, since, in that case, productivity would be partly passive and receptive, rather than being sheer activity (I, 204/44). 'However', he continues, 'if the ground of inhibitedness lies *in nature itself*, then nature [again] ceases to be *pure identity*' – pure self-identical activity – since it contains passivity as well. The only way to preserve the idea of nature's original spontaneity and productivity is to reconceive this productivity as being of a kind which works by dividing itself. 'Nature must originally be an object to itself; this transformation of the *pure subject* into an *object-to-itself* is unthinkable without an original diremption [*ursprüngliche Entzweiung*] in nature itself' (205/44). The mode in which natural productivity must originally operate is that of differentiating itself – a mode of operation which is distinct from sheer, energetic, dissipation, which typifies the form of productive activity into which original productivity, in part, splits.

Schelling's belief in the necessity of natural inhibition has implied an alternative conception of nature's original productivity, not as pure activity as opposed to passive inhibition, but as a productivity which proceeds by endlessly differentiating itself into purely active productivity and inhibition. This alternative conception of original productivity entails a changed model of how nature evolves (a model which has positive repercussions for rethinking Irigaray). If natural productivity is originally self-differentiating, then it will not seek to pass beyond particular products

---

[16] My argument draws on that of David Krell in 'Three Ends of the Absolute', pp. 62–7. Krell, having traced Schelling's reluctance to acknowledge original self-differentiation, concludes, 'he learns repeatedly . . . that heterogeneity can never be merely "introduced" into homogeneity. In order for heterogeneity and duality to advene they must always already have been there' (p. 65).

so as to restore its pure *activity* – as Schelling's actual model of natural evolution states, even in the introduction, where he continues to insist that 'in every opposition there must be a striving back toward identity' (I, 219/63).[17] Rather, this productivity will seek to transcend these products so as to reassert itself as the process of *differentiating* itself.

One might wonder whether Schelling's alternative conception of productivity implies that nature need no longer evolve. Perhaps, if natural productivity is self-differentiating, then polar products directly express it and it need not strain beyond them. However, for Schelling, the self-differentiating productivity of nature remains infinite, not exhaustible in any finite product. Every finite product has a *fixed* polar structure, which represents the cessation of the *process* of self-differentiation which is proper to productivity. Productivity therefore strains to go back to existing in the form of this process, not that of the fixed polarity which has resulted from it.

In what specific manner must productivity strain beyond its polarised products? Since nature is striving to return to engaging in the process of splitting, it must strive to go beyond any form in which it has become confined specifically by splitting up that form. But, because any form in which nature has become confined must be polar, consisting in two poles, nature must strive to break up each of these poles: to divide each pole into two elements, each of which must then become split in turn. Schelling's belief that nature is originally self-differentiating therefore implies a changed model of how nature evolves; on this model, nature evolves not by endlessly trying to return to unity but by endlessly breaking up the poles of oppositions into a multiplicity of new elements. (In speaking of Schelling's 'models' of natural evolution, I do not mean that these are intended as direct biological descriptions of the evolutionary process, such as natural scientists offer. These accounts of evolution are cast at a philosophical level and provide models for *conceiving* and understanding nature. It is a separate question how these models compare with scientific claims, and what reformulations of scientific claims these models might make possible.)

The implications of this transformed model of natural evolution for how Schelling conceives of sexual difference are profound. Sexual

---

[17] For instance, Schelling claims that the submerged *activity* within all products is what seeks to restore itself to freedom (FO, 34/100) and so drives on beyond those products, entering into an infinite development (18/83). He also asserts that this submerged productivity within products evinces a tendency to 'overcome [*aufheben*] all duality' and for its 'heterogeneity to pass [back] into activity' (140/209).

difference, to recall, is for Schelling found throughout organic nature and is the exemplary expression of polarity in nature. But, given his changed model of evolution, productivity will no longer strive to supersede the sexual opposition by 'return[ing] into the identity of the genus' (I, 231/74) and motivating the male, active sex to initiate reproduction. Rather, since the existence of a fixed sexual opposition limits natural productivity *qua* self-differentiating, this productivity must strive to divide up each pole of the sexual opposition, or, more concretely, to divide up each sex. This process must take place within a sexed individual, so that each individual develops a tendency to lose his or her sexed character – a tendency for this character to split up into a pair of characteristics, each of which, again, splits up, so that a plurality of characteristics results. The picture emerging here is that nature strives beyond sexual duality, not towards unity – as Schelling actually maintains, claiming that nature 'hates' sex, yet finds it 'unavoidable' (231/74) – but towards introducing internal multiplicity into each sexed individual.

This changed conception of sexual difference might seem still to be problematic from a feminist perspective, assuming that it retains the symbolisation of males as predominantly active and females as predominantly passive. In fact, though, the changed conception complicates that symbolism in several ways. In Schelling's revised framework, inhibition is no longer a secondary addition to pure activity, but an equally basic manifestation of nature *qua* self-differentiating. By implication, even if females are predominantly passive, this does not make them inferior to males but confers on them a distinctive way of being, of value in its own right. This aligns with Irigaray's claim that female passivity should be reinterpreted non-pejoratively, as a distinctive way of growing with its own worth:

> Woman's . . . so-called passivity would not then be part of an active/passive pair of opposites but would signify another economy, another relation to nature and the self that would amount to attentiveness and to *fidelity* more than *passivity*. It is therefore not a matter of pure receptivity but of a movement of growth. (ILTY, 38/71)

Irigaray suggests that what has been classified, negatively, as female 'passivity' is the pattern of growth which follows from their specific rhythm. Fusing Schelling's and Irigaray's frameworks, we might say that males, being predominantly active, have a compulsion to activity which occasionally becomes punctuated by rest (the interludes of 'release' which Irigaray attributes to men), while females tend to remain (faithfully or 'passively') within the specific stages of life which they have reached, while over time gradually moving towards the transition into a quite different stage.[18]

In any case, we should bear in mind that, on Schelling's changed conception of sexual difference, no human individual is exhaustively constituted by his or her sexed character. As we have seen, each male and female body also strives to break out of its sexed character, and to develop an internal diversity which – since it arises from the dissolution of the body's sexed character – makes that body *non*-sexuate. This is a process which happens within the life span of each sexed individual; it is not a question of a movement whereby the species so evolves as to abandon a formerly exhaustive sexuation. Moreover, since males and females tend towards this internal differentiation and not towards unification with the other sex, they will not inherently seek to reproduce together, nor, therefore, are males destined to occupy the position of reproductive activity in opposition to passive females.[19] Sexual activity can be rethought outside the context of reproduction.

At this juncture, we can helpfully recall the broader philosophical context in which Schelling's changed conception of sexual difference has emerged. As a whole, his recognition that inhibition is internal to productivity has implied that nature evolves by fixing itself in polarities and then reintroducing a movement of differentiation into each of its poles. This model of natural evolution has implied that, whenever nature produces sexual duality, nature will also strive to break up this duality and introduce internal diversity into sexed individuals. Since this conception of nature and sexual difference reconciles duality and multiplicity, it is helpful for feminism: it fleshes out how duality and multiplicity can co-exist, and it provides grounds to think that they really do co-exist in nature. To clarify this, let me first provide a reminder of why duality and multiplicity (as hitherto conceived) are incompatible, and then clarify how Schelling's implicit view of self-differentiating nature reconciles them.

---

[18] Since Irigaray does not engage with Schelling, I am not claiming that she herself views sexuate rhythms as (in Schellingian terms) inversely symmetrical balances of active and inhibiting forces. Rather, Schelling's (implied) conception of sexual difference in terms of these balances of forces independently comes close to Irigaray's view of sexuate rhythms. This proximity makes it possible to recast Irigaray's view of rhythms on a Schellingian basis.

[19] This changed version of Schelling need not have the – patently false – implication that sexual activity never takes place in nature. Rather, it could suggest that sexual activity is not inherently oriented to reproduction, and that sexual activity stems from desires which reflect the plurality of forces in each sexed individual, not only from desires which reflect the individual's sexed character.

Why are sexual duality and multiplicity incompatible? After all, one might think that individuals could both (1) have a range of characteristics (for example, a womb, breasts) which they share with only certain other individuals and which therefore form a natural group which defines all these individuals as sexed; and also (2) have other characteristics which they share with all other individuals (for example, a liver, a heart) and which, therefore, constitute that individual's multiplicity of non-sexed elements. However, the specific conceptions of rhythmic duality and multiple forces which I have been considering admit of no such straightforward reconciliation (and, moreover, these conceptions both have much to recommend them, as I have argued on phenomenological grounds). If a body has a sexually specific rhythm, then it retains no ontological room for (i) any non-sexed features – since all bodily forms and features must manifest the body's rhythm – or for (ii) multiple forces as independent centres of energy. Conversely, if a body has multiple forces, then (i) it retains no ontological room for any overarching rhythm which would regulate all these independent sites of force, and (ii) nor can any of these forces themselves contribute to defining a sexed character, since none of them naturally cluster together. Hence arises the need to rethink multiplicity and duality such that they are capable of co-existing within bodies.

Now, how does Schelling's and Hölderlin's (implicit) view of self-differentiating nature imply such a rethinking? According to this view, nature as a movement of self-differentiation, of self-division into pure activity and inhibition, necessarily concretises itself in polar products and processes (each pole of which embodies a determinate balance between pure activity and inhibition). The product which most fully manifests this polarity is the sexual difference that, Schelling asserts, obtains in all organic life. Given that many species reproduce asexually, this assertion is not tenable; instead, we could say that different kinds of organisms manifest natural polarity more or less fully in proportion to the extent of their sexual differentiation. Where it exists in organisms, sexual difference can be characterised, with Schelling, as a difference between those who are predominantly active and those who are predominantly passive, or, with Irigaray, as a difference between those with a linear and those with a cyclical rhythm of growth.

Now, as Irigaray has argued, once sexual difference has emerged, the male sex will become motivated to deny sexual difference and forbid it cultural expression. Here, though, mapping Schelling's view of nature onto that of Irigaray becomes more difficult: must we say that *all* male organisms – including non-human male organisms – develop this propensity to suppress sexual difference? Let us recall that, according to Hölderlin, humans are separated from nature because they are distinctively conscious and cultural beings. Irigaray agrees that humans are different from other animals in needing to express and realise themselves culturally. Consequently, although all male animals may have particular difficulties with birth, only human males will seek to resolve these difficulties by creating a (kind of) culture through which they separate themselves from the rest of nature (including from themselves *qua* natural).[20] This means, moreover, that the kind of culture which human males spontaneously create will be predicated on hostility to, and repression of, sexual difference.

To return to Schelling, nature necessarily strives to go beyond every polarity in which it becomes fixed. Hence, when nature generates sexual duality, it must press to split up the elements of this duality and, specifically, to split up each particular male or female body. Each sexed individual must therefore always acquire a diversity of internal characteristics which conflicts with his or her sexed character. What form, more concretely, must this diversity take? For Schelling, individuals are sexed insofar as they have a basic character where either activity prevails over passivity or vice versa. Since it is this fixed character which natural productivity strives to break up within each individual, productivity must strive to break down each of these balanced forces (activity and passivity) into a new pair of polarised forces. Productivity must then, in turn, strain to break up each of these forces, and so on indefinitely, generating a profusion of forces within each individual. Each sexed individual necessarily comes to acquire an ever-expanding number of forces, each of which, as a bodily force, must pursue expression and manifestation. These multiple forces, then, can be identified as the diverse, pre-volitional, bodily motivations which become reflected in individuals' diverse physical features. The movement of splitting which Schelling implicitly identifies in

---

[20] Irigaray's view that animals are non-cultural explains her apparently ambivalent attitude to them. In *The Way of Love*, she suggests at one point that animals are more 'advanced' than humans in their respect for differences (WL, 39); this is because animals do not separate themselves from their sexually differentiated nature through culture. But later in the same book, Irigaray tells us that humans are unique in being able to create relations of respect through dialogue, and that each animal is enclosed in its own world, so that animals cannot respect one another as humans can (167). Culture allows humans not only to suppress sexual difference (whereupon, Irigaray says, they fall below the level of animals) but also to realise this difference most fully; culture gives humans unique potential to maximally respect and develop sexual difference.

nature becomes, in each sexed individual, the source of a multiplicity of characteristics which conflicts with that individual's originally sexed character.

This multiplicity conflicts with the individual's sexed character (and so makes that individual non-sexuate) in two ways. Firstly, the multiplicity arises from the breakup of the individual's sexed character. The idea that an individual's sexed character could be dissolved may well seem perplexing. But recall that, according to Schelling, one's sexed character just consists in a pair of forces which regulate one's bodily growth and which occupy a particular balanced relationship to one another. This character can be broken down because its component forces are only forms into which natural productivity has settled. Natural productivity remains able to transform each of these forces, injecting activity into inhibition and vice versa (and then transforming again the new sets of forces which result from this injection, and so on). Secondly, multiplicity is non-sexuate because none of the forces which the individual hereby acquires are organised into the kind of stable pairing which defines a sexed character (on Schelling's view). Emerging as they do through nature's striving to break down any such stable pairings, these forces form a plurality, and one which has no fixed organisation, since it is continually shifting and multiplying due to nature's self-differentiating productivity.

I turned to Schelling to find a way of saying that sexed individuals necessarily have multiple bodily forces as well. However, it looks as if Schelling's implicit model of nature entails, more strongly, that sexed individuals necessarily *cease* to be sexed and become internally diverse instead. This conclusion would be problematic, since it would be empirically false to say that sexed bodies always spontaneously develop beyond sexuation. Part of the way to avoid this conclusion is to return to Irigaray's claim that human beings have long inhabited a culture which denies, and endeavours to suppress, sexual difference. This culture has prevented men and women from satisfactorily expressing their sexuate natures in their actions, feelings, or creations. Since nature has thereby been prevented from fully manifesting itself in sexually polar form, it has not, either, fully acquired the striving to pass on into the form of internally multiple bodies. At the same time, patriarchal culture has not *wholly* crushed sexual difference. By its very existence, this culture gives partial expression and realisation to sexual difference, since it is this difference that spontaneously leads men to erect this culture. Because nature has been partly able to realise itself in sexually polar form, it has partly developed the striving to break down each individual's sexed character into multiple characteristics. But because this striving has not emerged fully, it has not completely broken down our sexed characters. From Irigaray's perspective, sexual difference would have to gain cultural expression, and full self-realisation, before these multiple forces could fully emerge in response.

However, saying that multiplicity has been able to co-exist with sexuate character due to the repressiveness of patriarchal culture only pushes back our problem. For saying this seems to have the incredible implication that the inception of a sexuate culture would – by allowing multiple forces to emerge fully – precipitate the physical draining of sexual difference out of humanity. I suggested in Chapter 4 that we can escape this implication if we suppose that the tendency of bodies to become internally diverse is matched by a tendency of bodies to remain sexed. But why should we think that bodies have the latter tendency? Remember that, on Schelling's initial model, natural evolution would happen infinitely quickly unless something 'retarded' natural productivity. On his revised model of evolution, too, it seems that self-differentiating productivity would split up all the polarised products in which it manifests itself infinitely quickly unless it were retarded. But the only thing available to retard productivity is some resilience or resistance on the part of the natural products themselves. These products must, therefore, be supposed to have a tendency to persist in their polar form; more concretely, each sexed individual must have a tendency to retain its sexed character – even as this character also tends to break up into multiple forces. Sexuation and multiplicity, then, can co-exist in bodies as *opposed tendencies*.

Let us pause to review what we have learnt from Schelling as a whole. His premise is that nature is spontaneous – and must be so for human intellectual spontaneity to exist – but he also argues that this spontaneity must exist as productivity, and, moreover, as a specifically self-differentiating kind of productivity. So, since Schelling gives us grounds to think that nature really is spontaneous, we also have grounds to think that nature really does differentiate itself into polar forces and manifest itself in polar products, including sexual duality, before passing on to break down the sexed character of each individual. Unusual and speculative though this account of nature is, Schelling provides definite reasons to think that nature really does pass through this process of self-differentiation. His philosophy of natural productivity can therefore ground an account of human bodies which corrects Irigaray's one-sidedness by seeing sexuation as ever-accompanied by multiple forces.

We should now explore how this account of human bodies enables us to rethink Irigaray's proposals for a sexuate culture and law.

III. Irigaray's Politics Revisited: Multiplicity and Multiculturalism

The most serious problems with Irigaray's political proposals are that the culture she advocates, which accentuates our sexuate identities in every domain, seems threateningly constricting, and that she envisions the heterosexual, nuclear family remaining a key institution within this culture. By beginning from the account of human bodies as both dual and multiple which Schelling's philosophy generates, we can rethink Irigaray's proposals for a sexuate culture to relieve them of these problems. Her own recent work – especially *Between East and West* – begins to reformulate these proposals to overcome, specifically, the worry that a sexuate culture would be constricting. Her reformulation is unsatisfactory, but it deserves consideration, as it points to a way of rethinking her politics.

Many readers of Irigaray's political texts have worried that a culture organised by sexuate rights would promote normative and constraining images of women which seem dismayingly similar to existing patriarchal images.[21] I argued in the last chapter, though, that this worry need not arise, since sexuate rights must actually be understood not as sexually specific rights but as universal rights to express oneself in one's sexual specificity. Irigaray, therefore, does not envisage a law which promotes a unified set of images of femaleness, but a law which guarantees all women the conditions to develop cultural expressions of their individual female natures. These expressions would build on, and contribute to, traditions which make available multiple representations and conceptions of the female. Yet Irigaray always sees this multiplicity as reflecting the diversity of women as instances of the *same* sex or *genre*. At one point, for instance, she states that each woman should not 'fall into . . . dispersion, the multiplicity [*le multiple*] of her desires . . . [but should] gather herself within herself in order to accomplish the perfection of her *genre* for herself' (ILTY, 27/53). Women should explore their diverse forces and capacities only insofar as these make up their particular ways of instantiating the

---

[21] See, for instance, the criticisms by Nicola Lacey mentioned in Chapter 5, note 26. One place where Irigaray's proposed laws embody seemingly traditional imagery is when she suggests that girls should have a right to bodily integrity in the form of 'virginity'. As Alison Martin notes, this image 'has patriarchal ancestry and . . . association with a judgemental and commercial evaluation of the body' (*Luce Irigaray and the Question of the Divine*, p. 206).

female character. But women should not pursue the expression of any forces or capacities which might conflict with those which constitute them as women (and as members of the same *genre* as other women). At this point, Irigaray's proposed culture threatens to look restrictive. In *Between East and West*, she acknowledges this problem, emphasising more strongly than in previous work that individuals have multiple forces and capacities, all needing expression. We need to 'realiz[e] the complexity of human identity, the multiplicity of its subjective facets, its relational aspirations and difficulties' (BEW, 139/183). The question, though, is whether Irigaray now believes that the multiple forces of individuals trouble their sexed characters and make it necessary that individuals express themselves beyond, as well as through, sexuate practises and representations.

Irigaray discusses the need for culture to express our 'multiplicity' within the book's closing chapter, 'Mixing [*Mixité*]: A Principle for Refounding Community'. She begins by focusing on the family, arguing that it has changed and is no longer a geographically settled and culturally closed unit. Families are now often nomadic and composed of men and women of different races or ethnicities; the present-day family is 'crossed... by differences foreign to our customs and our knowledge', customs which fail to recognise these differences (133/176). Social and cultural institutions lag behind the family, whose members already respect diversity. Institutions need to be updated, Irigaray maintains, to recognise the value of 'multicultural cohabitation' and cultural difference (134/177). Her aim, then, is to derive from the current reality of family life principles of respect for difference following which social institutions can be reorganised. At this point, her argument takes a new turn. She maintains that 'society has need of a minimum of shared rules' (136/179), presumably to give its members a common sense of identity. These rules, she claims, must consist in legally enshrined sexuate rights. This is because such rights enable a common culture of respect for sexual difference, within which individuals can develop the capacity and motivation to respect other differences as well. She writes: 'the relation between the *genres* can serve as a relational paradigm for the refoundation of... a mixed society. Managing to respect the other of sexual difference... represents a universal path to attaining respect for other differences' (137/181). For Irigaray, the only way to bring about a social culture of respect for differences is to start by instituting a culture of sexual difference. Once this is done, she anticipates that this culture will directly engender a culture of 'generalised mixing'

(142/188), 'a culture of between-sexes, of between-races, of between-traditions' (139/183).

Appraising Irigaray's proposals in *Between East and West*, Penelope Deutscher concludes that they 'do represent an important modification in her work' since, with them, she 'effectively answers the question of why we must cultivate relations of sexual difference with the answer that they will better facilitate multiculturalism (as Irigaray understands this)'.[22] But is Irigaray really suggesting that sexual difference should become merely one among the various differences that a new, 'mixed', culture would respect? So she partly implies, suggesting – as Deutscher notes – that sexual difference must be recognised first, not because this recognition is fundamentally important, but because it is useful in leading to the recognition of differences generally. As Deutscher notes, *Between East and West* states that it is 'advantageous' to begin by recognising sexual difference (136/180). Still, Irigaray believes that recognising sexual difference serves this purpose *because* it is the most fundamental difference, cutting across all races and traditions, and rendering men and women irreducibly 'mysterious' to one another. Because this difference is most fundamental, once it is recognised, it is relatively easy to extend one's respectful attitude to cover other differences. Although Irigaray sees the recognition of those other differences as valuable in itself, for her it is possible only if sexual difference is seen as not merely one difference among others but the most basic. This damages her claim to abandon the 'integrationist' approach to cultural differences, for, on her proposals, various cultural traditions may be recognised only insofar as they respect the shared framework of a sexuate culture, but not if they depart from that common framework.

In order to define sexual difference as most fundamental, Irigaray must claim that cultural and racial differences between men or between women do not render them 'mysterious' to one another as men and women are. She therefore claims, as Deutscher observes, that racial or ethnic differences make individuals 'secret' to one another but not mysterious, where, by implication, a secret can potentially be discovered while a mystery can never be dissolved.[23] Irigaray offers no argument for this claim. She still appears, ultimately, to think that the differences between

---

[22] Deutscher, *Politics of Impossible Difference*, pp. 171, 165. However, Deutscher argues (as I do) that Irigaray eventually still considers cultural and racial differences secondary to sexual difference.

[23] Deutscher, *Politics*, p. 175.

women or between men only distinguish them as particular members of their sex, without ever making them so different from, and mysterious to, one another that they can feel greater commonality with (some of) those of the other sex.

Irigaray's persisting belief that sexual difference is most fundamental informs, too, her neglect of differences of sexuality in *Between East and West*. Because, from her perspective, sexual difference is the source of a mystery which generates natural attraction between men and women, her proposals for *mixité* continue to assume that heterosexuality is natural and that the multi-racial, rootless, families she praises centre on heterosexual couples. It is no coincidence that she imagines 'a couple formed by a white woman and a black man' as 'a site of civic education for the surpassing of instinct' (135–6/179). This assumption of heterosexuality is, indeed, central to her entire argument, since, for her, the contemporary family provides a template for social reorganisation insofar as, within it, respect for cultural or ethnic differences derives from respect for sexual difference – which the family can embody only if it is heterosexual.

Admittedly, Irigaray does occasionally say that women (and men) should not have to 'prefer one sexual choice to another' (DBT, 105) – 'sexual choice' meaning the same as the English 'sexual orientation'. Thus, in this passage from *Democracy Begins Between Two* Irigaray is conceding that, although the family is the primary site in which we must learn to respect differences, families need not be heterosexual to exemplify such respect. But she does not explain *how*, on her own terms, a lesbian or gay couple could possibly display the same level of respect for difference as a heterosexual couple, nor how lesbian or gay relationships could be understood other than as deviations from the natural norm. Evidently, Irigaray is aware of and uneasy about the heterosexism of her framework, but she lacks the philosophical resources to undo it.

It looked as if *Between East and West* might show Irigaray voicing new support for a culture which recognises multiplicity within and between individuals, without insisting that their differences always be understood as particular differences in how they instantiate their sexed character. However, because she insists that recognising sexual difference as fundamental is the appropriate way to create this 'mixed' culture, she ensures that this culture would, after all, only ever recognise multiplicity as multiplicity *within* a given sex. Irigaray herself, though, would deny that such a culture would be restrictive. In *I Love to You*, she claims that for a woman to identify with the male sex is impossible and self-deluding (ILTY, 61–2/105), implying that the reality of every woman's nature is such that it can be exhaustively expressed through female traditions. But this is simply implausible: we do have diverse forces and capacities which trouble our constitution as sexed and so, too, our ability to identify exhaustively with either male or female identity categories. The conclusion is inescapable that Irigaray's sexuate culture, as envisioned, would confine us in sexed identities which are unduly limiting.

IV. Rethinking Irigaray's Politics: Self-Critical Sexuate Culture

Irigaray's proposals for a mixed culture in *Between East and West* suggest, in places, that sexual difference should be recognised only as a way of initiating a cultural climate in which generalised recognition of differences becomes viable. Transposing this into the language of self-expression and self-realisation which she uses elsewhere, her suggestion is that a culture which gives expression to sexual difference, as a basic difference in kind, is necessary to provide the conditions in which other, varied, bodily forces can also come to expression. We have seen, though, that because these varied forces render individuals *non*-sexuate, they could not in fact attain full expression – in their inherently non-sexuate character – within a sexuate culture. Irigaray's suggestions concerning a mixed culture have therefore proved unworkable. Nonetheless, they indicate the direction to take in rethinking her politics.

Irigaray's suggestion that multiple forces could come to expression only via a sexuate culture is worth preserving. It is only if our sexuate nature becomes fully realised – through its cultural expression – that our multiple bodily forces can fully develop as well. (My argument for this, to recall, is that multiple bodily forces result from nature's striving to break down any sexuate form into which it has settled, a striving which can only fully emerge after nature has fully developed into its sexuate manifestations. Prior to this development, multiple bodily forces can only arise partially and incompletely.) Because multiple forces can fully develop only once sexual difference is fully realised, any attempt to express these forces directly – bypassing the stage of constituting a sexuate culture – cannot succeed: without a prior sexuate culture, these forces will lack the level of development and the strength to give themselves adequate expression. This is why, as I suggested in Chapter 4, these forces have historically only been able to introduce incessant shifts and moments of diversification into patriarchal culture, without transforming it (although they *have* introduced into this culture a level of diversity much greater than Irigaray acknowledges).

It appears, though, that these multiple forces, which can only develop fully within a sexuate culture, would *still* be unable to come to cultural expression in such a culture, because sexuate culture – as Irigaray defines it – recognises multiplicity only within sexuate categories. To overcome this problem, we need to reconceive the form that a sexuate culture should take. In particular, a *self-critical* sexuate culture could permit multiple bodily forces to express themselves. A sexuate culture of this type would provide representations of sexed identities which recognise their inherent insufficiency to capture our full nature as humans. These representations would embody an acknowledgement that they express only *part* of our nature – the sexuate part – and fail to accommodate our accompanying non-sexuate dimension. This acknowledgement of limitations must be constitutive of the content of these representations – not merely added on, but fundamental to how they depict sexuate identity. A sexuate culture of this type would still contain a duality of traditions and practises, making available to men and women images of their distinct identities for them to instantiate, and adapt, in particular ways. But now these images would always make explicit their own limitations. In taking up and expressing themselves through such images, men and women would be expressing not only their sexuate natures but also their *non*-sexuate forces, which would express themselves by appropriating and adapting the moment of self-criticism contained within the culturally available images. As men and women adapt these critical elements, their multiple forces could come to expression in their character as a diversity which actively opposes, and conflicts with, each individual's sexuate nature.

To illustrate what constitutively self-critical representations of female identity might be like, we can reconsider the historical development of feminist philosophy itself. Feminist philosophers began by criticising the masculinist symbolism that pervades the tradition and disciplines of philosophy, and by rethinking and revaluing 'female' or 'feminine' concepts or characteristics (these being taken to be 'female' or 'feminine' either – as for early Irigaray – because of their symbolism or because they reflected women's biological or socially conditioned experience).[24] This rethinking and revaluing work articulates a female identity in something like Irigaray's sense, where women contribute diverse, interrelated understandings of female identity which build into a tradition. But later feminists severely criticised this work for assuming that there is a common

---

[24] See, for example, the essays in Sandra Harding and Merrill B. Hintikka, eds., *Discovering Reality: Feminist Perspectives on Epistemology, Metaphysics, Methodology, and Philosophy of Science* (Dordrecht: David Reidel, 1984).

pattern of female experience (which, tacitly, was the pattern typical of white, middle-class women). That is, earlier feminist philosophers had neglected the multiplicity of women – their internal diversity and their deep differences from one another. In response, feminist philosophers and theorists re-examined the category of 'woman', producing the anti-essentialist understandings of women's diversity which have informed my own criticisms of Irigaray. On this basis, feminist thinkers went on to develop criticisms of masculinism in philosophy, and analyses of women's situations, which acknowledge the problematic status of the analytical categories they deploy and the instability of the phenomena being studied. This acknowledgement is not merely appended to otherwise unaffected analyses; rather, feminist thinkers now generally recognise that the limitations of their categories infect their analyses with definite and pervasive restrictions. This historical shift exemplifies the move from, and the difference between, the project of constituting a sexuate culture in Irigaray's sense and that of constituting a self-critical sexuate culture, which offers representations of male and female identity which inherently recognise their limitations and partiality.

A sexuate culture could, then, express multiplicity as well as duality if it constantly, and vigilantly, recognises that sexuation is only *part* of our nature. But besides her insufficiently self-critical vision of sexuate culture, the other problematic aspect of Irigaray's politics is her commitment to the heterosexual family. She thinks it vital to transform family life since, for her, it is here that male drives have been left to develop and manifest themselves spontaneously. But because she supposes that natural duality generates a natural attraction between the sexes, she assumes that this transformation of family life would leave the *heterosexuality* of the family intact. As I mentioned earlier, we can rethink this aspect of Irigaray's politics, having reconceived sexual duality as a mere stage in natural self-differentiation. The intra-familial re-education of male drives which Irigaray recommends would, she believes, make it possible not only for women to express their female nature, but also for men to express *all* the elements of their nature (not only that element of it which opposes the rest). But, in expressing their natures fully within these intimate relationships, men's and women's tendencies to develop multiple drives and capacities would be correspondingly strengthened. Now, according to Irigaray, 'desire is linked to energy, particularly sexual energy' (ILTY, 50/89), where 'energy' is synonymous with 'rhythm' for her. Thus, for Irigaray, men's and women's sexual desires manifest their rhythms: for example, as we saw earlier, she sees men's sexual desires as following a pattern of accumulating tension and returning to homeostasis, reflecting the general rhythm of men's growth. Since the multiple forces which tend to emerge in each body arise from the breakup of the balance of forces which defines its sexed rhythm, these multiple forces must lead to different patterns of sexual desire. What form do these patterns take?

Whereas sexuate rhythms, for Irigaray, lead to a natural heterosexual attraction, these multiple forces are non-sexuate, and so they must manifest themselves in desires whose direction cannot be specified in terms of sexuate identity categories. Let me try to clarify: these must be desires which are directed towards particular individuals, just in respect of their particular ways of embodying the character of non-sexuate diversity. These desires, then, are directed towards individuals without regard to whatever sexed character these individuals also have. These desires might be ones which someone who is also a woman has for someone who is also a man, but, even in this case, they are not properly classed as heterosexual, since they are desires for this person in virtue of 'his' *non*-sexuate character. Nor, if these are desires that someone who is also a woman has for someone else who is also a woman, are they properly classed as homosexual. These desires are better thought of as 'particularistic'.

Recognising natural multiplicity alongside duality challenges Irigaray's heterosexism in two ways. Firstly, it implies that, naturally, individuals have never been simply heterosexual but have always had desires of a particularistic kind as well. These particularistic desires must surreptitiously pursue fulfilment in even the most ostensibly heterosexual of relationships (in the sense that people must always be attracted to someone not only as the embodiment of a particular sex but also as someone who is irreducibly particular, in a non-sexuate way). Secondly, after the inception of a sexuate culture, the bodily forces which support these particularistic desires would be strengthened, which would propel more and more individuals to feel dissatisfied with the 'traditional' family and to seek out different familial – or non-familial – forms of life which can better accommodate the increasingly complex structure of their desires. A self-critical sexuate culture would *undermine*, not support, the heteronormative family.[25]

---

[25] This challenge to Irigaray's heterosexism might seem weak, since it retains her view that all individuals, *qua* sexed, are naturally attracted to those of the other sex. But notice that, if we say that, in some people, tendencies to multiplicity can be stronger than tendencies to sexuation, then these people's heterosexual desires will not prevail, nor will they be able to embrace heterosexuality as an identity. Still, Irigaray's view that sexuation implies heterosexuality undoubtedly limits how far her philosophy can think about sexual diversity; my point is only that these limits are less severe, and more malleable, than it might at first seem.

Let me address one last problem with my fusion of Schelling and Iri-garay. If all bodies must be both sexuate and non-sexuate, what room remains for the intersexed? Even if we say that the tendency to multiplicity is particularly strong in some bodies (namely, the intersexed), my fusion of Schelling and Irigaray might still seem to imply that the intersexed must be partly (if very weakly) sexed and so not genuinely *inter*sexed. This conclusion would be implausible and, potentially, oppressive, resonating with the traditional view that every intersexed person is really closer to one sex than the other and should be surgically 'perfected'. Actually, though, my rethinking of Irigaray does not claim that the tendency to sexuation in each individual is *more* real than each individual's tendency to internal diversity; the latter is equally real, and can be much stronger, as in the case of the intersexed. By implication, those in whom internal diversity predominates really are, by nature, intersexed – a view which departs from the traditional view which justifies coercive surgery. Admit-tedly, my rethinking of Irigaray implies that, even in the intersexed, there must be some residue of sexuation; if one still thinks that this unaccept-ably inflates how far we are all sexed, then one must reject, not rethink, Irigaray's later philosophy.

Against this, I recommend that we continue to engage in rethinking her ideas, since they can be adapted to recognise intersexed bodies much more fully than in Irigaray's original presentation. Part of this adaptation must consist in saying, based on the idea that sexuate culture should be self-critical, that one central way in which representations of male and female identity should acknowledge their limitations is by acknowledg-ing, and remaining sensitive to, the fact that they are especially inapplica-ble to the intersexed. Potentially, then, intersexed people could express themselves by drawing on these strands of criticism and self-limitation, and by adapting these to articulate an identity which consists in a mix-ing of these openly self-critical moments within sexuate identities. It is a strength of Irigaray's conception of sexuate culture that it at least admits of being rethought along these lines. In conclusion, I shall reassess the strengths of Irigaray's later philosophy as a whole, and I shall show how my rethinking of this philosophy can combine these strengths with the seemingly antithetical attractions of Butler's approach to sex and gender.

Conclusion

Reconciling Duality and Multiplicity

Drawing on Schelling, I have proposed a rethinking of Irigaray's philosophy according to which nature's process of self-differentiation becomes restricted by a culture which denies sexual difference, and would be released by a culture which recognises that difference. In conclusion, I want to bring together the strands of my argument in this book and show how my rethinking of Irigaray combines the strengths of her philosophy with those of Butler's – at least when Butler's philosophy is revised to recognise the natural multiplicity of bodies. By reviewing the respective strengths of these philosophies as a whole, and showing how the theory of self-differentiating nature can reconcile them, I aim also to provide a more integrated statement of this theory as a contribution to feminist thinking about nature, bodies, and culture.

I introduced Irigaray's philosophy of natural sexual duality by reassessing feminist debates surrounding her essentialism. I argued that her later writings affirm a form of realist essentialism according to which human bodies naturally have inherent characters, which they actively strive to express culturally. Opposing the widely held view that realist essentialism is untenable, I suggested that Irigaray's later position is appealing because it revalues bodies, and nature more generally, as active and self-expressive, intertwining the project of creating a sexuate culture with that of learning to 'respect the realities that compose the pre-given world: that of the macrocosm and that of living beings' (BEW, 16/27–8). Admittedly, this realist essentialist philosophy has problems: it sees sexual difference as the most fundamental of all differences, underestimates differences between women, and is heterosexist and potentially conservative in see-ing patriarchal culture as an outgrowth of nature. Yet Butler's theory of gender, often regarded as a preferable alternative to Irigaray's later thought, proved to have equally significant problems. Ultimately, Butler sees human bodies as passive vis-à-vis culture, and she ties her politics of subversion to this problematic view by justifying subversion with refer-ence to our bodily vulnerability to harmful forms of cultural moulding. More positively, though, she recognises the oppressiveness of dualistic gender norms, which she urges us to break down, in part by reconceiving women as a non-unified group. I proposed earlier that we can preserve these positive features of Butler's theory by setting out a revised version of this theory predicated upon the idea that bodies naturally consist of multiple, non-sexuate, forces, all striving actively for self-expression. But this raised the question of whether human bodies really are so composed, or whether they are naturally sexually dual as Irigaray holds.

With this question in mind, I explored how Irigaray supports her belief in natural duality with a philosophy of nature which leads her to redefine sexual difference as a difference in rhythms. She claims phenomenologi-cal justification for her conception of nature and of dual bodily rhythms. Yet equal phenomenological justification can be claimed for the idea that human bodies have multiple forces, an idea which is also supported by intersex, insofar as intersex is taken to manifest the general diversity of human bodily features and forces. The fact that the beliefs in natural duality and in bodily multiplicity both have phenomenological support suggests that we need to reconceive human bodies in a way which com-bines these attributes. In working towards this reconception, I reinterro-gated Irigaray's engagements with *Naturphilosophie*, eventually suggesting that sexuation and multiplicity can co-exist in human bodies if they are manifestations of self-differentiating nature. Nature first splits into sex-ual duality and then, in proportion as it achieves realisation – including cultural expression – in this dual form, it tends to pass beyond duality by breaking down the balances of forces which give individuals their sexed characters. The resulting profusion of forces within each sexed individ-ual's body can be identified with their non-sexuate multiplicity.

It might seem that this philosophy of self-differentiating nature only reconciles duality and multiplicity in a rather weak sense, by identifying them as consecutive manifestations of nature. But this is not so: firstly, even when sexual duality is only imperfectly expressed and realised, it still finds *some* realisation (minimally, via a culture which denies sexual difference), and so some level of multiplicity always emerges in bodies alongside sexuation. Still, multiplicity can only fully develop once a sexuate culture is created; therefore, to avoid restricting multiplicity, this culture must assume a specifically self-critical form. Secondly, although multiplicity emerges in bodies by breaking down their sexuation, bodies also have a tendency to retain their sexuation, and hence bodies become divided between two, opposing, tendencies. Having sketched this view of nature and sexuate culture in the last chapter, I now want to tease out how it reconciles the specific conceptions of the body, sex, and gender which are offered by Irigaray and by the revised version of Butler's thought which I have proposed.

Let us remind ourselves what these conceptions of the body are. For Irigaray, a body is sexuate in that it grows according to one of two rhythms. These rhythms regulate how the fluid physical elements of bodies enter into temporary forms, from which, in turn, derive the capacities and properties of those bodies and so, too, their ways of perceiving and acting. A body's rhythm also manifests itself more directly in the body's sexuality. In contrast, on the revised version of Butler's thought, each body consists of diverse forces, which pursue varied, sometimes conflicting, ends, and which co-exist in unstable relations of competition. The diversity of forces within any individual is manifest in the plurality of their bodily features, among which, according to Butler, none naturally cluster together to give that individual a sex. According to Butler's argument as it is elaborated by Warnke, our identifications of certain features as naturally grouping together, to make somebody sexed, reflect social expectations about the capacity of these features to jointly realise gender norms. Since these groupings are cultural, nothing like them can exist independently of social expectations; hence, sex cannot exist naturally. Irigaray's view of bodies and that which I have derived from Butler seem flatly opposed: one perceives natural duality where the other sees no natural sex at all; one sees a single rhythm orchestrating each body where the other sees only an unstable array of forces.

Rhythmic duality and diverse forces can, however, co-exist as manifestations of self-differentiating nature. In much of organic life, nature splits into sexual duality, where each sex embodies a definite – inversely symmetrical – balance of inhibiting and active forces. Just as, throughout organic nature, these forces shape the formation of particular organisms (according to Schelling), so the particular balance of forces which constitutes each sexed human body shapes its process of growth. These balances of forces thus act as do the rhythms which regulate the growth of bodies, according to Irigaray. That balance in which active forces prevail corresponds to males' linear rhythm; the balance in which inhibiting forces prevail corresponds to females' cyclical rhythm. Sexually dual rhythms may therefore be reconceived as manifestations of self-differentiating nature, and so as inversely symmetrical balances of forces which regulate bodies' emergence and growth. But, insofar as each individual has a fixed, stable, sexed character, nature will strain to break down the forces which define this character into further forces which each, in turn, will subdivide and seek expression. These new, more complicated, constellations of forces within bodies give them a character of internal diversity and instability, a character which makes bodies non-sexuate.

Inasmuch as sexual duality and multiplicity can co-exist, Irigaray and Butler are wrong to deny, respectively, multiplicity and natural sex. Irigaray denies bodily multiplicity because she assumes that affirming it means reasserting that there is a common human nature, which, she thinks, is overwhelmingly likely to be symbolised as male. The idea of bodily multiplicity averts this worry, since it asserts only a shared human character of internal *diversity*, where the various forces composing each body differ, to varying degrees, from those of other bodies. On this view, what human bodies share is the character of being, precisely, internally diverse and *dis*unified. Butler, for her part, has argued against the possibility of natural sex, but we can now identify a flaw in her argument. On that argument, any natural groupings of bodily features just cannot be like the groupings which we identify, in light of social expectations, and take to constitute sex. However, there could be natural groupings of bodily features which are wholly unlike those for which social expectations direct us to look, and yet which suffice to make bodies sexed, by giving them a character distinct from that of bodies of the other sex. Specifically, the rhythms which Irigaray postulates orchestrate the growth of bodies so that the movements of their fluids, their perceptions, and their sexuality are all sexed, where all these features differ in kind from the static, biological features for which we look when guided by (patriarchal) social expectations.

Having seen that duality and multiplicity can co-exist – dynamically and conflictually – in human bodies, I want, finally, to explain how this view of bodies enables a broader synthesis of the attractive elements in Irigaray's and Butler's political theories and in their understandings of culture and of women's status as a group. Politically, as I have suggested, the idea of self-differentiating nature implies that a culture of sexual difference must be self-critical, promoting representations of male and female identity which constitutively recognise their own partiality and which therefore allow multiplicity to express itself by drawing on this critical moment. This notion of a self-critical sexuate culture preserves Irigaray's valuable idea that our bodies need self-expression *qua* sexed; it also preserves Butler's recognition that dualistic sex categories are constricting and should be subverted – since self-critical sexuate categories would continually undermine and limit themselves.

We have observed that Irigaray underestimates the extent to which western culture not only suppresses sexual difference but also contains elements which revalue and redefine that difference. In contrast, Butler exaggerates the diversity of this culture, supposing that individuals constantly change the meaning of gender norms with respect to social circumstances and power relations. Against Butler, Irigaray is right that hierarchical conceptions of sexual difference are especially entrenched and resilient. For her, this persistently hierarchical construal – or repression – of sexual difference reflects and expresses men's self-opposing tendency. Because Butler denies that any such tendency inheres in the male body (which, for her, does not naturally exist), she sees no basis for cultural formations to endure and hence emphasises their instability. But because Irigaray denies multiplicity, she downplays the constant slippages and reversals in meaning which do occur within non-sexuate culture, and which (I have suggested) reflect the efforts of bodies' multiple forces to achieve self-expression by injecting change and diversity into culture. By recognising both duality and multiplicity, we can acknowledge that our culture *has* persistently denied sexual difference – but in a more fluctuating and uncertain way than Irigaray countenances.

Irigaray's and Butler's divergent conceptions of culture lead them to different views of the status of women (and men) as a group. For Butler, the meanings of gender norms shift whenever people enact them, so that women share no common understanding of femininity but differ, fundamentally, embodying different understandings of femininity. In contrast, for Irigaray, women share a common natural character and would, ideally, be able to experience themselves – in ever-particular ways – as people who exemplify a common female type. Further, for Irigaray, women *already* share a common cultural location, that of lacking an identity as members of a *sui generis* kind. But if there are endless shifts within patriarchal culture, then the extent and meaning of women's devaluation must itself shift over time. How far, and in what manner, women experience their identity as devalued will therefore vary greatly. We can thus say that, within patriarchal culture, women exist as a merely historical group, with each woman becoming a member of this group by reinterpreting received ideas of female identity – ideas, however, which will persistently tend to fall back (in differing ways) into being negative and pejorative, owing to the ongoing effects of male nature. Moreover, at the level of nature, women do not simply share a sexed character: they are always *non*-sexed as well. As a result, women can properly identify as members of the female kind only if the available representations of this kind enable women to recognise that they are not simply female, and that they do not unambiguously belong to the same identity category as other women.

Despite the antagonism between Irigaray's and Butler's feminist philosophies, we need not abandon, but can combine, their attractions. I have suggested a particular way of doing this, drawing on the philosophy of nature to rethink sexual duality as co-existing, conflictually, with bodily multiplicity. Since Irigaray's later philosophy admits of this rethinking, it should not be dismissed as irredeemably naïve, conservative, or heterosexist. Through its relationship to broader ideas of nature as *physis*, as rhythmic, and as self-opposing, Irigaray's later conception of sexual difference opens itself to being rethought based on an idea of self-differentiating nature. With this idea that nature manifests itself within us as both sexuation and multiplicity, requiring expression in a self-critical sexuate culture, we can remain faithful to Irigaray's injunction to 'refuse to let parts of ourselves shrivel and die which we could let blossom' (SG, 69/81).

Bibliography

Abraham, Nicolas. *Rhythms: On the Work, Translation, and Psychoanalysis.* Translated by Benjamin Thigpen. Stanford: Stanford University Press, 1995.

Alaimo, Stacy. *Undomesticated Ground: Recasting Nature as Feminist Space.* Ithaca: Cornell University Press, 2000.

Allison, Henry. *Kant's Transcendental Idealism.* New Haven: Yale University Press, 1983.

Allwood, Gill. *French Feminisms: Gender and Violence in Contemporary Theory.* London: UCL Press, 1998.

Ansell-Pearson, Keith. *An Introduction to Nietzsche as Political Thinker: The Perfect Nihilist.* Cambridge: Cambridge University Press, 1994.

Armour, Ellen T. *Deconstruction, Theology and the Problem of Difference: Subverting the Race/Gender Divide.* Chicago, Ill.: University of Chicago Press, 1999.

Bachelard, Gaston. *The Dialectic of Duration.* 1950. Translated by Mary McAllester Jones. Manchester, U.K.: Clinamen Press, 2000.

Bachofen, Johann Jakob. *Myth, Religion and Mother-Right.* 1861. Translated by Ralph Manheim. London: Routledge, 1967.

Barad, Karen. 'Posthumanist Performativity: Toward an Understanding of How Matter Comes to Matter'. *Signs* 28: 3 (2003): 801–31.

Barnes, Jonathan, ed. *Early Greek Philosophy.* Harmondsworth: Penguin, 1987.

Battersby, Christine. *The Phenomenal Woman: Feminist Metaphysics and the Patterns of Identity.* Cambridge, U.K.: Polity Press, 1998.

Beiser, Frederick. 'German Romanticism'. In *The Routledge Encyclopaedia of Philosophy,* edited by Edward Craig. London and New York: Routledge, 1998.

———. *The Romantic Imperative.* Cambridge, Mass.: Harvard University Press, 2004.

Benhabib, Seyla. 'Subjectivity, Historiography, and Politics: Reflections on the "Feminism/Postmodernism Exchange"'. In Benhabib et al., *Feminist Contentions.* London: Routledge, 1995.

Benhabib, Seyla, Judith Butler, Drucilla Cornell, and Nancy Fraser. *Feminist Contentions: A Philosophical Exchange.* London: Routledge, 1995.

Bernstein, J. M. Introduction to *Classic and Romantic German Aesthetics*, edited by J. M. Bernstein. Cambridge: Cambridge University Press, 2003.

Benveniste, Emile. *Problems in General Linguistics*. 1966. Translated by Mary Elizabeth Meek. Coral Gables, Fla.: University of Miami Press, 1971.

Bigwood, Carol. *Earth Muse: Feminism, Nature, and Art*. Philadelphia: Temple University Press, 1993.

Birke, Lynda. *Feminism and the Biological Body*. Edinburgh: Edinburgh University Press, 1999.

Bloodsworth, Mary K. 'Embodiment and Ambiguity: Luce Irigaray, Sexual Difference and "Race"'. *International Studies in Philosophy* 31: 2 (1999): 69–90.

Bordo, Susan R. *The Flight to Objectivity: Essays on Cartesianism and Culture*. Albany: SUNY Press, 1987.

Boulous, Walker, Michelle. *Philosophy and the Maternal Body: Reading Silence*. London: Routledge, 1998.

Bowie, Andrew. *Schelling and Modern European Philosophy: An Introduction*. London: Routledge, 1993.

———. *Introduction to German Philosophy: From Kant to Habermas*. Cambridge, U.K.: Polity Press, 2003.

Braidotti, Rosi. 'The Politics of Ontological Difference'. In *Between Feminism and Psychoanalysis*, edited by Teresa Brennan. London: Routledge, 1989.

———. *Patterns of Dissonance: A Study of Women in Contemporary Philosophy*. Translated by Elizabeth Guild. Cambridge, U.K.: Polity Press, 1991.

———. 'Feminism by Any Other Name'. Interview with Judith Butler. *differences: A Journal of Feminist Cultural Studies* 6: 2 + 3 (1994): 27–61.

———. 'Sexual Difference Theory'. In *A Companion to Feminist Philosophy*, edited by Alison M. Jaggar and Iris Marion Young. Malden, Mass.: Blackwell, 1998.

———. *Metamorphoses: Towards a Materialist Theory of Becoming*. Cambridge, U.K.: Polity Press, 2002.

———. 'Becoming Woman: Or Sexual Difference Revisited'. *Theory, Culture and Society* 20: 3 (2003): 43–64.

Bray, Abigail. 'Not Woman Enough: Irigaray's Culture of Difference'. *Feminist Theory* 2: 3 (2001): 311–27.

Burke, Carolyn, Naomi Schor, and Margaret Whitford, eds. *Engaging with Irigaray: Feminist Philosophy and Modern European Thought*. New York: Columbia University Press, 1994.

Butler, Judith. 'Sex and Gender in Simone de Beauvoir's *Second Sex*'. *Yale French Studies* 72 (1986): 35–49.

———. 'Foucault and the Paradox of Bodily Inscriptions'. *Journal of Philosophy* 86: 11 (1989): 601–7.

———. 'Sexual Ideology and Phenomenological Description: A Feminist Critique of Merleau-Ponty's *Phenomenology of Perception*'. In *The Thinking Muse: Feminism and Modern French Philosophy*, edited by Jeffner Allen and Iris Marion Young. Bloomington: Indiana University Press, 1989.

———. 'Sexual Difference as a Question of Ethics: Alterities of the Flesh in Irigaray and Merleau-Ponty'. In *Bodies of Resistance: New Phenomenologies of Politics, Agency, and Culture*, edited by Laura Doyle. Evanston, Ill.: Northwestern University Press, 2001.

————. 'Gender as Performance: An Interview with Judith Butler'. Interview with Peter Osborne and Lynne Segal. *Radical Philosophy* 67 (1994): 32–9.

————. 'Performative Acts and Gender Constitution: An Essay in Phenomenology and Feminist Theory'. In *Writing on the Body: Female Embodiment and Feminist Theory*, edited by Katie Conboy, Nadia Medina, and Sarah Stanbury. New York: Columbia University Press, 1997.

————. *The Psychic Life of Power: Theories in Subjection*. Stanford: Stanford University Press, 1997.

————. *Excitable Speech: A Politics of the Performative*. London: Routledge, 1997.

————. *Anniversary Edition of Gender Trouble*. London: Routledge, 1999.

————. *Antigone's Claim*. New York: Columbia University Press, 2000.

————. *Contingency, Hegemony, Universality: Contemporary Dialogues on the Left*. With Ernesto Laclau and Slavoj Žižek. London: Verso, 2000.

————. *Kritik der ethischen Gewalt*. Frankfurt: Suhrkamp, 2003.

Cavarero, Adriana. *In Spite of Plato*. 1990. Translated by Serena Anderlini-D'Onofrio and Áine O'Healy. Cambridge, U.K.: Polity Press, 1995.

Chanter, Tina. *Ethics of Eros: Irigaray's Rewriting of the Philosophers*. London: Routledge, 1995.

Chase, Cheryl et al. 'Intersexual Rights'. Letters section, *The Sciences* (July/August 1993): 3–4.

Cheah, Pheng, and Elizabeth Grosz. 'Of Being-Two: Introduction'. *Diacritics* 28: 1 (1998): 3–18.

Chodorow, Nancy. *The Reproduction of Mothering*. Berkeley: University of California Press, 1978.

Colebrook, Claire. Introduction to *Deleuze and Feminist Theory*, edited by Ian Buchanan and Claire Colebrook. Edinburgh: Edinburgh University Press, 2000.

————. 'From Radical Representations to Corporeal Becomings: The Feminist Philosophy of Lloyd, Grosz, and Gatens'. *Hypatia* 15: 2 (2000): 76–93.

Cornell, Drucilla. *Transformations: Recollective Imagination and Sexual Difference*. London: Routledge, 1993.

————. *At the Heart of Freedom: Feminism, Sex, and Equality*. Princeton: Princeton University Press, 1998.

Dastur, Françoise. 'Tragedy and Speculation'. In *Philosophy and Tragedy*, edited by Miguel de Beistegui and Simon Sparks. London: Routledge, 2000.

De Lauretis, Teresa. 'The Essence of the Triangle or, Taking the Risk of Essentialism Seriously: Feminist Theory in Italy, the U.S., and Britain'. In *The Essential Difference*, edited by Schor and Weed.

Deleuze, Gilles, and Félix Guattari. *A Thousand Plateaus: Capitalism and Schizophrenia*. Translated by Brian Massumi. London: Athlone, 1988. Originally published as *Mille Plateaux*. Paris: Minuit, 1980.

Descartes, René. *The Philosophical Writings of Descartes*. 2 vols. Translated by John Cottingham, Robert Stoothoff, and Dugald Murdoch. Cambridge: Cambridge University Press, 1985.

Deutscher, Penelope. 'French Feminist Philosophers on Law and Public Policy: Michèle le Doeuff and Luce Irigaray'. *Australian Journal of French Studies* 34: 1 (1997): 24–44.

————. *Yielding Gender: Feminism, Deconstruction and the History of Philosophy*. London: Routledge, 1997.

————. *A Politics of Impossible Difference: The Later Work of Luce Irigaray*. Ithaca: Cornell University Press, 2002.

Di Giovanni, George. 'Kant's *Metaphysics of Nature* and Schelling's *Ideas for a Philosophy of Nature*'. *Journal of the History of Philosophy* 17 (1979): 197–215.

Disch, Lisa. 'Judith Butler and the Politics of the Performative'. *Political Theory* 27: 4 (1999): 545–59.

Fausto-Sterling, Anne. 'How Many Sexes Are There?' *New York Times* March 12, 1993: A29.

————. 'The Five Sexes, Revisited'. *The Sciences* (July/August 2000): 19–23.

————. *Sexing the Body: Gender Politics and the Construction of Sexuality*. New York: Basic Books, 2000.

Field, Terri. 'Is the Body Essential for Ecofeminism?' *Organization and Environment* 13: 1 (2000): 39–60.

Fielding, Helen. 'Questioning Nature: Irigaray, Heidegger and the Potentiality of Matter'. *Continental Philosophy Review* 36: 1 (2003): 1–26.

Foucault, Michel. *The History of Sexuality: Volume One*. 1976. Translated by Robert Hurley. London: Allen Lane, 1979.

————. 'Nietzsche, Genealogy, History'. 1971. In *Nietzsche*, edited by John Richardson and Brian Leiter. Oxford: Oxford University Press, 2001.

Fraser, Nancy. 'False Antitheses: A Response to Seyla Benhabib and Judith Butler'. In Benhabib et al., *Feminist Contentions*.

Freud, Sigmund. *On Metapsychology: The Theory of Psychoanalysis*. Translated under the general editorship of James Strachey. Harmondsworth: Penguin, 1984.

————. *Civilization, Society and Religion*. Translated under the general editorship of James Strachey. Harmondsworth: Penguin, 1985.

Fuss, Diana. *Essentially Speaking: Feminism, Nature and Difference*. London: Routledge, 1989.

Gallop, Jane. '*Quand nos lèvres s'écrivent*: Irigaray's Body Politic'. *Romanic Review* 74: 1 (1983): 77–83.

Gardner, Sebastian. *Kant and the Critique of Pure Reason*. London: Routledge, 1999.

Gatens, Moira. *Imaginary Bodies: Ethics, Power and Corporeality*. London: Routledge, 1996.

Gilligan, Carol. *In a Different Voice*. Cambridge, Mass.: Harvard University Press, 1982.

Glazebrook, Trish. 'From *Physis* to Nature, *Technē* to Technology: Heidegger on Aristotle, Galileo, and Newton'. *Southern Journal of Philosophy* 38 (2000): 95–118.

Goethe, Johann Wolfgang von. *Scientific Studies*. Edited and translated by Douglas Miller. Princeton: Princeton University Press, 1995.

Grosz, Elizabeth. *Sexual Subversions: Three French Feminists*. Sydney: Allen and Unwin, 1989.

————. *Jacques Lacan: A Feminist Introduction*. London: Routledge, 1990.

————. *Volatile Bodies: Toward a Corporeal Feminism*. Bloomington: Indiana University Press, 1994.

———. *Architecture from the Outside: Essays on Virtual and Real Space*. London: MIT Press, 2001.

———. *The Nick of Time: Politics, Evolution, and the Untimely*. Durham: Duke University Press, 2004.

———. *Time Travels: Feminism, Nature, Power*. Durham: Duke University Press, 2005.

Hammond, Michael, Jane Howarth, and Russell Keat. *Understanding Phenomenology*. Oxford: Blackwell, 1991.

Haraway, Donna. 'A Cyborg Manifesto: Science, Technology, and Socialist-Feminism in the Late Twentieth Century'. In Haraway, *Simians, Cyborgs and Women: The Reinvention of Nature*. London: Routledge, 1991.

Hardimon, Michael. *Hegel's Social Philosophy*. Cambridge: Cambridge University Press, 1994.

Harding, Sandra, and Merrill B. Hintikka, eds. *Discovering Reality: Feminist Perspectives on Epistemology, Metaphysics, Methodology, and Philosophy of Science*. Dordrecht: David Reidel, 1984.

Haslanger, Sally. 'Feminism in Metaphysics: Negotiating the Natural'. In *The Cambridge Companion to Feminism in Philosophy*, edited by Miranda Fricker and Jennifer Hornsby. Cambridge: Cambridge University Press, 2000.

Hass, Marjorie. 'The Style of the Speaking Subject: Irigaray's Empirical Studies of Language Production'. *Hypatia* 15: 1 (2000): 64–89.

Hayles, N. Katherine. 'Gender Encoding in Fluid Mechanics: Masculine Channels and Feminine Flows'. *Differences: A Journal of Feminist Cultural Studies* 4: 2 (1992): 16–44.

Hegel, G. W. F. *Natural Law: The Scientific Ways of Treating Natural Law, Its Place in Moral Philosophy, and Its Relation to the Positive Sciences of Law*. 1802–1803. Translated by T. M. Knox. Philadelphia: University of Pennsylvania Press, 1975.

———. *Encyclopaedia Logic*. Third edition, 1830. Translated by T. F. Geraets, W. A. Suchting, and H. S. Harris. Indianapolis: Hackett, 1991.

———. *Philosophy of Nature*. 3 vols. Third edition, 1830. Edited and translated by M. J. Petry. London: Allen and Unwin, 1970.

———. *Philosophy of Mind*. Third edition, 1830. Translated by A. V. Miller and William Wallace. Oxford: Clarendon, 1971.

Heidegger, Martin. *Introduction to Metaphysics*. 1935. Translated by Ralph Manheim. New Haven: Yale University Press, 1959.

———. *Elucidations of Hölderlin's Poetry*. Translated by Keith Hoeller. New York: Humanity Books, 2000. Published in German as *Erläuterungen zu Hölderlins Dichtung*. Frankfurt: Klostermann, 1981.

———. 'On the Essence and Concept of *Physis* in Aristotle's *Physics* B, I'. 1939. Translated by Thomas Sheehan. In *Pathmarks*, edited by Will McNeill. Cambridge: Cambridge University Press, 1998. Published in German as '*Vom Wesen und Begriff der* Physis Aristoteles, *Physik B, 1*'. In *Wegmarken. Gesamtausgabe*, division 1, volume 9. Frankfurt: Klostermann, 1996.

———. 'Modern Science, Metaphysics, and Mathematics'. 1962. In *Basic Writings*, edited by David Farrell Krell. Second, revised, edition; London: Routledge, 1993.

Heinämaa, Sara. 'What Is a Woman? Butler and Beauvoir on the Foundations of the Sexual Difference'. *Hypatia* 12: 1 (1997): 20–39.

Heraclitus. *The Art and Thought of Heraclitus*. Edited and translated by Charles Kahn. Cambridge: Cambridge University Press, 1979.

Hodge, Joanna. 'Irigaray Reading Heidegger'. In *Engaging with Irigaray*, edited by Burke et al.

Hölderlin, Friedrich. 'Being Judgement Possibility'. 1795. In *Classic and Romantic German Aesthetics*, edited by J. M. Bernstein. Cambridge: Cambridge University Press, 2003.

———. *Hyperion and Selected Poems*. Edited by Eric L. Santner. New York: Continuum, 1990.

———. *Poems and Fragments*. Translated by Michael Hamburger. London: Anvil Press, 1994.

———. *Essays and Letters on Theory*. Translated by Thomas Pfau. Albany: SUNY Press, 1988.

———. *Sämtliche Werke und Briefe*. 2 vols. Edited by Günter Mieth. Munich: Carl Hanser Verlag, 1970.

Huntingdon, Patricia. *Ecstatic Subjects, Utopia, and Recognition*. Albany: SUNY Press, 1998.

———. Introduction to *Feminist Interpretations of Martin Heidegger*, edited by Nancy J. Holland and Patricia Huntingdon. University Park, PA: Penn State Press, 2001.

Irigaray, Luce. 'Women's Exile'. Translated by Couze Venn. *Ideology and Consciousness* 1 (1977): 62–76.

———. *Marine Lover of Friedrich Nietzsche*. 1980. Trans. Gillian C. Gill. New York: Columbia University Press, 1991.

———. 'Women-Mothers, the Silent Substratum of the Social Order'. 1981. In *The Irigaray Reader*, edited by Margaret Whitford. Oxford: Blackwell, 1991.

———. *Elemental Passions*. 1982. Translated by Joanne Collie and Judith Still. London: Athlone, 1992.

———. *To Speak is Never Neutral*. 1985. Translated by Gail Schwab. London: Continuum, 2002.

———. Interview with Elaine Hoffman Baruch and Lucienne J. Serrano. In *Women Analyze Women*, edited by Baruch and Serrano. New York: New York University Press, 1988.

———. 'From *The Forgetting of Air* to *To Be Two*'. In *Feminist Interpretations of Martin Heidegger*, edited by Nancy J. Holland and Patricia Huntingdon. University Park, PA: Penn State Press, 2001.

———. 'Why Cultivate Difference?' *Paragraph* 25: 3 (2002): 79–90.

———. 'Being Two, How Many Eyes Have We?' *Paragraph* 25: 3 (2002): 143–51.

———. 'Animal Compassion'. In *Animal Philosophy*, edited by Peter Atterton and Matthew Calarco. London: Continuum, 2004.

Joy, Morny. 'Love and the Labor of the Negative: Irigaray and Hegel'. In *Resistance, Flight, Creation: Feminist Enactments of French Philosophy*, edited by Dorothea Olkowski. Ithaca: Cornell University Press, 2000.

Kant, Immanuel. *Critique of Pure Reason*. 1781; second edition, 1787. Translated by Norman Kemp Smith. Basingstoke: MacMillan, 1929.

————. *Critique of Judgement.* 1790. Translated by Werner S. Pluhar. Indianapolis: Hackett, 1987.

Keltner, Stacy. 'The Ethics of Air: Technology and the Question of Sexual Difference'. *Philosophy Today* Suppl. 45:5 (2001): 53–65.

Kessler, Suzanne. *Lessons from the Intersexed.* Brunswick, NJ: Rutgers University Press, 1998.

Kirby, Vicki. *Telling Flesh: The Substance of the Corporeal.* London: Routledge, 1997.

Krell, David Farrell. 'Three Ends of the Absolute: Schelling on Inhibition, Hölderlin on Separation, and Novalis on Density'. *Research in Phenomenology* 32 (2002): 60–85.

Lacan, Jacques. *Écrits.* 1966. Translated by Alan Sheridan. London: Tavistock, 1977.

Lacey, Nicola. *Unspeakable Subjects: Feminist Essays in Legal and Social Theory.* Oxford: Hart, 1998.

Lacoue-Labarthe, Philippe. *Typography: Mimesis, Philosophy, Politics.* Edited by Christopher Fynsk. Stanford: Stanford University Press, 1998.

Lear, Jonathan. *Aristotle: The Desire to Understand.* Cambridge: Cambridge University Press, 1988.

Lefebvre, Henri. *Rhythmanalysis: Space, Time, and Everyday Life.* Translated by Stuart Elden and Gerald Moore. London: Continuum, 2004.

Lennon, Kathleen. 'Imaginary Bodies and Worlds'. *Inquiry* 47 (2004): 107–22.

Lloyd, Genevieve. *The Man of Reason.* Second edition. London: Routledge, 1993.

————, ed. *Feminism and History of Philosophy.* Oxford: Oxford University Press, 2002.

Locke, John. *An Essay Concerning Human Understanding.* 1690. Edited by John W. Yolton. London: J. M. Dent, 1976.

Lorrain, Tamsin. *Irigaray and Deleuze: Experiments in Visceral Philosophy.* Ithaca: Cornell University Press, 1999.

MacDonald, Mairi. 'Intersex and Gender Identity'. 2000. At: www.ukia.co. uk/voices/is_gi.htm

MacKinnon, Catherine. 'Feminism, Marxism, Method and the State: An Agenda for Theory'. *Signs* 7 (1982): 515–44.

Mader, Mary Beth. 'All Too Familiar: Luce Irigaray's Recent Thoughts on Sexuation and Generation'. *Continental Philosophy Review* 36: 4 (2003): 367–90.

Martin, Alison. *Luce Irigaray and the Question of the Divine.* Leeds: Maney Publishing, 2000.

McNay, Lois. *Gender and Agency: Reconfiguring the Subject in Feminist and Social Theory.* Oxford: Blackwell, 2000.

Merleau-Ponty, Maurice. *Nature: Course Notes from the Collège de France.* Translated by Robert Vallier. Evanston, Ill.: Northwestern University Press, 2003.

Miller, Elaine. *The Vegetative Soul: From Philosophy of Nature to Subjectivity in the Feminine.* Albany: SUNY Press, 2002.

Mills, Catherine. 'Efficacy and Vulnerability: Judith Butler on Reiteration and Resistance'. *Australian Feminist Studies* 32 (2000): 265–79.

Moi, Toril. *Sexual/Textual Politics: Feminist Literary Theory.* London: Methuen, 1985.

————. *Simone de Beauvoir: The Making of an Intellectual Woman.* Oxford: Blackwell, 1994.

Murphy, Ann V. 'The Enigma of the Natural in Irigaray'. *Philosophy Today*. Suppl. 45: 5 (2001): 75–82.

New, Caroline. 'Realism, Deconstruction, and the Feminist Standpoint'. *Journal for the Theory of Social Behaviour* 28: 4 (1998): 349–72.

Nicholson, Linda. 'The Myth of the Traditional Family'. In *Feminism and Families*, edited by Hilde Lindemann Nelson. London: Routledge, 1997.

Nietzsche, Friedrich. *On the Genealogy of Morality*. 1887. Translated by Carol Diethe. Cambridge: Cambridge University Press, 1994. Published in German as *Zur Genealogie der Moral*. In *Kritische Gesamtausgabe*, Division 6, Volume 2, edited by Giorgio Colli and Mazzino Montinari. Berlin: de Gruyter, 1967–.

———. *The Will to Power*. 1906. Translated by Walter Kaufmann and R. J. Hollingdale. New York: Random House, 1967.

Olkowski, Dorothea. 'Materiality and Language: Butler's Interrogation of the History of Philosophy'. *Philosophy and Social Criticism* 23: 3 (1997): 37–53.

———. *Gilles Deleuze and the Ruin of Representation*. Berkeley: University of California Press, 1999.

———. 'The End of Phenomenology: Bergson's Interval in Irigaray'. *Hypatia* 15: 3 (2000): 73–91.

———. 'Morpho-logic in Deleuze and Irigaray'. In *Deleuze and Feminist Theory*, edited by Ian Buchanan and Claire Colebrook. Edinburgh: Edinburgh University Press, 2000.

Patton, Paul, ed. *Nietzsche, Feminism, and Political Theory*. London: Routledge, 1993.

Pinkard, Terry. *Hegel's Phenomenology: The Sociality of Reason*. Cambridge: Cambridge University Press, 1996.

Plato. *Timaeus and Critias*. Translated by Desmond Lee. Harmondsworth: Penguin, 1977.

Plaza, Monique. '"Phallomorphic Power" and the Psychology of "Woman"'. *Ideology and Consciousness* 4 (1978): 5–36.

Poxon, Judith L. 'Corporeality and Divinity: Irigaray and the Problem of the Ideal'. In *Religion in French Feminist Thought: Critical Perspectives*, edited by Morny Joy, Kathleen O'Grady, and Judith L. Poxon. London: Routledge, 2003.

Richardson, John. 'Nietzsche's Power Ontology'. In *Nietzsche*, edited by John Richardson and Brian Leiter. Oxford: Oxford University Press, 2001.

Richards, Robert J. *The Romantic Conception of Life*. Chicago, Ill.: University of Chicago Press, 2002.

Ricoeur, Paul. *Freud and Philosophy: An Essay on Interpretation*. Translated by Denis Savage. New Haven: Yale University Press, 1970.

Riley, Denise. *'Am I That Name?': Feminism and the Category of 'Women' in History*. London: Macmillan, 1988.

Rose, Jacqueline. 'Introduction – II'. In Jacques Lacan, *Feminine Sexuality*, edited by Juliet Mitchell and Jacqueline Rose. New York: Norton, 1982.

Salih, Sara. *Judith Butler*. London: Routledge, 2002.

Sandford, Stella. 'Feminism Against "The Feminine"'. *Radical Philosophy* 105 (2001): 6–14.

Sayer, Andrew. *Realism and Social Science*. London: Sage, 2000.

Sayers, Janet. *Sexual Contradictions: Psychology, Psychoanalysis, and Feminism*. London: Tavistock, 1986.

Schelling, F. W. J. *Von der Weltseele. Eine Hypothese der höhern physik zur Erklärung des allgemeinen Organismus.* 1978. In Schelling, *Werke: Historisch-kritische Ausgabe Reihe 1.* Vol. 6, edited by Jörg Jantzen. Stuttgart: Frommann-Holzboog, 2000.

Schlegel, Friedrich. 'Dialogue on Poetry' (selections). Translated by Ernst Behler and Roman Struc. In *German Romantic Criticism*, edited by A. Leslie Willson. New York: Continuum, 1982.

Schoenbohm, Susan. 'Heidegger's Interpretation of *Physis* in *Introduction to Metaphysics*'. In *A Companion to Heidegger's Introduction to Metaphysics*, edited by Richard Polt and Gregory Fried. New Haven: Yale University Press, 2001.

Schor, Naomi. 'Previous Engagements: The Receptions of Irigaray'. In *Engaging with Irigaray*, edited by Burke et al.

———. 'This Essentialism Which Is Not One: Coming to Grips with Irigaray'. In *Engaging with Irigaray*, edited by Burke et al.

———. 'French Feminism Is a Universalism'. *differences: A Journal of Feminist Cultural Studies* 7: 1 (1995): 14–47.

Schor, Naomi, and Elizabeth Weed, eds. *The Essential Difference.* Bloomington: Indiana University Press, 1994.

Schrift, Alan. *Nietzsche and the Question of Interpretation: Between Hermeneutics and Deconstruction.* London: Routledge, 1990.

Schutte, Ofelia. 'A Critique of Normative Heterosexuality: Identity, Embodiment, and Sexual Difference in Beauvoir and Irigaray'. *Hypatia* 12: 1 (1997): 40–62.

Schwab, Gail. 'Sexual Difference as Model: An Ethics for the Global Future'. *Diacritics* 28: 1 (1998): 76–92.

Sen, Amartya. *Inequality Reexamined.* Oxford: Clarendon Press, 1992.

Shildrick, Margrit. *Leaky Bodies and Boundaries: Feminism, Postmodernism and (Bio)ethics.* London: Routledge, 1997.

Spelman, Elizabeth. *Inessential Woman: Problems of Exclusion in Feminist Thought.* London: The Women's Press, 1988.

Spivak, Gayatri Chakravorty. *Outside in the Teaching Machine.* London: Routledge, 1993.

———. 'Feminism, Criticism and the Institution'. *Thesis Eleven* 10/11 (1984/5): 175–87.

Sturma, Dieter. 'The Nature of Subjectivity: The Critical and Systematic Function of Schelling's Philosophy of Nature'. In *The Reception of Kant's Critical Philosophy: Fichte, Schelling, and Hegel*, edited by Sally Sedgwick. Cambridge: Cambridge University Press, 2002.

Summers-Bremner, Eluned. 'Reading Irigaray, Dancing'. *Hypatia* 15: 1 (2000): 90–124.

Van Lenning, Alkeline. 'The Body as Crowbar: Transcending or Stretching Sex?' *Feminist Theory* 5: 1 (2004): 25–47.

Vasseleu, Cathryn. *Textures of Light: Vision and Touch in Irigaray, Levinas and Merleau-Ponty.* London: Routledge, 1998.

Vasterling, Veronica. 'Butler's Sophisticated Constructionism'. *Hypatia* 14: 3 (1999): 17–38.

Vogel, Steven. 'Nature as Origin and Difference: On Environmental Philosophy and Continental Thought'. *Philosophy Today* 42 Suppl. (1998): 169–81.

Walsh, Lisa. 'Her Mother Her Self: The Ethics of the Antigone Family Romance'. *Hypatia* 14: 3 (1999): 96–125.

Warnke, Georgia. 'Intersexuality and the Categories of Sex'. *Hypatia* 16: 3 (2001): 126–37.

Webster, Fiona. 'The Politics of Sex and Gender: Benhabib and Butler Debate Subjectivity'. *Hypatia* 15: 1 (2000): 1–22.

Weir, Allison. *Sacrificial Logics: Feminist Theory and the Critique of Identity*. London: Routledge, 1996.

Weiss, Gail. *Body Images: Embodiment as Intercorporeality*. London: Routledge, 1999.

Whitford, Margaret. *Luce Irigaray: Philosophy in the Feminine*. London: Routledge, 1991.

———. 'Irigaray, Utopia and the Death Drive'. In *Engaging with Irigaray*, edited by Burke et al.

———. 'Reading Irigaray in the Nineties'. In *Engaging with Irigaray*, edited by Burke et al.

———, ed. *The Irigaray Reader*. Oxford: Blackwell, 1991.

Williams, Raymond. *Keywords: A Vocabulary of Culture and Society*. Revised, expanded, edition. London: Flamingo, 1983.

Wirth, Jason. *The Conspiracy of Life: Meditations on Schelling and His Time*. Albany: SUNY Press, 2003.

Wood, David. 'Thinking With Cats'. In *Animal Philosophy*, edited by Peter Atterton and Matthew Calarco. London: Continuum, 2004.

Wright, Elizabeth, ed. *Feminism and Psychoanalysis: A Critical Dictionary*. Oxford: Blackwell, 1992.

Xu, Ping. 'Irigaray's Mimicry and the Problem of Essentialism'. *Hypatia* 10: 4 (1995): 76–89.

Young, Iris Marion. *Throwing Like a Girl and Other Essays in Feminist Philosophy and Social Theory*. Bloomington: Indiana University Press, 1990.

———. 'Gender as Seriality: Thinking about Women as a Social Collective'. *Signs* 19: 3 (1994): 713–38.

Index

www.ingramcontent.com/pod-product-compliance
Ingram Content Group UK Ltd.
Pitfield, Milton Keynes, MK11 3LW, UK
UKHW010038140625
459647UK00012BA/1465